"I found [Ragen's] work particularly instructive in its detailed analysis of the themes of the automobile and the literary-theological myth of the Adamic American man. I am sure that students of O'Connor will find it equally illuminating."

—Sally Fitzgerald, editor of
*The Habit of Being*

"Brian Abel Ragen's new study of Flannery O'Connor is an original and significant contribution to the analysis of one of America's foremost writers of fiction. By placing her in the context of American literary traditions, he sheds new light on O'Connor's sense of the Incarnation and the ways in which she consciously wanted her fiction to work."

—Arthur F. Kinney, author of
*Flannery O'Connor's Library: Resources of Being*

"With great sensitivity to O'Connor's texts and with impressive learning in theology and biblical exegesis, Ragen discovers new dimensions to her work and provides us with superb new interpretations. This is must reading for students and lovers of O'Connor."

—Professor Emory Elliot
Chair, Department of English
Princeton University

"I teach a "Bible and Literature" course, and I am quite familiar with the recent work in that field. Much of it is very exciting. I must say that Ragen's book, in that context, is one of the most truly illuminating biblical studies of a modern author known to me. What is new about this book is the depth and subtlety of Ragen's biblical reading. He perfectly matches the modern author, who is his subject, both in the breadth of his knowledge of the Catholic exegetical tradition and in his playful attitude toward it. Time after time Ragen offers us truly illuminating readings—readings which enrich our understanding of the writer's mind and art."

—John V. Fleming
Visiting Fellow at The Institute for Advanced Study

"The two strengths of *A Wreck on the Road to Damascus* are its illuminating discussion of the automobile as a spiritual symbol in American life and its discovery of O'Connor's reinvention of Christian iconography for the twentieth century. Ragen's treatment of the automobile as a symbol of freedom from the taint of Original Sin adds a new chapter to the story of the American Adam and his not-so-innocent trek to the West. Ragen's acute insights into the biblical archetypes, that give structure to O'Connor's bizarre narratives of 'life in the South,' add a new dimension to the so-called violence of her fiction, and promulgate a world of Christian understanding beyond that violence."

—Professor Thomas P. Roche, Jr.
Department of English
Princeton University

# A Wreck on the Road to Damascus

Flannery O'Connor's Self-Portrait, courtesy of Regina O'Connor

# A Wreck on the Road to Damascus:

*Innocence, Guilt, & Conversion
in Flannery O'Connor*

**Brian Abel Ragen**

Loyola University Press
Chicago, Illinois

Library of Congress Cataloging in Publication Data

Ragen, Brian Abel
    Wreck on the road to Damascus:  innocence, guilt, and
conversion in Flannery O'Connor/Brian Abel Ragen.
        p.  cm.—(A Campion Book)
        Bibliography: p. 223
ISBN: 0-8294-0605-0
        1. O'Connor, Flannery—Criticism and Interpretation.  2.
Innocence (Theology) in literature.  3. Guilt in literature.  4. Con-
version in literature.  I. Title
PS3563.C57Z84  1989            813'.54—dc19            89-2470

Unpublished writing of Flannery O'Connor © 1989 by Regina
O'Connor and used by permission of the Literary Executor. Ac-
knowledgment is also made in appreciation for permission to
reprint passages from previously published works to the following
authors and their publishers: Excerpts from *All the King's Men*,
© 1946 and renewed 1974 by Robert Penn Warren, reprinted by permission of Harcourt Brace Jovanovich, Inc.; excerpts from "The Life
You Save May Be Your Own" in *A Good Man is Hard to Find and Other
Stories*, © 1953 by Flannery O'Connor and renewed 1981 by Mrs.
Regina O'Connor and reprinted by permission of Harcourt Brace
Jovanovich; Alfred A. Knopf, Inc., for *The Collected Poems of Wallace
Stevens*, © 1923 and renewed 1951 by Wallace Stevens; Oxford Uni-
versity Press for *The  Allegory of Love*  by C. S. Lewis, © 1936; Van-
guard Press, a Division of Random House, Inc. for *The Mechanical
Bride*, © 1951 by Marshall McLuhan; Stein and Day for *Love and Death
in the American Novel*, © 1966 by Leslie Fiedler; University of Chicago
Press for *The American Adam* , © 1955 by R. W. B. Lewis; and *American
Quarterly Magazine*  for excerpts from "Melodramas of Beset Manhood: How Theories of American Fiction Exclude Women Authors," © 1981 by Nina Baym.

*To*
*Nancy Manning*

# Contents

# Foreword

We would pack up our belongings, the moving van would pull away, and we would be on the road one more time, following the map to the new duty station—an air base in Montgomery or Sumter or Valdosta or Macon. On two-lane roads we'd pass the Newborn Baptist Church, the road signs announcing Jesus' imminent return, and at one point a huge red cross erected near the "Yield" sign. One of my earliest memories is of fields of kudzu sending out tentative feelers along the telephone lines, overtaking abandoned shacks and even whole trees.

"I wanted this car mostly to be a house for me," Hazel Motes says to the salesman in *Wise Blood*. I remember our Hudson, which was our home between homes—complete with venetian blinds in the back window and an armrest large enough to be a child's throne in those pre-seatbelt days.

What was permanent in our lives? Only our car, our furniture which arrived at each new base with a few more nicks and scratches, and Grandma's house in Florida, where we'd stay sometimes for months at a time when Dad was on TDY in Okinawa or Omaha. Grandpa's rose-and-black Plymouth sat in his garage where the tropical air created an eternal stickiness on the vinyl seats. The smell of an old garage—oil cans, kerosene, dust and tar—permeated the inside of the car and whenever we'd ride with Grandpa for a couple of miles to Lake Killarney for a swim or to Robert E. Lee Junior High School where we were temporarily enrolled, we'd emerge with that pungent mustiness in our hair and on our clothes.

The memories of our cars follow us forever, perhaps because the automobile is an extension of ourselves, taking us places, giving us freedom, always making us feel more powerful than we really are. In a sense one's car becomes more than oneself. It is the twentieth-century horse—both companion and enabler. In the first stanza of his poem "Buick," Karl Shapiro captures the physical nature of this relationship.

> As a sloop with a sweep of immaculate wings on her delicate spine
> And a keel as steel as a root that holds in the sea as she leans,
> Leaning and laughing, my warmhearted beauty, you ride, you ride,
> You tack on the curves with parabola speed and a kiss of goodbye,
> Like a thoroughbred sloop, my new high-spirited spirit, my kiss.*

The freedom of the seas is transferred to land when one is behind the wheel of an automobile.

My friend Bill Brown recently visited the Ford Museum in Dearborn, Michigan, where amidst the collection, which includes favorite cars of ex-presidents, sits the vehicle in which President John F. Kennedy was assassinated. Identified only by a small sign, this is the automobile that the whole world watched, following the blur of Jackie's pink suit as she stretched across the back to help a Secret Service man into the car. At that point in our history as a nation, the ship of state was a black limousine, "a sloop with a sweep of immaculate wings," but now carrying a fatally wounded captain. My friend stood there in a confounding rush of memory and felt that old sorrow all over again. He walked away, turned a corner, and there it was—another part of himself from an even earlier time: a 1956 turquoise and ivory Chevy convertible, his first new car—the exact model, color, design. He stepped over the barrier, opened the car door whose handle felt so familiar in his hand, and remembered himself as he had been then. When he closed the door again, it thunked reassuringly.

As the twentieth century drives us forward to its finish, we realize that it is in the automobile graveyards that future archaeologists will find sociological, anthropological, psychological, and even theological evidence of our values, our vision, and our failures. What we drive, drives us.

What is it about the automobile that makes it such a peculiarly American symbol—even now when most of the world drives cars made in other countries? Brian Abel Ragen identifies the feeling of freedom that the automobile has encouraged, and links it with the myth of the American Adam, which has permeated our literature from Natty Bumppo to Huck Finn to Jay Gatsby. The American Adam always sets out for new territory without an Eve, without a

* Copyright 1941 by Karl Jay Shapiro, from *Poems 1940-1953* by Karl Shapiro. Random House.

God, with no obligations or responsibilities. This is, Ragen contends, a myth with which Flannery O'Connor's fiction is violently at odds. Hazel Motes's attempts to escape from Jesus are supported by his contention that "Nobody with a good car needs to be justified." But his car keeps stopping, often in front of those roadside signs advising immediate repentance.

The test of a sound thesis lies, I believe, in its applicability outside the boundaries of the work being analyzed. Professor Ragen's thesis—that O'Connor's heroes repeatedly encounter the impossibility of escape from God, even in their own automobiles—is also evident in recent novels by Michael Malone, Frederick Buechner, and Walker Percy, writers with profoundly sacramental and incarnational sensibilities. O'Connor, then, becomes one of the chief, though not the only purveyor of a tradition that began with Hawthorne and that runs counter to that of the American Adam. There is freedom for the heroes of these Christian novelists, but it is not the freedom of escape. The hound of heaven pursues and the freedom Hazel Motes has is to allow himself to be caught, to acknowledge his sinfulness, and to stand facing the scandal of the cross. In T. S. Eliot's "Journey of the Magi" one of the three kings asks if they were "led all that way for Birth or Death?" It is both a "hard and bitter" birth and an agonizing death they encounter. The Incarnation can be described only with such paradoxical statements and is, perhaps, a sign that discursive language can contain truth only by turning back on itself, and only by approaching truth indirectly through metaphor and through story.

In *A Wreck on the Road to Damascus*, Professor Ragen never loses sight of O'Connor's characters, her metaphors and her stories—a feat that is too rare in current literary criticism. Flannery O'Connor would have been pleased, I think, to discover that every now and then in academia appears an English teacher with clear vision and Worded words.

Jill P. Baumgaertner
Associate Professor of English
Wheaton College

# Preface

Whenever I wanted to escape my work in college, I would get into a beat-up '67 Valiant, and drive. I would start down Indian Hill Boulevard toward the decaying city of Pomona, turn right at Indian Hill Village, a half-abandoned shopping center, and head west, past used car lots, Freak's Head Shop, Big Momma's Bail Bonds, and the Central Baptist Church. I never felt freer than when making that drive for a midnight hamburger. I was in the driver's seat. I might be traveling through dangerous territory, but I could always keep the car moving and the windows rolled up. I was not entangled in any complicated human relationships while I was in the car. I was anonymous. Behind the tinted windows I could sing or scream or talk as I pleased. I could turn up the radio and drown the world out. I was free.

It was, of course, an illusion. The freedom for sale at the used car lots was as temporary as the liberation offered at Freak's and Big Momma's. And I was not really my own master even behind the wheel. The state had me tagged front and back. The red lights stopped me even on the empty streets. The car itself—the possession of my father's that I used most regularly after his death—tied me to the past. And the Valiant might have betrayed me on one of those midnight drives instead of waiting for a 90° afternoon halfway up route 101. But while I moved through the empty streets, I felt no constraints.

Those drives were my small participation in the old American dream of freedom and escape. The classics of our literature—and the songs I heard on the Valiant's AM radio—tell of many men who light out for nowhere in particular and escape all that ties them down. Like the frontiersman or the outlaw trucker, I was escaping all restrictions. I was enjoying, for a few minutes, a dream of freedom that I recognized, even then, as attractive, powerful, and profoundly false.

I often think of those midnight drives when reading Flannery O'Connor. In several works O'Connor uses the automobile to embody the idea of perfect freedom; the rush of liberty that even those of us who drive utilitarian cars and obey the speed limits can experience on an empty highway shows how appropriate that identification is. In O'Connor's stories—as in real life—the liberation a driver feels is all too temporary, but extremely powerful while it lasts. O'Connor uses the automobile as an emblem for the philosophies celebrating the individual's absolute freedom and autonomy that have dominated our culture during the last two centuries. She can do so because those ideas have often been associated with physical motion—and with automobiles—in American literature and popular culture and because, when we are behind the wheel and there is nothing to slow us down, they feel true.

When I began studying Flannery O'Connor, I was struck by her vivid images of beat-up cars, either traveling on into the sunset or wrecked beside a country road, for they seemed to be building on the celebration of the automobile in American culture while, at the same time, criticizing it. But it was clear to me that the car was not the main issue. As I studied the use of the image of physical motion in the American tradition, it became clear that O'Connor's real quarrel was with the myth of innocence and freedom that has so often appeared in American literature. O'Connor uses automobiles to attack other schools of thought that have celebrated absolute freedom in one form or another. Especially in *Wise Blood*, automobiles are linked with Existentialism, the philosophy that makes the isolated, anguished individual sovereign in an empty universe. But the myth of perfect freedom native to the American tradition was more important to O'Connor than its modern French counterpart.

Much American literature and popular culture is dominated by the figure of the solitary man, who is burdened by no past, forms no ties in the present, and is always able to create himself anew and assume a fresh identity. He enjoys this perfect freedom because he is not involved in any history—he gives himself his own name and remembers no parents. His triumph is to avoid the limits that might be imposed on his freedom by involvement in society or by entanglements with domesticating women. He begins his career in perfect innocence, and needs to atone for no sins—he has no more use for a savior than for a father or a wife, and runs from God as from women and the past. His perfect freedom is embodied in the image of physical movement—travel westward or out to sea or, in this century, down the highway in a beat-up car.

O'Connor is at odds with this tradition for several reasons, including its treatment of women as mere impediments to the hero's freedom. But she opposes the tradition primarily on theological grounds, for it denies all the Christian doctrines O'Connor believed in so fervently: Original Sin, Redemption, the Incarnation. The moving man admits no guilt, and accepts no savior. In accepting the illusory promise of perfect freedom, he refuses the real offer of redemption.

What makes O'Connor so fascinating is her ability to at once describe a recognizable world, attack a philosophical tradition, and make manifest the action of grace. Her stories work by fusing elements that seem very different—images from popular culture, echoes of biblical stories, and grotesque acts of violence. I began my study of O'Connor by examining the fusion of the image of the automobile with the story of St. Paul in *Wise Blood*. When Hazel Motes is behind the wheel, he feels all the liberation a car can offer, and his Essex embodies most clearly several traditions that celebrate perfect freedom and deny Original Sin and the need for a savior. Motes's car also takes its place in Motes's story of a latter-day Saul. When Motes attacks the church of Christ, the Essex is his pulpit. When he kills a man because he believes in Jesus, the car is the instrument of martyrdom. When he goes to persecute the church of Christ in a new city, the automobile is his vehicle. And when Motes is stopped on that journey, it is the destruction of his car that leads to his blindness and conversion. The moment when Motes sees his car wrecked is at once the completion of an attack on the philosophies that declare man utterly free, an echo of Paul's story, and an offer of grace to Motes.

In many essays and lectures, O'Connor describes how such disparate elements can be joined in a work of fiction, and my exploration of O'Connor's fusion of biblical stories and images from popular culture naturally led me to a study of her theory of fiction. O'Connor built her theory from elements taken from both the New Critics and medieval commentators on Scripture. What she found attractive in both schools of thought was the idea that a work can convey many meanings, including the most spiritual, by accurately describing the physical world.

The medieval exegetes claimed that many senses were contained in the literal level of the sacred text, and O'Connor claimed that this was also true of fiction. The elements in her stories that make them so strange and even shocking—the surprising echoes of biblical characters, the unexpected violence—are devices that guide the reader to those other senses. O'Connor's stories could be said to contain all the senses that the exegetes find in Scripture—there is no lack of allegorical or moral elements—but the sense she stressed most was the anagogical, the sense that describes "the divine life and our participation in it." In O'Connor's stories, the anagogical sense appears as an offer of grace to a character, a call to conversion, and those offers of grace are usually made violently. For O. E. Parker, the offer comes in a wrecked tractor and the vision of a burning tree; for Hazel Motes, it comes as the sight of a car smashed into many pieces. If the reader has his eyes open for the anagogical sense in O'Connor's stories, both these wrecks will appear not as accidents, but as epiphanies.

Underlying O'Connor's stories are the essential Christian doctrines—Original Sin, the need for a savior, the Savior's Incarnation. In my readings of "Parker's Back," "The Life You Save May Be Your Own," and *Wise Blood*, I try to show how those doctrines animate O'Connor's work. In all three of these stories, O'Connor shows men attracted by the dream of innocence and freedom—moving men who are on the run from women, responsibility, and God, who admit no guilt and accept no Redeemer. Motes and Parker—whose vehicles are wrecked—are converted. Motes stops professing his innocence, and begins practicing penances; the redemptive mystery of the Incarnation is enacted in Parker's own flesh. Mr. Shiftlet accepts no offer of grace and drives off into the West, protected from redemption by the dream of freedom offered by a car and an empty highway. In all three works, the character's reaction to the awful offer of grace is tightly bound up with O'Connor's exploration of Christian mysteries and her attack on recent intellectual movements. All are embodied in a visual image, often that of a beat-up car.

Although I began my study of O'Connor with *Wise Blood*, and it was her first book, I present my reading of that novel last. I hope that the exploration of O'Connor's theory in chapter one, and the study of O'Connor's place in the American tradition in chapter two, will be a good preparation for my reading of the novel. In my reading of "Parker's Back," I show how O'Connor uses typology, the echoes of Moses in Parker's conversion. In chapter two, I show some of the meanings automobiles have acquired in the American tradition and examine how O'Connor manipulates the image in "The Life You Save May Be Your Own." In the final chapter, I try to show how all the various elements—automobiles and typology—work together in the story of Hazel Motes, a St. Paul struck down from an Essex.

I have received a good deal of assistance in completing this book. I would like to thank Nancy Davis Bray of the Ina Dillard Russell Library at Georgia College, for her assistance when I was working with O'Connor's manuscripts, and Jeanette Ertel of Loyola University Press, for her editing of my manuscript. I am grateful to several scholars who were all generous in listening to my ideas and in sharing their learning with me, including Sally Fitzgerald, and Professors Horton Davies and Albert Raboteau of Princeton's Religion Department.

I would like to thank the members of Princeton's English Department who were willing to read my work, especially Professors A. Walton Litz and Thomas P. Roche, Jr., who together commented on every draft and put up with more discussions of automobiles and theology than anyone can be expected to undergo. Professors Willard Thorp, John Fleming, and Emory Elliott all read the manuscript, and provided helpful comments on my work. And I thank my friends who were willing to help me at various stages of this project, especially Beth Harrison, Steven Justice, Christine Krueger, Nancy Manning, Michelle Preston, Richard Preston, Nancy Ruff, and Scott Wayland.

I finished the first draft of this book only a few months before the death of my guardian, Professor Katherine Ragen of the History Department at San Diego State University. Katie, whose bedtime stories were often anecdotes from American history, was my first introduction to the study of American culture. I regret she did not live to see the publication of the work she encouraged in so many ways.

# A Wreck on the Road to Damascus

# Introduction

## An Incarnational Art

"... fiction is so very much an incarnational art."
—"The Nature and Aim of Fiction"

When Flannery O'Connor called fiction an incarnational art, she meant that in fiction every idea—even the most exalted and mysterious—must take a physical form. Her insistence that ideas must be embodied in things was not at all revolutionary for an author writing when the prestige of the New Criticism was at its height. What makes O'Connor's formulation of the critical doctrine so striking is the theological justification she finds for her position. For O'Connor, the writing of fiction, like everything else, is best understood in the light of the Incarnation. If the Word became flesh and dwelt among us, the material world, even at its humblest or most sordid, can be a sign of the Divine life. This is a blessing for the novelist, since his purpose is to describe faithfully the world as he sees it. Without transforming his stories into philosophical essays or theological treatises, the novelist can probe the same mysteries the philosophers and theologians explore.

While the Incarnation provides O'Connor with a justification for her technique, it also gives her her subject, for the mysteries that O'Connor shows embodied in the actions of her characters are those that grow out of the Incarnation. Her characters are often driven—even tormented—by the idea that they have been redeemed, that the Son of God became Man and died to take away their sins. Some of them, like Hazel Motes in *Wise Blood*, try to escape the terrifying promise of Salvation by denying that they need to be redeemed—by rejecting the doctrine of Original Sin. But whether they finally accept the promise of redemption, as Motes does, or reject it, as does Mr. Shiftlet in "The Life You Save May Be Your Own," they are confronted with an offer of grace from the Incarnate Savior.

When defending her conception of fiction as an incarnational art, O'Connor drew on authorities as diverse as Thomas Aquinas and Joseph Conrad. O'Connor wanted her fiction to at once do justice to visible reality—to the real South of beat-up cars and CCC snuff signs—and to reveal the motions of grace. What she found useful both in medieval commentators on Scripture and in the modern critics who built on James and Conrad was their emphasis that the deepest—or most spiritual—meanings are conveyed through concrete images. If the writer could accomplish Conrad's task and make the reader see, he might give the reader "a glimpse of the truth for which he had forgotten to ask."[1] For O'Connor, that truth would be one of the mysteries of the Christian faith. For fiction might share what Aquinas and Gregory the Great said was the peculiar excellence of Holy Scripture, "that while it describes a fact, it reveals a mystery."[2]

When describing her conception of fiction, O'Connor often uses the terminology that the medieval theologians developed to describe the different kinds of meaning they found in the literal level of Scripture. The concrete actions described in fiction can reveal a spiritual sense just as the historical actions in the biblical text do. (Like Aquinas, O'Connor emphasizes that the spiritual senses of a text are contained in its literal level, not separate from it.)  Of the different senses the medieval exegetes describe—the allegorical, the moral, the anagogical, and all their subdivisions—the one O'Connor most emphasizes is the anagogical. For the anagogical, which she defines as the sense of scripture which has "to do with the Divine life and our participation in it," can be considered the sense in which the faithful renderings of the visible universe that make up a piece of fiction give a glimpse of the mysterious workings of grace in the world.

What makes O'Connor's work so different from that of her contemporaries is her conscious attempt to reveal an anagogical sense, to show the intervention of grace in human lives. While in the medieval exegetes "anagogical" often refers to that which prefigures eternal glory in the life to come, in O'Connor the anagogical element is what shows the intervention of the Divine in this life. That intervention is often shown in the humblest sorts of people and the most grotesque situations, and it is revealed by the most physical acts. For in O'Connor's theology, as in her literary theory, what is highest and most mysterious works through what is most physical.

It is because they ignore the anagogical sense of her work that many of O'Connor's critics see her world as without love or devoid of goodness. O'Connor does describe a world full of sordidness and real evil—though no more sordid or evil than the world of the Old Testament prophets or of the Gospels. But the depravity and the violence in her work, like the marriage of Hosea to the harlot or the Crucifixion itself, reveal love and goodness of the most overwhelming kind, and perhaps of the kind modern critics are least ready to recognize—the love of God for unworthy men. Just that sort of love is what animates both "Parker's Back" and *Wise Blood*. Neither O. E. Parker nor Hazel Motes can finally escape Jesus. O'Connor shows God's love hounding both men despite all their efforts to ignore it. The reader who is not attentive to the signs of the anagogical action—or who is unwilling to suspend any disbelief in the action of grace—will miss the point. O'Connor does a great deal to make the anagogical sense plain, but the reader has to be willing to accept that even what seems most grotesque, even the most shocking act of violence, can bring an offer of God's love—and perhaps a great triumph. One must accept the unprovoked destruction of a car by a highway patrolman or a man's self-blinding, as one accepts the horrific tortures in saints' lives, as moments of glory.

Other critics misunderstand O'Connor's works because they treat them as simple allegories. O'Connor does use allegory, especially in the form of typology, the echoing of biblical figures, but she uses it, like the distortion of the grotesque, to guide the reader to the more important anagogical sense. Her characters never become simple signs for ideas or types of biblical figures. Instead, the allegorical element helps to show how the character "participates in the Divine life."[3] It is a signpost that marks the offer of grace, which is the central action of the story.

That offer of grace is often conveyed or received by a freakish character, and this presents one of the difficulties in reading O'Connor. She herself realized that it would be difficult to make some readers understand how she was using her freaks, "to get across to the modern reader that you take these people seriously, that you are not making fun of them, but that their concerns are your own and, in your judgment, central to human life." O'Connor uses her deformed and freakish characters, not primarily as images of privation, but as reminders of what a whole man is. O'Connor's conception of the whole man is grounded in the doctrines of the Creation, the Fall, the Incarnation, and the Redemption. Her characters must be understood, not simply as victims of this or that unfortunate mental or social condition, but as souls who share humanity's common dignity, suffer from its common calamity, and are faced with the same terrifying promise that is offered to all. They are made in the image and likeness of God, that image and likeness has been effaced by Original Sin, and the hope of being made whole again is offered through the Incarnate Savior. The freak is less able to ignore the message than the man who thinks he is undamaged and therefore never admits that his situation is ultimately as desperate as that of the man whose deformity is manifest. O'Connor uses the very things that mark her characters as freaks to show both what they lack and what will make them whole.

O'Connor at times describes her freakish characters as prophets and identifies their prophetic function with her own function as a novelist. Both the freakish character and the grotesque novelist can present a double message: They can both show us what we lack and what will make us whole, both describe our fallen condition and offer a savior. The prophetic messages that O'Connor's freakish characters bring grow out of the doctrine of the Incarnation, for that is the basis of the promise of help. O. E. Parker in his last tattoo reminds his wife that the word became flesh; the dying Hazel Motes turns Mrs. Flood's desires toward the star that heralded the Incarnation. One message is rejected, the other may be heard; in both, the good news of the Word become flesh is made manifest through bizarre and freakish acts.

O'Connor's freakish characters are marked as prophets by the typology that underlies her stories. The biblical echoes that inform their stories will not allow the reader to see characters like O. E. Parker and Hazel Motes simply as madmen. Parker goes to have Jesus tattooed on his back after receiving a call like that given to Moses. His reaction to the burning bush is not as grand as Moses's, but neither is it as mad as trying to oppose a mighty king. Hazel Motes's every attack on the Church of Christ is reminiscent of Saul of Tarsus, and his self-blinding makes sense only as the culmination of a story like Saint Paul's. The reader has to see Motes and Parker reacting to God's terrifying love, and the biblical echoes are what let him see it. Typology, O'Connor believed, allows the fiction writer to invest his story with a standard beyond the secular one.

> To be great storytellers, we need something to measure our-
> selves against, and this is what we conspicuously lack in this age.
> Men judge themselves now by what they find themselves doing.
> The Catholic has the natural law and the teaching of the Church
> to guide him, but for the writing of fiction, something more is nec-
> essary.
>
> For the purposes of fiction, these guides have to exist in con-
> crete form, known and held sacred by the whole community. . . .
> It takes a story to make a story. It takes a story of mythic dimen-
> sions, one which belongs to everybody, one in which everybody
> is able to recognize the hand of God and its descent. In the Prot-
> estant South, the scriptures fill this role.[4]

When the barefoot Parker sees the burning tree, when Hazel Motes
is stopped on his way to harry the Church in a new city, the reader
has to see the descent of the hand of God.

If men judge themselves today by anything beyond "what they
find themselves doing," it is often by the myth that dominates the
American literary tradition and American popular culture, and
O'Connor also uses biblical stories to attack that myth. Our tradition
celebrates a perfect freedom—a freedom so complete that the past is
unimportant and a fresh start is always possible, so complete that a
man need be bound by no ties or responsibilities, so complete that he
needs no savior. Critics have often recognized O'Connor's attacks
on existentialism. They have not paid so much attention to her
opposition to the myth of freedom native to our country. O'Connor,
I think, found Emerson a more dangerous influence than Sartre, and
while she occasionally attacks the modern European movement, the
old American tradition is her constant enemy.

O'Connor is at odds with this tradition for many reasons. Most
importantly, she attacks it because it denies the Christian doctrines
she considers vital: Original Sin, the Redemption, and the Incarnation. The mainstream of the American literary tradition grows out
of New England Unitarians and Transcendentalists. Its foundation
is the idea of Original Innocence: men today are not stained by
Adam's sin. There was no Fall and there is no Original Sin. The ever-
moving Adamic American hero becomes an image of this doctrine.
He bears no stain, for the past and his race's history have nothing to
do with him. Since man is unfallen, he needs no redeemer. There is
no place in this view of man for an Incarnate Savior. Indeed, the

freedom and self-sufficiency of each man is so perfect that he can ignore God almost entirely. For O'Connor, this celebration of the goodness of man is false from beginning to end, for man is fallen, in need of a savior, and saved.

Beyond her theological opposition to the American Adam tradition, O'Connor opposes it because it leaves hardly any more room for women than for God. The hero of our myth is always male. Women hardly have any role in his story. His biblical image seems to be Adam, not only before the Fall, but before the very creation of Eve. The only role women can play in this myth is that of entrapper and domesticator, the representative of the things that it is the glory of our hero to escape. Women represent the ties and responsibilities of society, and they represent history. If they become important to the story, the American myth is spoiled. The solitary male's freedom will be lost in the duties of marriage and family. And with procreation original innocence disappears, for new generations will be involved in their father's history. Our ever-moving hero can only use women or escape them. If they become too important, his story is over.

As both a woman and a Catholic, O'Connor opposes the Adamic American myth. She instead allies herself with the schools of American writing that oppose the mainstream of the New England tradition. She considered herself a disciple of Hawthorne, both because he wrote romances instead of novels and because he hated the Transcendentalists[5] and remembered the sins of the fathers. A grotesque writer whose subject is sin and guilt—and whose daughter became a nun and devoted herself to caring for real-life freaks at a cancer home—Hawthorne is as perfect a master for O'Connor as can be imagined. And in his work, alone among the classic American novels, a woman—a sexually mature woman—plays the central role. O'Connor also identified with the tradition of Southern writing, for other Southern writers of the first half of this century have as little patience for the myth of the innocent, ever-moving male as O'Connor does herself. In both Faulkner and Robert Penn Warren, O'Connor found characters who cannot escape the past or pretend that they are perfectly free and innocent, who remember the sins of their fathers. They cannot play the role of the American Adam, for there is no escape from the burden of the past and no perfectly fresh start.

O'Connor embodies the tradition she attacks—the myth of the innocent, ever-moving male—in the image of the automobile. The image is perfectly appropriate. Both in our literature and in popular culture, the celebration of movement, and of all that movement has represented, that proceeded on foot and by water in the nineteenth century now travels down the highway in a beat-up car. The old flight from women, society, and God—from the past, responsibility, and guilt—continues in thousands of stories and songs about driving down the highway. The solitary male is still moving on, still trying to create himself anew, escape entanglements with women, deny his past, and avoid facing God.

An automobile dominates O'Connor's own version of the American Adam. Her Adam is a charlatan—but then most of them are. Like many of his predecessors, Mr. Shiftlet in "The Life You Save May Be Your Own," constantly creates himself anew. He gives himself a name and a past as he needs it. The story describes his escape from the danger that always confronts the American Adam: a domesticating female. With little trouble, Mr. Shiftlet reasserts his mobility, and, having forsaken women and responsibilities for the open road, he follows the route of countless Americans playing the Adamic role, and heads west. In my reading of this story, I show both how O'Connor's despicable hero fits the paradigm of the American Adam, and how O'Connor attacks the myth.

*Wise Blood* is the story of another man who is trying to play the role of the innocent, ever-moving male. Hazel Motes very much wants to be the American Adam, and his desire grows out of the theology that first gave rise to the Adamic figure in our literature. Motes rejects the idea of Original Sin, because he is terrified by the prospect of having been redeemed by an Incarnate Savior. He preaches a doctrine of perfect freedom—freedom from the past, from sin, from the awful possibility of salvation—and he preaches it from atop an automobile. Again, the automobile and the mobility it brings embody a denial of Original Sin and a flight from women, from responsibility, and, most importantly, from God. But Motes is not in the end an American Adam figure like Mr. Shiftlet, because he cannot ignore the Divine love that so terrifies him, and because his running is stopped.

When Motes's car is destroyed on the road out of Taulkinham, and Motes goes back to town and blinds himself, the myth of the Adamic American is fused with a very different story. The running man who has been playing the unconverted Saul—attacking the Church not to uphold the old law but to defend his own perfect freedom—becomes the blinded and converted Paul. By joining the story of Paul's violent conversion on the road to Damascus with the image of the automobile, O'Connor at once attacks the philosophical schools she abhors and shows grace working in the life of her tormented character. Her use of typology makes it possible both to attack the myths of freedom embodied in the car, since they are what make Motes, like Saul, an enemy of Christ, and to show God's love even for His persecutor. If the destruction of Motes's car and his blindness are seen in the light of the blindness and conversion of Paul, they reveal an offer of grace. The biblical echoes in *Wise Blood* guide the reader to the anagogical sense that reveals a terrifying love even in a wrecked car and an act of self-mutilation.

In the appendix, "The *Wise Blood* Manuscripts." I point out how O'Connor's fusion of the story of Saint Paul and the image of the automobile emerges in the course of manuscripts of the novel. In the earlier drafts, there are no references to Paul and the automobile is unimportant. Haze, whose last name is not yet Motes, is troubled by the ideas of sin and cleanness, but he is not hounded by the fear that he has been redeemed. Asa Hawks, the blind prophet, is not a fraud, and there is no mention of self-blinding. Motes buys the Essex, but none of the passages in which he identifies the car with freedom and innocence are present. Between finishing a draft in 1949 and writing the final version of the novel, O'Connor read the Theban plays of Sophocles, and her novel snapped into focus. The Oedipus story gave her the idea of self-blinding, and in the juxtaposition of a false blind man and a true one, she found a way to show her hero assuming the role he had earlier rejected. In Saint Paul she found a model for an enemy of Christ who is dogged by redemption, and in his violent conversion a way of representing her hero's transformation. In the automobile she found an embodiment for the idea that man is so free that he needs no redeemer. The completed novel owes its power to the interplay of these disparate elements.[6]

In his self-blinding, Motes becomes a physically grotesque and freakish figure. All the same, during his last months as a blind and almost silent man practicing extreme penances, he acts as a prophet. Like O'Connor's other freaks, he conveys some hint of God's love to another person. In his death, Motes makes a sensible and selfish materialist, Mrs. Flood, want something beyond herself. At first the object of her desire is Motes himself, but after he is gone it becomes a point of light, like the star on a Christmas card. O'Connor can reveal an anagogical sense in the banal as well as in the violent, and in the end the dying Motes has led Mrs. Flood to begin to want

Christ's love—to want the grace brought by the Incarnation the star on the Christmas card announces.

In much American literature, men stand alone. They may find themselves enjoying solitude in a benevolent wilderness or fighting against a hostile society, but they enjoy the dignity, and suffer the terror, of perfect freedom. O'Connor's works allow no such isolation. Her characters often have to face the frightful idea that God loves them and will go out of his way to save them. Sometimes they even find themselves unwillingly bringing the news of God's inescapable love to others. In this work, I explore the techniques O'Connor uses to make that love manifest—to reveal the "participation in the Divine life" that is the anagogical sense. Using everything from echoes of biblical stories to descriptions of horrible acts of violence to force her reader to see the descent of the hand of God, O'Connor shows characters who cannot be perfectly alone or enjoy perfect freedom. At the same time, she attacks the dominant myths of our culture, myths that promise us absolute freedom: freedom from the past, from responsibility, and from the love of an Incarnate Savior.

# 1

## The Burning Bush and the Illustrated Man

Henry James said that Conrad in his fiction did things in the way that took the most doing. I think the writer of grotesque fiction does them in the way that takes the least, because in his work distances are so great. He's looking for one image that will connect or combine or embody two points; one is a point in the concrete, and the other is a point not visible to the naked eye, but believed in by him firmly, just as real to him, really, as the one that everybody sees.
— "The Grotesque in Southern Fiction"

When describing the writer of grotesque fiction, Flannery O'Connor devotes as much attention to his vision of reality as to his fictional technique. What separates the grotesque writer from other novelists is precisely his view of reality: "the realism of each novelist will depend on his view of the ultimate reaches of reality."[1] The writer who does not believe in anything beyond the physical world will try only to represent concrete reality; the writer who "believes that our life is and will remain essentially mysterious" will try to use his descriptions of the physical world to embody the mystery. He will distort concrete reality in order to present an image that will link the physical and the mysterious. In her story "Parker's Back,"[2] O'Connor finds such an image in a woman wounding her husband's tattooed flesh.

O'Connor is, of course, describing her own technique when she talks about the writer of the grotesque. Other writers of grotesque fiction may use distortion for different ends or use different means to guide the reader to the mystery beyond the concrete image. What makes O'Connor's work so unusual in modern American fiction is that she consciously uses the grotesque to write on what she called the anagogical level: her goal is to show the intervention of grace in human lives. Comparing "Parker's Back" with the story that probably gave O'Connor the germ for her tale of the woes of a tattooed man illuminates both O'Connor's own methods and the differences between her work and other kinds of grotesque writing.

Ray Bradbury's story "The Illustrated Man"[3] appeared in *Esquire* in 1950, more than ten years before O'Connor began work on "Parker's Back." O'Connor never mentions Bradbury's story in her published letters. She tells one correspondent that she is learning about tattooing from *Memoirs of a Tattooist,* a book she found in a Marboro sale catalog.[4] It seems almost certain, however, that O'Connor read "The Illustrated Man" and that it was the ultimate source for "Parker's Back." The parallels between the two stories are striking. Both stories describe men who have had themselves almost completely covered with tattoos; both turn on the quarrels between the tattooed man and his wife. In both, the wife wounds her husband's tattooed flesh, and at the end, the tattoo on the man's back is revealed. Tattoos are not unknown in American literature, but I can think of no other works dominated by the image of tattooed flesh being wounded in a domestic quarrel.[5]

Of course, the plots of the two stories are not very similar beyond these central events. Bradbury describes a carnival roustabout who, in his sorrow over the arguments that have dominated his short marriage, has taken to eating and put on a mass of fat. He is in danger of losing his job with the carnival, since he is no longer much good at tent work and the show has no need for another Fat Man. But the recent death of Gallery Smith has left one opening: the carnival needs a tattooed man. William Philippus Phelps goes off to have himself tattooed, but the artist who illustrates his flesh is no ordinary operator of some dockside tattoo parlor. Phelps's skin is decorated by a witch, whose eyes and ears are stitched shut and who already has a portrait of Phelps tattooed on her own palm. Besides the pictures that cover most of Phelps's body, she gives him two special tattoos, one on his chest and one on his back. She covers these with bandages, and tells Phelps that he must wait a week before uncovering his chest and another week before revealing his back. The special tattoo will show the future: "I put ink on your flesh and the sweat of you forms the rest of the picture, the Future—your sweat and your thought" (*Vintage Bradbury*, p. 256). Phelps returns to the carnival, only to hear his wife exclaim, "My God . . . My husband's a freak."

A large crowd is attracted to witness the unveiling of the "Mysterious Portrait upon the Illustrated Man's Chest." The audience is impressed by the intricate and vivid tattoos that are already visible, but when Phelps's chest is unveiled they are appalled, for on it there is a horribly real picture of the illustrated man killing his wife. Phelps's quarrels with his wife only become worse after the picture is revealed. Phelps tries to have it removed, but it is indelible. What is more, the carnival boss thinks that the image is too revolting to be shown, and only lets Phelps appear with it covered up. Hoping that the other special tattoo will be a better draw for the carnival, the boss looks under the bandage on Phelps's back, but he sees nothing. That night, while Phelps is trying once again to remove the tattoo, his wife returns and tells him that she is leaving him. Phelps tries to embrace her, but she responds violently. She beats and scratches her husband's chest until blood runs from the picture on his chest. When his wife screams, Phelps puts his fingers around her neck and cuts the shriek off.

The other carnival freaks have been attracted by the scream, but Phelps leaves his trailer calmly and walks past them. They soon discover the dead woman and, taking lanterns and tent stakes with them, begin to follow the tattooed man. Phelps does not want to escape, and they soon catch up with him and attack him with their tent stakes. The freaks roll Phelps onto his stomach and tear the bandage from his back. The illustration on Phelps's back shows "a crowd of freaks bending over a dying fat man on a dark and lonely road, looking at a tattoo on his back which illustrated a crowd of freaks bending over a dying fat man on a . . ." (*Vintage Bradbury*, p. 265). The horror of the tattoos is how they do show the future.

Bradbury's tale, with its witch and its magic tattoos, is fantasy. O'Connor in her version of the grotesque does not employ fantasy. There is no element of the magical—or even of the strictly miraculous—in her story of a tattooed man. That a man might, like O. E. Parker, have a Byzantine Christ tattooed on his back in order to please his hard-shell Protestant wife, and that his wife would then reject both him and the tattoo out of horror at his idolatry, is at least possible in a way that witches with eyelids sewn shut and prophetic tattoos that grow out of ink and sweat are not. But there are more significant differences between the two stories than that one is limited by physical possibilities and one is not. Bradbury and O'Connor make use of the grotesque image of an unhappy tattooed man for different ends.

Bradbury's story seems intended to produce a frisson of horror—and it does. The reader shares the freaks' shock at the image revealed on the fat man's back. But the story also captures the mingled feeling of wonder and terror that lingers around any circus or carnival. Carnivals are full of splendid things, but they are somehow hollow. They sometimes seem like a sham controlled by some unknown power—and not necessarily a benevolent power. In "The Illustrated Man," the splendid and terrifying atmosphere of the carnival is matched with the horrifying vision of a malevolent fate. Phelps's destiny is spelled out in his tattoos; there is nothing he can do about it, any more than he can remove the horrible image the witch has left on his chest. That Phelps may be in part the creator of his destiny only makes the final images more terrible. How awful, not only to have your thought form pictures on your skin, but to see in the pictures the violence you want to deny! It is as if Dorian Gray's picture were emblazoned on his flesh instead of hidden in his attic. In the end "The Illustrated Man" captures the horrible feeling of emptiness that lies beneath the pleasure at most carnivals. Behind the amazing images and the scraps of mystery, there may be nothing—or something real and horrible.

Flannery O'Connor could also make use of a carnival scene, and she could show the feeling of emptiness that the sideshow can produce. But O'Connor uses the carnival to reveal a depth even greater than what is seen from day to day. A visit to a carnival tent— and the strange feeling it leaves him with—leads Hazel Motes face-to-face with Original Sin. A story about a sideshow freak leads the little girl in "A Temple of the Holy Ghost" to the mysteries of Providence and purity. In "Parker's Back," the fourteen-year-old O. E. Parker first begins to feel a hint of wonder when he sees an illustrated man at a fair. But Parker himself is not a sideshow freak. And O'Connor is trying to do more with her version of the tattooed man than to capture the hint of terror in a carnival. She is trying to embody the mystery of the Incarnation in the tattoo on a man's back.

O'Connor believed that a writer needs to have the sort of vision that can connect things as seemingly remote from each other as a tattooed man and the mysteries of the Christian faith. When she describes this vision, which is certainly the vision she hoped would illuminate her own works, O'Connor often uses the term "anagogical." Her model for the writer of fiction is the medieval reader of scripture:

> The kind of vision the fiction writer needs to have, or to develop, in order to increase the meaning of his story is called anagogical vision, and that is the kind of vision that is able to see different levels of reality in one image or one situation. The medieval commentators on Scripture found three kinds of meaning in the literal level of the sacred text: one they called allegorical, in which one fact pointed to another; one they called tropological, or moral, which had to do with what should be done; and one they called anagogical, which had to do with the Divine life and our participation in it. Although this was a method applied to biblical exegesis, it was also an attitude toward all of creation, and a way of reading nature which included most possibilities, and I think it is this enlarged view of the human scene that the fiction writer has to cultivate. . . . ("The Nature and Aim of Fiction," *Mystery and Manners*, p. 72)

It is significant that O'Connor takes the ideal of the four senses of scripture not only as a model for her method—as did earlier writers, like Dante and Spenser—but as the view of all creation that opens to the writer the most possibilities.

O'Connor takes her description of the four senses of scripture from Aquinas. As the many references to Saint Thomas and Thomism in her letters show, O'Connor not only found Aquinas one of the most attractive saints but also discovered that his thought, especially as expounded by Etienne Gilson and Jacques Maritain, provided her with a basis for defending or explaining her work. [6] What O'Connor would have found useful for a fiction writer in Aquinas's description of the four senses of scripture is his emphasis that the spiritual senses are contained in the literal. Any spiritual sense "is based on the literal, and presupposes it." [7] While most writers who discuss the four senses (or levels) of interpretation acknowledge the primacy of the literal, some make the four senses seem almost equal. [8] Thomas's justification of the multiple senses of scripture can be easily adapted into a description of how the writer of fiction can join two realms of experience in a single image. Aquinas explains that the sacred text can coherently and without confusion or contradiction bear more than one meaning because God, who inspires the text, is not limited to words for signifiers. The things the words describe are also God's creation—Genesis would give ample justification even for saying that they are also his utterance—and therefore He can use the things signified, as well as the words themselves, to convey His meaning. "That signification whereby things signified by words have themselves also a signification is called the spiritual sense." God could so arrange the world, and the history of his chosen people, that a literal description of them would also reveal spiritual meanings.  In his more limited sphere, the author can so arrange the things he describes and the events he narrates that they lead the reader to a recognition of some spiritual meaning.[9]

Aquinas's description of the spiritual sense being conveyed more by the thing than by the word lends support to some of O'Connor's other beliefs about the nature of fiction.  Both the critical traditon in which O'Connor was educated and the theology she tried to embody in her fiction emphasize that meaning comes from the thing as well as from the word.  When explaining or defending her fiction, O'Connor invokes both literary theories taken from Conrad or the New Critics and the sacramental theology of the Catholic Church. O'Connor knew quite well that in writing fiction she was using a form that had been molded by her predecessors.  As the New Critics had taught her, one of the things that made the modern novel different from its ancestors was that the author had stopped entering his fiction to guide the reader to its significance.  Instead, he began to let the story's significance be conveyed by the things he describes.

> [A]llong about the time of Henry James, the author began to tell his story in a different way.  He began to let it come through the minds and eyes of the characters themselves, and he sat behind the scenes, apparently disinterested.  By the time we get to James Joyce, the author is nowhere to be found in the book.  The reader is on his own, floundering around in the thoughts of various unsavory characters.  He finds himself in the middle of a world apparently without comment.
>
> But it is from the kind  of world the writer creates, from the kind of character and detail he invests it with, that a reader can find the intellectual meaning of a book.  ("The Nature and Aim of Fiction," *Mystery and Manners,* pp. 74–75)

That the author conveys his meaning through concrete images became the basis of much of O'Connor's commentary on fiction. Like Conrad, Ford, and their successors, she demanded that things be shown, not told; rendered, not reported. What a fiction writer had to have, according to O'Connor, was the ability to make what he describes visible to the senses.

The writer O'Connor most often invokes to support her view of fiction is Joseph Conrad. In both her letters and her lectures, she often quotes Conrad's description of art from the Preface to *The Nigger of the "Narcissus"*: "art itself may be defined as a single-minded attempt to render the highest kind of justice to the visible universe."[10] The idea of rendering justice to the physical universe supports O'Connor in the belief that in fiction—at least in fiction after Henry James—as much as possible must be shown, rather than told; rendered, rather than reported.

This emphasis on showing over telling was, of course, the reigning dogma when O'Connor began to write. The assertion, growing out of James and Conrad, that "The novelist was not to 'tell the reader' about what happened but to *render* it in action"[11] had become an accepted truth. But it was a belief O'Connor made her own. She often describes how the novelist must make everything in his work appeal to the senses.

> No reader who doesn't actually experience, who isn't made to feel, the story is going to believe anything the fiction writer merely tells him. The first and most obvious characteristic of fiction is that it deals with reality through what can be seen, heard, smelt, tasted, and touched. ("Writing Short Stories," *Mystery and Manners*, p. 91)

And when she laments that a novel whose title has piqued her interest has turned out not to be very good, she says, "dear Lord, it's all reported" (*The Habit of Being*, p. 128). There is little more to say about a book that claims to be fiction.

But O'Connor takes more from Conrad than the importance of showing rather than telling. She also invokes Conrad when arguing that by doing justice to the visible world the fiction writer can also give his readers evidence of things not seen. When she quotes Conrad's famous description of his aim in writing—"My task . . . is, before all, to make you *see*"— O'Connor explains that in rendering the visible, Conrad was also presenting something beyond it:

> Conrad said that his aim as a fiction writer was to render the highest possible justice to the visible universe. That sounds very grand, but it is really very humble. It means that he subjected himself at all times to the limitations that reality imposed, but that

reality for him was not simply coextensive with the visible. He was interested in rendering justice to the visible universe because it suggested an invisible one... ("The Nature and Aim of Fiction," *Mystery and Manners*, p. 80)

O'Connor remembers that Conrad promises his readers a great deal if he can accomplish the task of making them see:

If I succeed, you shall find there, according to your deserts: encouragement, consolation, fear, charm—all you demand—and, perhaps, also that glimpse of truth for which you have forgotten to ask.[12]

When O'Connor claims that the purpose of fiction is to embody a mystery in a physical image, she is not going much farther than Conrad himself. Conrad says the artist's task is to make the reader see, but that by doing so "he speaks to our capacity to delight and wonder, to the sense of mystery surrounding our lives."[13] O'Connor understood every sense of the word "mystery," but the religious was always primary. By making the reader see the visible world, she hoped to give him some sense of the mysteries of the Christian faith.

O'Connor found a good deal of support for her enterprise in the theology of the Church. As Aquinas's description of the various senses of scripture shows, the Catholic tradition gives ample support to the position that ideas can be conveyed by things as well as words. O'Connor drew on both this long tradition in Catholic thought and the fairly recent critical preference for showing over telling when defending her methods.

Saint Augustine wrote that the things of the world pour forth from God in a double way: intellectually into the minds of the angels and physically into the world of things. To the person who believes this—as the western world did up until a few centuries ago—this physical, sensible world is good because it proceeds from a divine source. The artist usually knows this by instinct; his senses, which are used to penetrate the concrete, tell him so. When Conrad said that his aim as an artist was to render the highest possible justice to the visible universe, he was speaking with the novelist's surest instinct. The artist penetrates the concrete world in order to find at its depths the image of its source, the image of ultimate reality. ("Novelist and Believer," *Mystery and Manners*, p. 157)[14]

The world is good and worth showing.[15]   Moreover, the things of the world point to something.  Fidelity to visual detail can lead beyond the surface to some truth about the creator of all things visible and invisible.

The belief that creation is good leads to the idea that there is no radical separation between the physical and the spiritual. The flesh is not evil, nor is the spirit always good. Both are good and both can be corrupted. O'Connor sees the separation of matter and spirit not only as a heresy but also as an obstacle to the writing of fiction.

> The Manicheans separated spirit and matter.  To them all material things were evil.  They sought pure spirit and tried to approach the infinite directly without any mediation of matter. This is also pretty much the modern spirit, and for the sensibility infected with it, fiction is hard if not impossible to write because fiction is so very much an incarnational art. ("The Nature and Aim of Fiction," *Mystery and Manners*, p. 68)

The writer's use of material things to represent spiritual truths is justified by more than the goodness of all things formed by the hand of a benevolent creator. Christian writers will also believe that God Himself entered the material world, and by suffering in the flesh saved His people. As O'Connor points out, a belief in Christ's Incarnation must affect the artist who works by representing the physical world.

> Whatever the novelist sees in the way of truth must first take on the form of his art and must become embodied in the concrete and human. If you shy away from sense experience, you will not be able to read fiction; but you will not be able to apprehend anything else in this world either, because every mystery that reaches the human mind, except in the final stages of contemplative prayer, does so by way of the senses. Christ didn't redeem us by a direct intellectual act, but became incarnate in human form, and he speaks to us now through the mediation of a visible Church. All this may seem a long way from the subject of fiction, but it is not, for the main concern of the fiction writer is with mystery as it is incarnated in human life. ("Catholic Novelists and Their Readers," *Mystery and Manners*, pp. 175–76)

The Incarnation gives the fiction writer a theological basis for presenting his deepest meanings through physical images. Christ

Himself redeemed the world through His physical body, and that body is now glorified with Him. There is therefore no radical division between the things of this world and the spiritual realm. Rather the world of things can reveal the most profound mysteries. The novelist can take God's entry into the material world as a warrant for using things to embody spiritual truths and physical human actions to reveal the actions of the Spirit.

O'Connor also argued that the Catholic novelist would find support for his art in the sacramental theology of the Church. The Church teaches that Christ's involvement with the physical world did not end when He saved mankind through His Incarnation in a material body. He still touches His people's lives through material signs. Most importantly, he is really present in the Eucharist. The physical bread becomes Christ's body, and the material act of eating becomes a channel of grace. The other sacraments are also physical acts that bring grace. A sacrament is "an outward sign of inward grace," but the sign is always physical—bread and wine or water or oil or some human act. O'Connor saw this theology as a help to the novelist, since it reminds him that the most important events must be represented physically.

> [T]he real novelist, the one with an instinct for what he is about, knows that he cannot approach the infinite directly, that he must penetrate the natural human world as it is. The more sacramental his theology, the more encouragement he will get from it to do just that. ("Novelist and Believer," *Mystery and Manners*, p. 163)

O'Connor would not accept the charge that the Church limits the writer; rather she asserted that the

> Catholic sacramental view of life is one that sustains and supports at every turn the vision that the storyteller must have if he is going to write fiction of any depth. ("The Church and the Fiction Writer," *Mystery and Manners*, p. 152)

In other words, the sacramental theology of the church encourages the writer to see with an anagogical vision, since it finds in physical things signs for our participation in the Divine life. The Church's teaching makes it easier for the novelist to write fiction that does justice to both the surface of reality and whatever lies beyond.

Although O'Connor's defenses of fiction draw largely on Catholic theology, to some extent her arguments could be applied to stories that are not written from a Christian perspective. Any fiction that uses the world of things to reveal hidden truths might be said to be written with an anagogical vision. One might say that Hermann Hesse, for example, writes anagogical fiction from a Buddhist perspective. The things of this world lead the reader to a vision of a higher reality that makes the visible seem like an empty sham. A reader taking O'Connor's view might argue that such a vision is not as well adapted to fiction as is the Christian vision that can invest the world with an importance derived from the Incarnation and the sacraments. But fiction such as Hesse's is shaped by a vision that uses physical things to lead to spiritual truths, and therefore might be called anagogical.

While O'Connor sometimes speaks of the fiction writer's vision as anagogical, at times she even goes so far as to call it prophetic, and thus to make a talent for creating stories almost a spiritual gift.[16]

> The fiction writer should be characterized by his kind of vision. His kind of vision is prophetic vision. Prophecy, which is dependent on the imaginative and not the moral faculty, need not be a matter of predicting the future. The prophet is a realist of distances, and it is this kind of realism that goes into great novels. It is the realism which does not hesitate to distort appearances in order to show a hidden truth. ("Catholic Novelists and Their Readers," *Mystery and Manners*, p. 179)

Here O'Connor makes fiction a form of prophecy, and hence closely akin to scripture. Even if there were no justification for reading the whole world as one reads scripture, one might all the same be justified in seeking an anagogical sense in fiction, since it is in some way informed by the same vision as the sacred text. O'Connor describes the prophetic vision as one that joins the two qualities she demands of fiction: realism and a willingness to distort in order to reveal the hidden truth. The prophets of the Old Testament are certainly capable of telling stories that are at once true to the visible world, grotesque in their distortion, and rich in spiritual meanings. Hosea, for instance, describes the prophet's marrying a harlot at the Lord's command and then remaining true to her despite her continual returns to her sinful life. It is a story seamy enough to be one of O'Connor's own. But in it the marriage of harlotry is a sign of something that cannot be shown directly: God's unfailing love for his sinful people. The image of a marriage to a whore contains the anagogical sense of God's love for each sinner.

In her own fiction, O'Connor seeks to find an action or gesture that will reveal spiritual senses in just the way that Hosea's fidelity to the harlot Gomer does.

> I often ask myself what makes a story work, and what makes it hold up as a story, and I have decided that it is probably some action, some gesture of a character that is unlike any other in the story, one which indicates where the real heart of the story lies. This would have to be an action or gesture which was both totally right and totally unexpected; it would have to be one that was both in character and beyond character; it would have to suggest both the world and eternity. The action or gesture I'm talking about would have to be on the anagogical level, that is, the level which has to do with the Divine life and our participation in it. It would be a gesture that transcended any neat allegory that might be intended or any pat moral categories a reader could make. It would be a gesture which somehow made contact with mystery. ("On Her Own Work," *Mystery and Manners,* p. 111)

To fulfill all these requirements, O'Connor has to find an action that is at once appropriate on the most literal level—for she must do justice to the visible world—and also suggestive of something beyond. And she does find such gestures. It is both right and unexpected that the grandmother in "A Good Man Is Hard to Find" recognizes the man who is about to murder her as one of her own babies. It is both shocking and predictable that Hazel Motes blinds himself after he loses his car. And both actions do lead to some spiritual truth.

They do so, however, through the psychology of the characters who perform them, and for this reason they are not so easy to interpret as the actions of a figure who is simply allegorical. O'Connor does use symbolism and allegories of various kinds, but she does not allow the reader to rest after he has perceived their significance. Rather, she uses the allegorical element to illuminate the offer of grace made to her character. The actions on which her stories turn transcend any neat allegory because the allegory only points toward the real mystery that is being revealed anagogically. For instance, some of O'Connor's characters are identified with biblical characters, but perceiving the parallels only begins to show what is happening. While in a writer like Spenser one can perhaps be satisfied after perceiving that Red Cross Knight's three days of fighting with the dragon is like Christ's struggle with Death during His three days in the tomb, in an O'Connor story seeing the parallels between a character like O. E. Parker and Moses or Francis Marion Tarwater and Jonah only begins to illuminate the offer of grace being made to each character, and the character's response to that offer.

O'Connor realized that the very distortion that enabled her to guide her readers to the anagogical sense of her stories might predispose them not to look for it.

> When you write about backwoods prophets, it is very difficult to get across to the modern reader that you take these people seriously, that you are not making fun of them, but that their concerns are your own and, in your judgment, central to human life. It is almost inconceivable to this reader that such could be the case. It is hard enough for him to suspend his disbelief and accept an anagogical level of action at all, harder still for him to accept its action in an obviously grotesque character. He has the mistaken notion that a concern with grace is a concern with exalted human behaviour, that it is a pretentious concern. It is, however, simply a concern with the human reaction to that which, instant by instant, gives life to the soul. It is a concern with a realization that breeds charity and with the charity that breeds action. Often the nature of grace can be made plain only by describing its absence. ("The Catholic Novelist in the Protestant South," *Mystery and Manners*, p. 204)

In "Parker's Back," the main character is a freak—a tattooed man with Elizabeth II and Prince Philip over his stomach and liver, and Jesus on his back. He has made himself into a grotesque, but not a grotesque that is unimaginable. The real world includes many men who have their bodies covered with incongruous images. But Parker's freakishness points toward something more important. In the course of the story, the tattoos that make him a freak become the sign of something more important. They come to embody the action of grace in his soul and the redeemer who offers that grace. To understand O'Connor, the reader has to accept the freak as the representative of every soul.

For O'Connor, the freak is the image of both the author and the reader—and of all human beings. The freak in his distortion is able to reveal what ordinary people carefully hide. The wounds and needs manifest in the freak will point up the deficiencies carefully hidden by most ordinary people. The freak's very distortions allow the author to present some image of the whole person.

> A sense of loss is natural to us, and it is only in these centuries when we are afflicted with the doctrine of the perfectibility of human nature by its own efforts that the vision of the freak in fiction is so disturbing. The freak in modern fiction is usually disturbing to us because he keeps us from forgetting that we share his state. The only time he should be disturbing to us is when he is held up as a whole man. ("The Teaching of Literature," *Mystery and Manners*, p. 133)

One of the reasons O'Connor was happy to be a Southern writer was that she believed that in the South there was still some conception of the whole man. That conception, like her own, was theological.

> To be able to recognize a freak, you have to have some conception of the whole man, and in the South the general conception of man is still, in the main, theological.... I think it is safe to say that while the South is hardly Christ-centered it is most certainly Christ-haunted. The Southerner who isn't convinced of it, is very much afraid that he may have been made in the image and likeness of God. ("The Grotesque in Southern Fiction," *Mystery and Manners*, pp. 44–45)

The whole person is recognizable by the image and likeness of God. All people are freaks because that image is clouded first by Original Sin and then by each person's own sins. The grotesque character by his manifest deformities recalls each person's unfinished state.

O'Connor feared a South in which the vision of the whole which made possible the grotesque would have disappeared.

> I hate to think that in twenty years Southern writers too may be writing about men in gray-flannel suits and may have lost their ability to see that these gentlemen are even greater freaks than what we are writing about now. ("The Grotesque in Southern Fiction," *Mystery and Manners*, p. 50)

The obvious freak serves a prophetic function. He reminds those who would like to think they are whole that in fact they lack something vital. An author needs just such figures in order to speak to a generation that takes itself as the measure of all things and has lost the balance provided by some transcendental value.

> The novelist can no longer reflect a balance from the world he sees

around him; instead he has to create one .... When such a writer
has a freak for his hero, he is not simply showing us what we are,
but what we have been and what we could become. The prophet-
freak is an image of himself. ("On Her Own Work," *Mystery and
Manners*, pp. 117–18)

The author of grotesque fiction, like the freak, reminds the reader of
his incomplete state. If he writes anagogically, he may even bring
him some hint of the mysteries that would make him whole.[17]

O'Connor certainly believed that people who seem freakish in
real life may bring others a hint of those mysteries. In her introduction to *A Memoir of Mary Ann*, a book the sisters at the Dominican
Cancer Home in Atlanta wrote about a child who had been under
their care from the age of three until her death at twelve, she deals
with the possibilities presented by just such a real-life freak. The
child was born with a tumor on the side of her face, and one eye had
to be removed. She was in some ways "plainly grotesque." Yet she
seems to have had a wonderful effect on those around her. In her
letters about the sisters' project, and in the introduction itself,
O'Connor shows that despite her initial unwillingness to help a
group of nuns tell the story of a pious child, she came to see in Mary
Ann's story something like what she tried to embody in her fiction.
After she had completed her introduction, she saw it as a key to her
work:

> In the future, anybody who writes anything about me is going to
> have to read everything I have written in order to make legitimate
> criticism, even and particularly the Mary Ann piece. (Letter to
> "A," June 10, 1961, *The Habit of Being*, p. 442)

O'Connor makes this comment while explaining why she did not
want to write an extended introduction to the new edition of *Wise
Blood*. Evidently she thought her piece on Mary Ann illuminated all
her work, even the very earliest.

In the introduction to *A Memoir of Mary Ann*, O'Connor describes one of the sisters asking her why she writes about grotesque
characters, "why the grotesque (of all things) was my vocation."
Another guest tells the sister, "It's your vocation too." O'Connor
goes on to describe how this linking of her grotesque characters and
the maimed humans the Dominicans care for shaped her thinking
about the grotesque.

This opened up for me also a new perspective on the grotesque. Most of us have learned to be dispassionate about evil, to
look it in the face and find, as often as not, our own grinning
reflections with which we do not argue, but good is another
matter. Few have stared at that long enough to accept the fact that
its face too is grotesque, that in us the good is something under
construction. The modes of evil usually receive worthy expression. The modes of good have to be satisfied with a cliché or a
smoothing-down that will soften their real look. When we look
into the face of good, we are liable to see a face like Mary Ann's,
full of promise. ("Introduction to *A Memoir of Mary Ann,*" *Mystery
and Manners,* p. 226.)

In O'Connor's grotesque characters—in the Misfit, in Tarwater, in
Hazel Motes, and in O. E. Parker—O'Connor shows the twisted face
of good under construction.

In *Wise Blood,* O'Connor describes the heavens over Taulkinham
as a "black sky . . . underpinned with long silver streaks that looked
like scaffolding and depth on depth behind it were thousands of
stars that all seemed to be moving very slowly as if they were about
some vast construction work that involved the whole order of the
universe and would take all time to complete" (*Wise Blood,* p. 37). No
one in Taulkinham is looking at the sky, but in both *Wise Blood* and
the introduction to *A Memoir of Mary Ann* , the idea of the universe
and of the human as a construction project implies that each is directed toward some end. O'Connor will never accept that the world
is chaotic; despite the seeming disorder, the project is moving toward some fulfillment.

The acts on which O'Connor's works turn, the gestures that
reveal the anagogical sense, show good growing in some terrible
form. When the grandmother calls the Misfit one of her children,
when Hazel Motes begins practicing penances, when Tarwater
baptizes the child he is drowning, good is under construction. The
same building project is underway when O. E. Parker has Jesus
tattooed on his back.

In "Parker's Back" the things that come to reveal the growing good
in Parker are the very things that make him seem freakish: the tattoos
that cover most of his body. Parker's tattoos are all tacky enough to
be true to life. His tattoos are not in any way magical, like the ones

that illustrate William Phillipus Phelps. Parker has had himself decorated with an eagle perched on a cannon, his mother's name, portraits of the Royal Family and other things that manage only to be mundane in their attempt to be grand and beautiful. But the tattoos soon come to embody a great deal. The decorations on his flesh come to stand for Parker's soul.

Simply on the level of character, tattoos are what first bring Parker to the dim realization that there is something more in life than the ordinary. The sight of the tattooed man at the fair awakens in Parker an aesthetic longing that prepares the way for his spiritual transformation. The vision of the rich arabesque of colors on the tattooed man's skin plays much the same role in Parker's life that the discovery of the Norse myths played in the young C. S. Lewis's: they awake a longing that does not find its goal until, after years of resistance, a reluctant convert accepts Christ.[18]   In the sideshow tent, Parker is surprised by joy.

The tattooed man, as Parker sees him, is a wonder.

> Except for his loins, which were girded with a panther hide, the man's skin was patterned in what seemed from Parker's distance—he was near the back of the tent, standing on a bench—a single intricate design of brilliant color. The man, who was small and sturdy, moved about on the platform, flexing his muscles so that the arabesque of men and beasts and flowers on his skin appeared to have a subtle motion of its own. Parker was filled with emotion, lifted up as some people are when the flag passes. He was a boy whose mouth habitually hung open. He was heavy and earnest, as ordinary as a loaf of bread. When the show was over, he had remained standing on the bench, staring where the tattooed man had been, until the tent was almost empty. (*Complete Stories*, pp. 512-13)

The sideshow freak brings Parker the realization that there is something missing in his life. The boy who is as ordinary as a loaf of bread begins to see that there is something more than the ordinary. And Catholics of course believe that a loaf of bread can be transformed in the Eucharist into something a great deal more than the ordinary.[19]

The tattooed man gives Parker the first hint that he can be—that in fact he already is—something more than the ordinary.

> Parker had never before felt the least motion of wonder in

himself. Until he saw the man at the fair, it did not enter his head that there was anything out of the ordinary about the fact that he existed. Even then it did not enter his head, but a peculiar unease settled in him. It was as if a blind boy had been turned so gently in a different direction that he did not know his destination had been changed. (P. 513)

Parker's unease grows out of two perceptions. The first is that there is something wonderful about his very existence; the second is that there is some more wondrous thing that he can just sense but has not grasped. In the wonder he feels at the tattooed man, Parker begins to sense both the glory of being made in the image of God—of being a whole man—and the burden of bearing that image in a form that is twisted and defaced. Parker does not realize why he feels either the wonder or the attendant unease, but he soon begins trying to capture the wonder he has begun to feel by having himself tattooed.

When Parker gets his first tattoo, "it hurt very little, just enough to make it appear to Parker worth doing." Parker's reaction to the pain is the beginning of another transformation. Up to this point, "he had thought that only what did not hurt was worth doing" (p. 513). With the new sense of wonder, Parker is also gaining a new attitude toward suffering. When he finally reaches the goal to which his vague longings are leading him, he finds himself suffering more severe pains and mysteriously participating in the greatest sufferings.

But when he is getting his first tattoos he does not know that his longing is leading him anywhere. Like the blind boy, he does not realize that his direction has been changed. The idea that his longing has anything to do with Jesus certainly never enters his head. When his mother, who weeps over what is becoming of her son—a son who is drinking and fighting and getting himself covered with tattoos—tries to take him to a revival meeting, Parker runs away, lies about his age, and joins the navy. The navy is more than an escape from his mother; it also gives him an opportunity to acquire exotic tattoos from around the world.

The tattoos are Parker's reaction to the "peculiar unease" that has settled on him, but they only provide a temporary relief from it.

Parker would be satisfied with each tattoo about a month, then something about it that had attracted him would wear off. Whenever a decent-sized mirror was available, he would get in front of it and study his overall look. The effect was not of one intricate arabesque of colors but of something haphazard and botched. A huge dissatisfaction would come over him and he would go off and find another tattooist and have another space filled up. The front of Parker was almost completely covered but there were no tattoos on his back. He had no desire for one anywhere he could not readily see it himself. As the space on the front of him for tattoos decreased, his dissatisfaction grew and became general. (P. 514)

Parker's longing cannot be satisfied by tattoos, and as it becomes harder for him to gain even the temporary relief given by each new one, he becomes more and more uneasy. He does not lose his feeling of dissatisfaction until he finds a different goal for his longing.

After five years in the navy, Parker goes AWOL. O'Connor describes the rage that drives him to jump ship in terms of his tattoos:

His dissatisfaction, from being chronic and latent, had suddenly become acute and raged in him. It was as if the panther and the lion and the serpents and the eagles and the hawks had penetrated his skin and lived inside him in a raging warfare. (P. 514)

With similes like this one, O'Connor begins to make the tattoos the sign of Parker's inward life. They become more than the expression of the longing that animates Parker's soul; they become the symbol of his soul itself.[20]

In "The Illustrated Man," Bradbury uses the tattoos that cover Phelps as signs of his interior life. The roses on Phelps's hands bloom and wither with his changing emotions, and, what is more, the magic tattoos that develop on his chest and back may reveal the feelings that he will not even admit to himself. O'Connor's symbolic use of the tattoos begins in this way, with the tattoos as the expression of Parker's longing. One might even say that in choosing living images instead of inanimate ones—and then often beasts of prey—Parker is also expressing his rage. But O'Connor's use of the tattoos goes beyond this. The tattoos become the sign of more than Parker's feelings. By the end of the story, the botched tattoos that cover Parker come to stand not only for his soul, but for a soul transformed by grace.

Parker's tattoos can come to embody so much because O'Connor weaves through her story reminders of biblical stories that help

make the meaning of Parker's actions manifest. O'Connor thought
that living in the South gave the Catholic writer several advantages.
One of these was that while

> [i]t becomes more and more difficult in America to make belief
> believable . . . the Southern writer has the greatest possible advan-
> tage. He lives in the Bible Belt. ("The Catholic Novelist in the
> Protestant South," *Mystery and Manners*, p. 201)

With that region for his subject, the novelist can convincingly present believers as diverse as Sarah Ruth Cates, Old Tarwater, and the
rest of O'Connor's bizarre Christians.

But O'Connor thought the South offered another advantage:
Southerners still remember the Bible. While the Catholic imagination had been too little nourished by the concrete images of faith the
Bible presents, the South is still full of people whose faith is based
solely on the Bible.

> To be great storytellers, we need something to measure our-
> selves against, and this is what we conspicuously lack in this age.
> Men judge themselves now by what they find themselves doing.
> The Catholic has the natural law and the teaching of the Church
> to guide him, but for the writing of fiction, something more is
> necessary.
> For the purposes of fiction, these guides have to exist in con-
> crete form, known and held sacred by the whole community.
> They have to exist in the form of stories which affect our image of
> ourselves. Abstractions, formulas, laws will not serve here. We
> have to have stories in our background. It takes a story to make
> a story. It takes a story of mythic dimensions, one which belongs
> to everybody, one in which everybody is able to recognize the
> hand of God and its descent. In the Protestant South, the scrip-
> tures fill this role. ("The Catholic Novelist in the Protestant
> South," *Mystery and Manners*, p. 202)

The guides that help the reader see what is happening in "Parker's
Back" are the stories of Moses and the Burning Bush and of Jonah, the
reluctant prophet.

After Parker has filled the front of his body with tattoos, his
dissatisfaction begins to grow again. He has by this time married
Sarah Ruth Cates, a strict Protestant with no taste for the tattoos
Parker already has. Parker cannot understand why he stays with

Sarah Ruth—he "understood why he had married her—he couldn't have got her any other way—but he couldn't understand why he stayed with her now" (*Complete Stories*, p. 510)—but he does stay with her. Now he begins to think of getting a tattoo for his back that will please his wife—or at least stop her censorious tongue for a while.

> Dissatisfaction began to grow so great in Parker that there was no containing it outside of a tattoo. It had to be his back. There was no help for it. A dim half-formed inspiration began to work in his mind. He visualized having a tattoo put there that Sarah Ruth would not be able to resist—a religious subject. He thought of an open book with HOLY BIBLE tattooed under it and an actual verse printed on the page. This seemed just the thing for a while; then he began to hear her say, "Ain't I got a real Bible? What you think I want to read the same verse over and over for when I can read it all?" He needed something better even than the Bible! He thought about it so much that he began to lose sleep. (P. 519)

This is the first time that Parker has wanted a tattoo that would please someone else. When he was young he had got a tattoo of his mother's name, but that was only because it was the only thing she would pay for—and no one had to know that *Betty Jean* was his mother. Now he is interested in a tattoo that he will not even be able to see without two mirrors. He wants it for another person—if only "to bring Sarah Ruth to heel." But he cannot think of an appropriate subject.

Parker realizes what he must do about that tattoo for his back only after he runs a tractor into a tree. He has been negligently baling hay in a field with a large tree standing in its center. The old woman who owns the farm has told Parker to be careful of the tree and to carry any rocks he finds in his way to the edge of the field, but as soon as she is gone Parker begins running over the smaller rocks and just kicking the bigger ones out of the way. He is not paying attention to the tractor he is driving.

> As he circled the field his mind was on a suitable design for his back. The sun, the size of a golf ball, began to switch regularly from in front to behind him, but he appeared to see it in both places as if he had eyes in the back of his head. All at once he saw the tree reaching out to grasp him. A ferocious thud propelled him into the air, and he heard himself yelling in an unbelievably loud voice, "GOD ABOVE!"

He landed on his back while the tractor crashed upside down into the tree and burst into flame. The first thing Parker saw were his shoes, quickly being eaten by the fire; one was caught under the tractor, the other some distance away, burning by itself. He was not in them. He could feel the hot breath of the burning tree on his face. He scrambled backwards, still sitting, his eyes cavernous, and if he had known how to cross himself he would have done it. (P. 520)

That Parker would cross himself if he knew how is one sign that he is beginning a conversion, as in his shout of "GOD ABOVE." The shout especially is described as if it is more a message to Parker than a blasphemy he has himself committed. But the biblical story that lies behind Parker's tractor wreck tells the reader more than either the shout he hears himself making or the gesture he would perform if he knew how. Parker has taken on the role of Moses standing before God on Mount Horeb.

As Exodus describes it, Moses received his call from God when he drove Jethro's flocks "to the inner parts of the desert" and came to Horeb, "the mountain of God."

And the Lord appeared to him in a flame of fire out of the midst of a bush: and he saw that the bush was on fire and was not burnt. And Moses said: I will go and see this great sight, why the bush is not burnt. And when the Lord saw that he went forward to see, he called him out of the midst of the bush and said: Moses, Moses. And he answered: Here I am. And he said: come not nigh hither, put off the shoes from thy feet: for the place whereon thou standest is holy ground. (Exodus 3: 1-5)[21]

Parker is receiving a call much like that of Moses, and his call comes through the vision of a burning bush. Like Moses he cannot keep his shoes in the presence of the vision, and like Moses, he is never the same after it.

Moses, after some bargaining with God over the terms of his assignment, returns to Egypt to lead the Children of Israel out of bondage. Parker's response to the sight of the burning bush may have no great consequences for his people, but it is more immediate. Even before he can stand up, he begins moving toward his truck, and without a single hesitation he begins driving toward a tattoo parlor in a city fifty miles away. He does not even stop to find something to put on his bare feet. He now knows what he has to do.

Parker did not allow himself to think on the way to the city. He only knew that there had been a great change in his life, a leap forward into a worse unknown, and that there was nothing he could do about it. It was for all intents accomplished. (P. 521)

As a result of this great change, Parker knows what he must have tattooed on his back.

Parker goes to an artist who has decorated him before, but the tattooist at first does not "recognize Parker in the hollow-eyed creature before him" (p. 521). When the barefoot man asks to see "the book you got with all the pictures of God in it," the artist replies "I don't put tattoos on drunks." But Parker soon convinces him to do the work. He asks Parker what he is interested in, "saints, angels, Christs or what?"

> "God," Parker said.
> "Father, Son or Spirit?"
> "Just God," Parker said impatiently. "Christ. I don't care. Just so it's God." (Pp. 521-22)

The artist brings him the book of religious pictures, and Parker begins looking through it, starting "at the back where the most up-to-date pictures were." Some of the images are familiar to him, saccharine images of a friendly Jesus.

> [B]ut he kept turning rapidly backwards and the pictures became less and less reassuring. One showed a gaunt green dead face streaked with blood. One was yellow with sagging purple eyes. Parker's heart began to beat faster and faster until it appeared to be roaring inside him like a great generator. He flipped the pages quickly, feeling that when he reached the one ordained, a sign would come. He continued to flip through until he had almost reached the front of the book. On one of the pages a pair of eyes glanced at him swiftly. Parker sped on, then stopped. His heart too appeared to cut off; there was absolute silence. It said plainly as if silence were a language itself, GO BACK.
>
> Parker returned to the picture—the haloed head of a flat stern Byzantine Christ with all-demanding eyes. He sat there trembling; his heart began slowly to beat again as if it were being brought to life by a subtle power. (P. 522)

The pictures that attract Parker's attention are not those that show

Jesus as simply an idealized man—a human being with an extra supply of compassion and all the rough edges removed. They are instead the images that emphasize the sterner elements in the doctrine of the Incarnation, the parts of Christian doctrine that scandalized the gnostics and the pagans. The images of Christ that catch Parker's eye show Jesus as fully human, in that he suffers and dies in a physical body, or as Lord—an all-demanding Lord. Parker finds himself choosing to have the image of Jesus as Pantocrator, Christ as Sovereign of the world, tattooed on his back.

The tattooist warns Parker that reproducing this image will be difficult and suggests simplifying it. Parker, however, wants it just as it is. He is willing to pay for it—ten dollars down and ten dollars for each of the two days it will take to complete the tattoo. Once the bargain has been struck, the artist tells Parker that they will start the next morning, but Parker demands that he begin immediately. The artist goes along with him.

> Anyone stupid enough to want a Christ on his back, he reasoned, would be just as likely as not to change his mind the next minute, but once the work was begun he could hardly do so. (P. 523)

Parker shows no sign of changing his mind. That he must have this tattoo put on his back seems to be the one thing he is sure about.

After the day's work the artist shows Parker how the work has been progressing with two mirrors. Most of the outline is there, but the eyes have not been drawn in yet. "The impression for the moment was almost as if the artist had tricked him and done the Physician's Friend" (p. 524). Without the "all-demanding eyes," the Christ on Parker's back seems almost like the saccharine images of Jesus he flipped past.

Parker spends the night thinking about those eyes. He is staying in the Haven of Light Christian Mission, since the place is free and provides a meal. He has also been given a pair of shoes. He lies awake all night in the dormitory, haunted by the images that have filled his mind during the day.

> The only light was from a phosphorescent cross glowing at the end of the room. The tree reached out to grasp him again, then burst into flame; the shoe burned quietly by itself; the eyes in the book said to him distinctly GO BACK and at the same time did not utter a sound. (P. 524)

In this swirl of memories, images that link Parker to Moses called by God from the burning bush are joined with images of Jesus in both his passion and his glory. The memory of the burning tree is juxtaposed with a cross of light; the burning shoes, with the Christ who says "GO BACK." "Take off your shoes," is the first instruction the Lord gives to Moses, as "GO BACK" is the first command Parker hears from the silent face of Christ. O'Connor uses a fusion of these images to show that Parker is being called to a devotion to Jesus the suffering Lord, almost as Moses was called to lead his people out of bondage. The words "GO BACK" seem to be a call to repent.

Parker is not particularly pleased to have received any call. As he lies in the Haven of Light Mission, he wishes that he were back with Sarah Ruth. The Jesus he is having emblazoned on his back seems even more demanding than his wife.

> Her sharp tongue and icepick eyes were the only comfort he could bring to mind. He decided he was losing it. Her eyes appeared soft and dilatory compared with the eyes in the book, for even though he could not summon up the exact look of those eyes, he could still feel their penetration. He felt as though, under their gaze, he was as transparent as the wing of a fly. (P. 524)

Parker has spent his life decorating the outside of his body. Now he faces the awful prospect of someone looking into his soul.

When the artist arrives at his studio the next morning, Parker is waiting for him. He has decided that once the tattoo is finished, he will not look at it—"that all his sensations of the day and night before were those of a crazy man and that he would return to doing things according to his own sound judgement." Parker is trying to convince himself that what has happened does not matter. He is attempting to ignore the call he has begun to hear. When the artist asks why he is getting this odd tattoo, Parker continues to pretend that he is not doing it because he has been called to.

> "One thing I want to know," [the artist] said presently as he worked over Parker's back, "why do you want this on you? Have you gone and got religion? Are you saved?" he asked in a mocking voice.
>
>     Parker's throat felt salty and dry. "Naw," he said, "I ain't got no use for none of that. A man can't save his self from whatever it is he don't deserve none of my sympathy." The words seemed to leave his mouth like wraiths and to evaporate at once as if he had never uttered them. (Pp. 524-25)

Parker is fighting the idea of salvation. He is talking against it, even though he is coming to believe in it. His own words cannot convince him that he does not care about Jesus now.

When the artist keeps asking why he is having Jesus tattooed on his back, Parker claims it is all because of his wife.

> "I married this woman that's saved," Parker said. "I never should have done it. I ought to leave her. She's gone and got pregnant."
>
> "That's too bad," the artist said. "Then it's her making you have this tattoo."
>
> "Naw," Parker said, "she don't know nothing about it. It's a surprise for her."
>
> "You think she'll like it and lay off you for a while?"
>
> "She can't hep herself," Parker said. "She can't say she don't like the looks of God." (P. 525)

Parker ends this conversation by saying that he wants to go to sleep. As the artist finishes his work, Parker lies awake, imagining Sarah Ruth's reaction to his holy tattoo. He has no inkling that she will not, after all, like the looks of God. But even in his fantasy he cannot keep the real reason for his action from creeping in.

> He lay there, imagining how Sarah Ruth would be struck speechless by the face on his back and every now and then this would be interrupted by a vision of the tree of fire and his empty shoe burning beneath it. (P. 525)

The Mosaic echoes of the burning bush and the empty shoes keep reminding the reader that Parker has acted because he has been called, not because of his own plans.

When the artist finishes the tattoo, Parker says he does not want to see it. But the artist, proud of his work, grabs Parker and makes him stand between the two mirrors and look.

> Parker looked, turned white and moved away. The eyes in the reflected face continued to look at him—still, straight, all-demanding, enclosed in silence. (Pp. 525-26)

Parker says nothing. He is still shocked by the all-demanding eyes on his back, and he makes one more attempt to ignore them.

After leaving the artist without a word, Parker goes to a package shop, buys a pint of whiskey and drinks it all in five minutes. He then goes to a pool hall where many people know him. Someone greets him with a slap on the back, and when he says, "Lay off . . . I got a fresh tattoo there," his friends demand to see what he has chosen to decorate his back with. He resists, but they grab him and pull up his shirt.

> Parker felt all the hands drop away instantly and his shirt fell again like a veil over the face. There was a silence in the pool room which seemed to Parker to grow from the circle around him until it extended to the foundations under the building and upward through the beams in the roof. (P. 526)

After this brief moment of natural reverence, someone says "Christ" and everyone begins to talk at once. The silence was bad enough, since the demands of the eyes on his back come to Parker in silence, but in the uproar Parker again has to explain why he has had Jesus put on his back—and again he does not want to admit the real reason.

The men in the poolroom wonder if Parker has got religion.

> "O. E.'s got religion and is witnessing for Jesus, ain't you, O. E.?" a little man with a piece of cigar in his mouth said wryly. "An o-riginal way to do it if I ever saw one." (P. 526)

Parker will not take much of this. He soon tells his friends to shut up. Then one of them asks him directly why he did it.

> "For laughs," Parker said. "What's it to you?"
> "Why ain't you laughing then?" somebody yelled. Parker lunged into the midst of them and like a whirlwind on a summer's day there began a fight that raged amid overturned tables and swinging fists until two of them grabbed him and ran to the door with him and threw him out. Then a calm descended on the pool hall as nerve shattering as if the long barnlike room were the ship from which Jonah had been cast into the sea. (P. 527)

This final simile makes explicit the other biblical story that underlies Parker's story. Like Jonah, Parker is a reluctant prophet. He hears the call of the Lord, and then runs from it. Even as a boy, Parker has played the role of Jonah. He runs off and joins the navy and travels to the ends of the earth rather than go into the revival tent with his mother. Like Jonah taking the ship to Tarshish, he tries to escape from the Lord. And as the crewmen on board Jonah's ship, even though they are pagans, can tell that Jonah is fleeing the Lord, Parker's friends, who are also more or less pagans, can tell that he is more serious about the Jesus on his back than he admits.

In Jonah, O'Connor finds the figure by which to judge many of her characters. Jonah is by no means the only prophet who accepts his call reluctantly. Even Moses hesitates when the Lord calls him and delays accepting his mission until the Lord has given him many assurances of assistance. But Jonah is the only prophet whose story is dominated by his resistance to the Lord's will. He first refuses to go to Nineveh and warn its citizens of the doom their sins have brought upon them. Jonah only performs his mission after being driven to it by storm and three days in the belly of a fish. And after he has preached at Nineveh, he grows angry at God because the Lord is merciful and does not inflict the punishment Jonah has threatened. From first to last, Jonah resists his call and quarrels with God. Yet, he is still a prophet, and even a type of Christ. When Jesus speaks of his coming sufferings, he speaks of them as "the sign of Jonah."[22] Many of O'Connor's characters resist the Lord as Jonah did, but finally bend to his will. Hazel Motes and Tarwater and O. E. Parker all try to escape the call they hear before finally accepting it.

After Parker has been thrown out of the pool hall, he sits on the ground and does something he has not done before: he examines his soul.

> He saw it as a spider web of facts and lies that was not at all important to him but which appeared to be necessary in spite of his opinion. The eyes that were now forever on his back were eyes to be obeyed. (P. 527)

His soul has been affected somehow by the act of having Jesus tattooed on his back. The all-demanding eyes of Jesus are altering his life forever. Parker is sure he must obey the eyes that have told him to "GO BACK."

> He was as certain of it as he had ever been of anything. Throughout his life, grumbling and sometimes cursing, often afraid, once in rapture, Parker had obeyed whatever instinct of this kind had come to him—in rapture when his spirit had lifted at the sight of the tattooed man at the fair, afraid when he had

joined the navy, grumbling when he had married Sarah Ruth.

All these events have helped lead him to accepting Jesus in the form of a tattoo.

The thought of Sarah Ruth gives Parker some idea of what to do. Despite the general unhappiness of his marriage, Parker has missed Sarah Ruth while he has been in the city getting his new tattoo. Now he thinks that if he goes back to her, she will know what to do.

> She would clear up the rest of it, and she would at least be pleased. It seemed to him that, all along, that was what he wanted, to please her.

Though pleasing Sarah Ruth has not been Parker's motive, he now does want to please her. A change is being worked in Parker despite himself.

Parker finds his truck and begins to drive back home. During the drive he discovers that all that has happened to him has made him feel very different.

> His head was almost clear of liquor and he observed that his dissatisfaction was gone, but he felt not quite like himself. It was as if he were himself but a stranger to himself, driving into a new country though everything he saw was familiar to him, even at night.

Parker is in the process of becoming a new man, of being converted into something more completely himself.

When he reaches home, Parker has to admit who he is. After he arrives at his house he makes as much noise as he can "to assert that he was still in charge here, that his leaving her for a night without a word meant nothing except it was the way he did things" (pp. 527-28). But when he tries to open the door, he finds it locked. He shouts for Sarah Ruth to open the door, but she will not respond. Finally she asks, "Who's there?" Parker answers "Me ... O. E." and repeats his name several times, but Sarah Ruth will not answer. Finally she says, "I don't know no O. E."

While Parker was courting her, Sarah Ruth discovered Parker's full name. He introduced himself only as "O. E. Parker."

> "You can just call me O. E.," Parker said. "Or Parker. Don't nobody call me by my name."

"What's it stand for?" she persisted.

"Never mind," Parker said. "What's yours?"

"I'll tell you when you tell me what them letters are the short of," she said. There was just a hint of flirtatiousness in her tone and it went rapidly to Parker's head. He had never revealed the name to any man or woman, only to the files of the navy and the government, and it was on his baptismal record which he got at the age of a month; his mother was a Methodist. When the name leaked out of the navy files, Parker narrowly missed killing the man who used it. (P. 517)

After some further hesitation, Parker whispers his name into Sarah Ruth's ear.

"Obadiah," she whispered. Her face slowly brightened as if the name came as a sign to her. "Obadiah," she said.

The name still stank in Parker's estimation.

"Obadiah Elihue," she said in a reverent voice.

"If you call me that aloud, I'll bust your head open," Parker said.

Sarah Ruth is evidently pleased to find that Parker has a biblical name. Now when Parker is trying to get back into his house, Sarah Ruth wants to hear him call himself by that name before she admits him.

Parker is standing on a porch like the one on which he sat when courting Sarah Ruth. The long view troubled Parker even then.

The view from the porch stretched off across a long incline studded with iron weed and across the highway to a vast vista of hills and one small mountain. Long views depressed Parker. You look out into space like that and you begin to feel as if someone were after you, the navy or the government or religion. (P. 516)

After his marriage Parker continued to feel that something might be after him. "Once or twice he found himself turning around abruptly as if someone were trailing him" (p. 520). Now, as he stands on the porch of his own shack just before dawn, all that he has been running from catches up with Parker.

Sarah Ruth again asks, "Who's there?" in "the same unfeeling

voice." Before he gives the answer, Parker comes to see himself
clearly for the first time.

> Parker turned his head as if he expected someone behind him
> to give him the answer. The sky had lightened slightly and there
> were two or three streaks of yellow floating above the horizon.
> Then as he stood there, a tree of light burst over the skyline.
> Parker fell back against the door as if he had been pinned there
> by a lance.
> "Who's there?" the voice from inside said and there was a
> quality about it now that seemed final. The knob rattled and the
> voice said peremptorily, "Who's there, I ast you?"
> Parker bent down and put his mouth near the stuffed keyhole.
> "Obadiah," he whispered and all at once he felt the light pouring
> through him, turning his spider web soul into a perfect arabesque
> of colors, a garden of trees and birds and beasts.
> "Obadiah Elihue!" he whispered. (P. 528)

In this description of the light of the rising sun shining on Parker,
most of the elements important to "Parker's Back" reach fulfillment.
Parker's conversion is almost complete.

While he waits on the porch, the things that Parker has both been
seeking and trying to escape catch up with him. The tattoos that have
been the expression of his longing for something beyond his mundane life are finally identified with his soul. He has thought of his
soul as a mass of cobwebs, but now in the light it is turned into what
he has wanted his tattoos to be—"a perfect arabesque of colors."
And what works this transformation is a "tree of light," like the
burning tree that sent him off to have Jesus tattooed on his back.
What transforms Parker is the call he has finally heard, the strange
theophany that he, like Moses, has received in the form of a burning
shrub.

Parker's identification with Moses at this point makes plain the
offer of grace that is being made to him. Parker can be transformed
and become a new man. Since he is finally admitting the name he
received at his baptism, he is becoming the man he was meant to be.
In the same way, Parker's similarities to Jonah reveal the offers of
grace made to him. God keeps calling him: if he will not listen to his
mother and a revivalist, he may listen to a burning tree and a tattoo
with all demanding eyes, just as Jonah, who would not listen to the
Lord, had to listen to the storm. That the biblical story is used to point

out the present offer of grace is what makes O'Connor's use of biblical figures different from most other versions of biblical figuralism.

Typology, the sense of scripture in which a person or event from the Old Testament prefigures a corresponding person or event in the New Testament, is a form of allegory. When Aquinas describes the allegorical sense, he discusses typology: "so far as the things of the Old Law signify the things of the New Law, there is the allegorical sense."[23]  When the reader sees the crucifixion prefigured in the sacrifice of Isaac or the water that flowed from Christ's side prefigured in the water that flows from the rock after Moses strikes it with his rod, he has reached the spiritual sense. And in writers who adapt typology from biblical exegesis to literature, it continues to be a form of allegory. When the reader sees the biblical figures in the characters in medieval or Renaissance writers, he has found the grain under the husk. The allegorical senses and the literal may play on each other in many different ways, but the biblical figure is not used to illuminate the life of the character. The character is being used to recall the biblical figure.

O'Connor, on the other hand, weaves biblical echoes through her stories because she wants them to illuminate the lives of her characters. The biblical echoes give the reader something to measure the character against. O'Connor uses typology to reveal the anagogical sense. The parallels between her characters and biblical figures help reveal how modern people still respond to the same grace that transformed the lives of the prophets of old. The biblical echoes remind the reader that part of the story he is being told has to do with how the character "participates in the Divine life." But the character participates in the Divine life only in the ways made possible by his own psychology. In allegory the characters are not burdened with internal lives, much less internal lives as strange as those of O. E. Parker and Hazel Motes. O'Connor's characters, however, respond to the offer of grace in the ways their minds and experiences allow them to. The biblical echoes help the reader see the acceptance of grace even in acts as grotesque or appalling as Parker's final tattoo or Motes's self-blinding.

That she uses biblical echoes to point out the present offer of grace is what makes O'Connor different from the many modern writers who have used biblical stories to structure their fiction. O'Connor's biblical echoes are not a pattern imposed on chaotic reality to give it some shape; they are signs pointing out the action of grace. When other twentieth-century writers build their works on biblical stories, the biblical analogue is largely a structure that gives shape to a narrative and a bit of thematic material that makes possible a certain kind of irony—an irony very different from O'Connor's; it is not an indication that any real contact between the Divine and the human is being made. In Faulkner's *Light in August,* for example, Joe Christmas is clearly a parallel with Jesus. The seamy events of his life have their counterparts in the life of Christ. But there is never any indication that this parallel reveals a real intervention of grace in any character's life. By the end of the novel it seems that all that has been transformed is the Rev. Hightower's literary taste.

The biblical analogues give shape to temporal actions; they do not make any link between the temporal and the eternal. The pattern imposed on modern events might as well be taken from some other classic text as from the Bible. The way Faulkner uses the story of Christ is not very different from the way Joyce uses the story of Ulysses. The myth in the background gives the squalid actions in the modern story some depth, but it does not make any connection with a spiritual reality. As Theodore Ziolkowski writes, the biblical echoes provide the writer primarily with a form.

> [T]he prefigurative pattern can supply a form for the modern work. This is what T. S. Eliot had in mind, in his essay *"Ulysses, Order, and Myth"* when he argued that Joyce's "Parallel use of the *Odyssey"* had the importance of a scientific discovery. "In using myth, in manipulating a continuous parallel between contemporaneity and antiquity, Mr. Joyce is pursuing a method which others must pursue after him. . . It is simply a way of controlling, of ordering, of giving a shape and a significance to the immense panorama of futility and anarchy which is contemporary history."[24]

But O'Connor does not believe that history—even contemporary history—is a panorama of futility and anarchy. If it seems so, it is only because people cannot perceive the final structure that is growing out of the present construction. In her stories, therefore, old patterns are not repeated to give some form to a chaotic present. The old stories are echoed because the same sort of intervention of grace in human lives is taking place.

One of the great differences between O'Connor works and those of other modern writers who make use of biblical stories is that O'Connor does not write about "Christ Figures." There is no equivalent of Joe Christmas in her stories. Her works are full of characters who are in some ways Christ-like or who share in Christ's suffering, but only in the ways that a Catholic would believe that all people can be imitators of Christ and participate in his passion. There are no characters who take on the role of Christ's surrogate throughout a story, as there are in many other modern novels. O'Connor evidently thought the attempt to create Christ-figures in fiction was in the end an impossible one. She ends a review of a study of Christ-figures, by calling it "an interesting study of attempts which by their nature must fail."[25]

Such efforts must fail because they reduce Christ to the level of a purely human character, and thus lose half the truth about His nature. What is more, they must find analogues for a unique being. While it is not difficult to create parallels for other biblical characters, since one creature can easily share characteristics with another, it is impossible to find a parallel for the only Son of God. Therefore fictional versions of Jesus must be failed Messiahs, who cannot rise again except by sleight of hand, and who can bring only the most ambiguous kinds of redemption.

Instead of showing characters who take on the role of Jesus, O'Connor shows the encounter of her characters with Jesus Himself. The Christian believes that Jesus is still active in the world, that he still offers salvation, and people still do answer his call. O'Connor shows modern people answering the call of Jesus as they hear it, not through their interactions with some imitation or substitute. The theology on which O'Connor built her stories taught her that Jesus did not need to be presented through a figural substitute, since he was literally present.

Soon after Parker feels his soul transformed by the tree of light, he takes some part in the sufferings of Christ, but he does not become a Christ figure. He simply becomes a Christian.

Sarah Ruth lets Parker in after he has called himself by his full name. She has heard all about the wrecked tractor, discovered the truth about some of her husband's lies, and is ready to tell Parker all about the long talk she has had with his employer. But Parker only responds by lighting a lamp and unbuttoning his shirt. Sarah Ruth tells him that there is no need for the light—or for his undressing.

"Shut your mouth," he said quietly. "Look at this and then I don't want to hear no more out of you." He removed the shirt and turned his back to her.

"Another picture," Sarah Ruth growled. "I might have known you was off after putting some more trash on yourself."

Parker's knees went hollow under him. He wheeled around and cried, "Look at it! Don't just say that! *Look* at it!"

"I done looked, " she said.

"Don't you know who it is?" he cried in anguish.

"No, who is it?" Sarah Ruth said. "It ain't anybody I know."

"It's him." Parker said.

"Him who?"

"God!" Parker cried.

"God? God don't look like that!"

"What do you know how he looks?" Parker moaned. "You ain't seen him."

"He don't *look*," Sarah Ruth said. "He's a spirit. No man shall see his face."

"Aw listen," Parker groaned, "this is just a picture of him."

"Idolatry!" Sarah Ruth screamed. "Idolatry! Enflaming yourself with idols under every green tree! I can put up with lies and vanity but I don't want no idolator in this house!" and she grabbed up the broom and began to thrash him across the shoulders with it.

Parker was too stunned to resist. He sat there and let her beat him until she had nearly knocked him senseless and large welts had formed on the face of the tattooed Christ. Then he staggered up and made for the door. (P. 529)

The violence Parker suffers is unexpected, but it is completely in character for Sarah Ruth. The attack on his tattoo completes Parker's conversion. He has had some inkling from the time he received his first tattoo that the wonder he was seeking came with suffering. Now that he has been transformed, turned, at least inwardly, into the rich pattern of arabesques he has always hoped for, he must undergo an even greater suffering. He has to endure not only the physical pain of the wounds on his back but also rejection from Sarah Ruth after he has finally come to truly care for her.

Parker's conversion begins and ends with violence—with the tractor wreck and with Sarah Ruth's attack on the tattoo. O'Connor's work is full of violence, but the violence serves much the same purpose as the echoes of biblical stories: it points out the actions of grace.

> Our age not only does not have a very sharp eye for the almost imperceptible intrusions of grace, it no longer has much feeling for the nature of the violences that precede and follow them. . . .
>
> I suppose the reasons for the use of so much violence in modern fiction will differ with each writer who uses it, but in my own stories I have found that violence is strangely capable of returning my characters to reality and preparing them to accept their moment of grace. Their heads are so hard that almost nothing else will do the work. ("On Her Own Work," *Mystery and Manners*, p. 112)

The reality that Parker is returned to is the reality of his call from God. That is what he sees in the burning tree at the tractor wreck. The final violence done by Sarah Ruth brings Parker back to several other realities. To begin with, he is left with no motive for transforming his life beyond obedience to the "all-demanding eyes" of Jesus. The other hopes he had harbored when he had Jesus tattooed on his back are stripped from him: this image will not please Sarah Ruth, much less "bring her to heel."

More importantly, the wounds on Parker's tattooed back return him to the reality of a mystery. Christ has to suffer, and the believer is saved by sharing in Christ's Passion. The images that caught Parker's attention in the artist's book were those that showed Jesus either as Lord or as victim. Now he is brought back to the reality that Christ must be both: He can save only because He suffers. One might even say that Parker is receiving his stigmata. He is bearing in his own body the wounds of Christ's—Christ's because they mar His face; Parker's because they tear his back.

Finally the mystery embodied in "Parker's Back" is that of the Incarnation. Christian dogma teaches that the Son of God saved his people by becoming a man and suffering in the flesh. As her comments even on the art of fiction show, the Incarnation was at the very center of all O'Connor's thinking. For her, the world was a different place than it would have been because God became flesh and endured crucifixion. The Incarnation, moreover, was not simply a momentous event in the past. For O'Connor it was an ever-present reality, continually made manifest in the Eucharist. The real presence of Christ in the sacrament was of the utmost importance to her. She had no patience with any view that made the sacrament merely into a beautiful symbol: she reports in one of her letters that when someone began to talk about the Eucharist in that way she replied,

"Well, if it's a symbol, to hell with it" (p.125). That Christ's body was really present—and that grace was really being conveyed under the accidents of something as material as bread—was to O'Connor true in the most literal way. Spiritual meanings grew only out of that literal fact.

O'Connor believed that the doctrine of the Incarnation was one of the basic facts about the world. She explains it to one correspondent in this way:

> To see Christ as God and man is probably no more difficult today that it has always been, even if today there seem to be more reasons to doubt. For you it may be a matter of not being able to accept what you call a suspension of the laws of the flesh and the physical, but for my part I think that when I know what the laws of the flesh and the physical really are, then I will know what God is. We know them as we see them, not as God sees them. For me it is the virgin birth, the Incarnation, the resurrection which are the true laws of the flesh and the physical. Death, decay, destruction are the suspension of these laws. I am always astonished at the emphasis the Church puts on the body. It is not the soul she says that will rise but the body, glorifed. I have always thought that purity is the most mysterious of the virtues, but it occurs to me that it would never have entered the human consciousness to conceive of purity if we were not to look forward to a resurrection of the body, which will be flesh and spirit united in peace, in the way they were in Christ. The resurrection of Christ seems the high point in the law of nature. (Letter to "A," September 6, 1955, *The Habit of Being*, p. 100)

Here O'Connor seems to be giving another definition of the whole man of whose existence her freaks remind us. Their bodies and spirits are not united in peace, but their very strife suggests the possibility of wholeness.

Parker's tattoo is an embodiment of the doctrine of the Incarnation: Christ is again become flesh, and again suffers in it. Parker slowly works out the paradox that Jesus is both God and man. The artist's pictures show him as both, and Parker is finally stopped by one that shows Christ primarily as Lord. That this tattoo is attacked is a reminder that the Messiah had to suffer—a doctrine that shocked those to whom Jesus announced it, was rejected by the Gnostics and the Manichees, and still troubles those who wish for a purely spiritual faith.

Sarah Ruth becomes the representative of those who find the doctrine of the Incarnation too fleshly. She evidently does not accept the doctrine that God became man, that the Divine and the human are still perfectly joined in Him, and that one day we will see him face to face. Instead she wants to worship in pure spirit. "He don't *look* ... He's a spirit. No man shall see his face." Evidently Sarah Ruth reads the Old Testament of her Bible more often than the New. She remembers the language of the prophets when rebuking Parker for "enflaming himself with idols under every green tree," but she forgets Paul's promise that we will one day see God "face to face" (1 Cor. 13:12). O'Connor quoted with pleasure a letter which Caroline Gordon sent her praising "Parker's Back" for dramatizing a heresy—"Sarah Ruth was the heretic—the notion that you can worship in pure spirit" (Letter to "A," July 25, 1964, *The Habit of Being*, p. 594).

Some of the heretics in the early Church attacked the idea of the Incarnation outright—the Gnostics held that the body on the cross was but an illusion; God could not really suffer. But one of the most troubling heresies questioned the Incarnation by making the charge of idolatry against most orthodox Christians, just as Sarah Ruth makes the charge against Parker. The Iconoclasts who split the Eastern Church asunder during the eighth and ninth centuries rejected any representation of God—or even of men—as idolatrous.

> The struggle was not merely a conflict between two conceptions of Christian art. Deeper issues were involved: the character of Christ's human nature, the Christian attitude towards matter, the true meaning of Christian redemption.[26]

The question was, as the orthodox saw it, whether Christ was truly man as well as truly God. If so, he could be represented physically. What is more, if God had really become incarnate in matter, matter must therefore be good, and worthy of reverence when it represents the Divine. The Iconoclasts saw a more radical division between the physical and the spiritual. To try to represent the Divine in the merely physical was idolatry.

Sarah Ruth shares the Iconoclasts' position, and she is also linked to them by the kind of image she attacks. It is significant that the image Parker chooses to have tattooed on his back is a Byzantine Christ. It is even a mosaic: the artist tells Parker that he doesn't really want "all those little blocks though, just the outline and some better features" (p. 522), but Parker wants it just as he sees it. When the artist shows him the work in progress, he sees his back "covered with little red and blue and ivory and saffron squares" that form the outlines of the face. Sarah Ruth, therefore, is attacking just the sort of image the Iconoclasts destroyed. O'Connor has marked Sarah Ruth's heresy by making so explicit the form of orthodoxy she attacks. And Parker is, when defending his tattoo, orthodox. The response of the opponents of the Iconoclasts was, more or less, "Aw listen . . . this is just a picture of him." To represent the Divine materially is not to make some lump of matter into an idol.

Sarah Ruth takes her mistrust of matter to the point of heresy, but O'Connor also uses her to point up the differences between Catholic and Protestant attitudes toward the Incarnation.[27] Though both groups believe in the doctrine, Catholics have taken the attitude towards matter founded on the Incarnation much farther than most Protestants do. The points of controversy are in fact often the very theological postions O'Connor used to defend her fiction. The question is to what extent God's entry into the material world gives us justification for using the material to represent the spiritual, and how far can matter be a means of grace.

Catholics have traditionally allowed the material to represent the spiritual to a much greater extent than have Protestants. A Protestant writer like C. S. Lewis can even see the disagreement over how far to press the incarnational principle as the root of the disagreements between the churches.

> It would appear that all allegories whatever are likely to seem Catholic to the general reader, and this phenomenon is worth investigation. . . . The truth is not that allegory is Catholic, but that Catholicism is allegorical. Allegory consists in giving an imagined body to the immaterial; but if, in each case, Catholicism claims already to have given it a material body, then the allegorist's symbol will naturally resemble that material body. . . . No Christian doubts that those who have offered themselves to God are cut off *as if* by a wall from the World, are placed under a *regula vitae*, and "laid in an easy bed" by "meek Obedience;" but when the wall becomes one of real bricks and mortar, and the Rule one in real ink . . . then we have reached the sort of actuality which Catholics aim at and Protestants deliberately avoid. Indeed, this is the root out of which all other differences between the two religions grow. The one suspects that all spiritual gifts are falsely claimed if they cannot be embodied in bricks and mortar, or official positions, or institutions; the other, that nothing retains its

spirituality if incarnation is pushed to that degree and in that way.... In the world of matter, Catholics and Protestants disagree as to the kind and degree of incarnation or embodiment which we can safely try to give the spiritual. . .[28]

Lewis goes on to say that Protestants are justified in giving spiritual things imagined physical form in allegories; he seems to have grave doubts about Catholics giving them actual physical form in real life.

Since the Reformation, Catholics and Protestants have often battled over "what degree of incarnation or embodiment we can safely give the spiritual." Many Protestants, like Sarah Ruth and the Iconoclasts, have answered, None. While some Catholics have at times allowed physical manifestations of the spiritual to become actually idolatrous—forgetting that "it's just a picture"—some Protestants have at times attacked all representation, acting, from the Catholic view, as if Christ's entry into the material world had made no difference to our view of it. Many Protestants became actual Iconoclasts, and their view of the separation of matter and spirit is still to be found embodied in the ruined statues and empty niches of many English cathedrals.[29] When Sarah Ruth attacks the image on her husband's back, she is continuing a long tradition of opposition to religious art among radical Protestants.

But in this dispute the morality of religious art is secondary. The real question is how to view the body—and the rest of the material world—in the light of the Incarnation. The Catholic view has been to pronounce both the body and the material world good, though marred by sin, and to take each as a means of grace. Protestants have treated both the body and the world with much more suspicion, and emphasized, almost exclusively, the more spiritual channels of grace. To Protestants grace comes from faith and hearing the word. For Catholics it comes as well from good works and from sacraments in which some material thing is a sign of inward grace.

The Catholic Church at its moments of greatest solemnity tries to involve all the body's senses. At an Easter vigil, for example, a Catholic will smell incense, hear music, see rich vestments and ritual actions, taste the bread and wine consecrated in the Eucharist, and feel himself sprinkled with water after he has renewed the vows made at his baptism. He will stand and kneel and sit, bow, cross himself, and shake his neighbor's hand in the sign of peace. Even today, a Protestant will find much less to appeal to his senses when he worships on the same occasion. His service will be much more simple, his body will be called on to do much less—and he will probably hear a sermon that has been prepared with much more care than has been expended on the homily his Catholic brother hears.[30] The Catholic will also have fasted the day before he comes to this vigil, and in requiring such mortifications the Church also shows that it considers the body a vehicle of grace. All its actions are important, both its fasts and its feasts. To the Protestant, however, neither will have nearly so much spiritual meaning. Fasting will rarely be required; great liturgical celebrations will not often be called feasts. What the body does on such a mundane level as eating will not be seen as having much spiritual importance. O'Connor uses the quality of Sarah Ruth Parker's cooking—she "just threw food in the pot and let it boil." (p. 519)—to suggest her disregard for the significance of the body. For Sarah Ruth, the physical body is just not worth bothering about all that much.

A similar contrast between Catholic and Protestant views of the body appears in the churches' attitudes toward sexuality. Both teach the same morality—marriage or abstinence—but each group views the two alternatives very differently. Catholics have traditionally both celebrated virginity and considered marriage a sacrament. Protestants have both attacked the idea of consecrated virginity and denied the sacramental nature of marriage. For the Catholic the purely animal act of procreation, like the animal act of eating, can be an outward sign of inward grace. God's entry into human form has transfigured the physical to such an extent that one of the seven special channels of God's grace is dependent on the physical act of intercourse. The sacrament is not complete until it has been physically consummated.[31]

The sacraments in general are, of course, one of the main battlegrounds between Catholics and Protestants. To begin with, Catholics admit more of them than do Protestants. The Catholic Church teaches that there are seven, while many Protestants accept only two. Catholics are willing to see many more material acts and objects as special channels of grace than are Protestants. What is more, the Catholic Church emphasizes the physical nature of the sacramental sign. There is a real presence in the Eucharist, not just a symbolic one. The material thing is important enough for it to be worth maintaining the doctrine that bread does substantially change into the body of Christ.

Parker and Sarah Ruth are cut off from most of the sacraments. Parker has been baptized, and part of his transformation involves his return to his baptismal name, but most of the other six are not open to him. The only exception is marriage. Sarah Ruth would doubtless deny that marriage is a sacrament. She insists on getting married, for she will not sin, but she does not marry in a church or even in the presence of a minister. "They were married in the County Ordinary's office because Sarah Ruth thought churches were idolatrous" (p. 518). Sarah Ruth, with her contempt for the material body, will not admit that any material building could be the house of God, and doubtless she would find any church decorations as idolatrous as her husband's back.

The marriage solemnized with the words "Three dollars and fifty cents and till death do you part!" (p. 518) does present both Parker and Sarah Ruth with an offer of grace all the same. For Sarah Ruth, Parker is an opportunity to move beyond her rigid righteousness to active charity. He needs her love; and after he receives his tattoo, he is ready to accept it. But Sarah Ruth is not willing to love her husband after he returns with the tattoo he thinks will finally please her. She sees what Parker has done only as another offense, an outright idolatry worse that all his previous blasphemies. Sarah Ruth rejects both her husband and the Jesus represented on his back: her husband is an idolator and the picture is of nobody she knows. Her faith is concerned more with the law than with the person of Jesus. She is a Pharisee; she means to keep the law, but does not know Jesus. Her marriage might have led her to an active love, but she will not let it. Parker, however, accepts the offer of grace the marriage brings. Sarah Ruth does bring Parker to Jesus.

Parker's marriage to Sarah Ruth is one of the things he does out of obedience to some instinct, and like getting his first tattoos and joining the navy, it helps lead him to his final conversion. Before meeting Sarah Ruth, Parker moves aimlessly through the world, not finding anything to quiet his dissatisfaction for very long. He has not wanted to get tied up with a woman permanently, but somehow he not only finds himself marrying Sarah Ruth but even staying with her. It is with Sarah Ruth in mind that he gets the tattoo that begins his transformation; it is from Sarah Ruth that he receives the wounds that complete it.

From the beginning to the end, Parker shocks Sarah Ruth's reverence for the commandments against false idols and taking the name of the Lord in vain. When she first meets him she condemns him as a blasphemer; when the story ends she rejects him as an idolator. The first charge is, at least, accurate. When Parker first sees the girl he tries to get her attention—and sympathy—by pretending that he has hurt himself while fixing his truck.

> He doubled over and held his hand close to his chest. "God dammit!" he hollered, "Jesus Christ in hell! Jesus God almighty damn! God dammit to hell!" (P. 511)

Instead of sympathy, Parker gets slammed in the side of the head. "You don't talk no filth here!" Sarah Ruth tells him. Despite her harshness, Parker is fascinated by the woman. Perhaps because she shows no interest in his bravado, or even his tattoos—in his mottled skin or the cobwebs with which he has filled his soul—he keeps coming back to her, and finally finds himself married in the County Ordinary's office.

The marriage is not happy, and Parker keeps thinking of leaving. Nevertheless, Parker's marriage is one of the things that leads him to his conversion. It is his desire to bring Sarah Ruth to heel that starts Parker thinking about a tattoo for his back. It is his longing for Sarah Ruth after he gets the tattoo that sends him back home to show it to her. Sarah Ruth makes him admit who he is, and it is while making that admission that his cobweb soul is transformed into "a perfect arabesque of colors, a garden of trees and birds and beasts," an image of the Paradise from which man is exiled. And it is Sarah Ruth who completes Parker's moment of grace by rejecting him and wounding his tattooed back. Thanks to that rejection, and thus to the marriage that allows it, Parker participates in the sufferings of Christ. The marriage, in a strange way, has been a channel of grace at least for Parker.

In the end Sarah Ruth's attack on the tattoo completes O'Connor's embodiment of the mystery of the Incarnation in fiction. The mystery tells that the Son of God had to take flesh, and to suffer and be rejected in the flesh in order to save his people. Parker's transformation comes through a tattooed image of Jesus that appears in human flesh and is torn in human flesh. His conversion is brought about by the Jesus who is finally rejected. The image of a wounded tattoo is grotesque, but through her echoes of the stories of Moses and Jonah, O'Connor shows that the tattoo is in some way the sign of the acceptance of a call from the Lord—a call that leads to suffering, as did many of the calls to prophets and apostles. Contained within the grotesque surface is an offer of grace. An anagogical sense is revealed even by a wounded tattoo.

# 2

## The Automobile and the American Adam

> ". . . the spirit, lady, is like an automobile: always on the move."
>
> —Mr. Shiftlet in "The Life You Save May Be Your Own"

Flannery O'Connor often made the plots of her stories turn on what happens in—or even to—a car. A wreck brings the Misfit and his victims together; the loss of his Essex transforms Hazel Motes; an old car is what interests Mr. Shiftlet at Mrs. Crater's farm; the bull impales Mrs. May against the hood of her automobile; and Tarwater accepts his calling after he has been molested by the man in the lavender and cream-colored car. O'Connor did not make such frequent use of automobiles because she herself had any great interest in them. She in fact only learned to drive late in her life and sometimes needed assistance when describing the parts of a car in her stories.[1] What attracted O'Connor to the automobile was the abundance of meanings that have become associated with it in the American mind.

O'Connor uses the automobile most often as an image of complete personal freedom—freedom from the past, freedom from responsibility, freedom even from God. This association is not at all inappropriate: freedom of some kind is certainly what the car means to many Americans. O'Connor also takes advantage of the connections that have grown up between the driver's ability to travel where he pleases and several ideas that have been powerful in America.

The first of these is the primarily masculine dream of always being able to chuck it all and walk away from whatever ties you down. America has heard many stories of men running or walking or sailing away from confining homes or responsibilities; in this century the hero of the same story is usually, like Jack Burden in *All the King's Men,* behind the wheel of a car as he makes his break for freedom. In some ways, the myth of the frontier lives on in our automobiles. If they had no association with the dream of leaving it all and starting fresh somewhere beyond all ties and memories, why would American cars be named for wild animals (Mustangs, Cougars), or for our first explorers (La Salles, De Sotos, Cadillacs), or for the explorers' goal (El Dorados)?

The automobile is also linked with the literary tradition that grows out of the memory of the frontier. To use R. W. B. Lewis's term, our literature is dominated by the myth of the American Adam. The quintessentially American hero is one who owns no ties to the past, and is constrained by few in the present. He is mobile and can go where he pleases. In nineteenth-century literature he must walk or sail through a wilderness, but this "hero in space" seems almost made for the automobile, which finally allows him to travel the continent at his whim, attached to no place or person. The tradition of the American Adam is the same one Leslie Fiedler sees in the history of the American Novel: men running from women and society. The frontiersmen on the prairie, the sailors out at sea, the escapees on their raft, all live on in drivers traveling on America's endless highways.

Finally, the automobile is linked with the theological premise that is at the root of these literary traditions. As both Lewis and Fiedler admit, the pattern they see in American literature grows out of a denial of Original Sin. Man—or the American man—is free, innocent, and unfallen. He is not bound by the past and his nature is not flawed. Left to himself, he will live nobly and innocently. Corruption only comes from entanglement with society—and with the women who restrict the man's freedom. It follows from this belief in Man's essential innocence that he needs no Redeemer. Indeed, the American hero is running from God, or at least from religion, as much as from women and society.

All these ideas are associated with the car, at one level or another, in the American mind. Flannery O'Connor is at odds with them all. Through her manipulation of the image of the automobile in several novels and stories, she develops a critique of the myth of the American hero free from the constraints imposed by women, society, and God, along with the literary tradition that grew from the myth and the theological premise from which the myth sprang. O'Connor shows American heroes neither so free nor so innocent as the frontier myth would make them.

## A Tradition of Movement

"Drive—Because Mobility is Freedom"
—Spare-tire cover on a van seen traveling down the Pennsylvania Turnpike.

At least since they became so common that almost everyone could have something that would run, cars have meant freedom to many Americans, especially American men. Automobiles have been used as symbols of liberation in songs and stories and sold as liberators in many advertisements. This is not to say that they have not meant other things as well. Cars often stand for a simple materialism: when we see Babbitt buying a new cigar lighter for his car early in Sinclair Lewis's novel, we recognize it as a sign of a man absorbed—perhaps even enslaved—by his possessions. And the expense and burden of an automobile is part of its meaning in the American mind. But even though a new or expensive car—or even an old one being kept in shape—may represent materialism or the burdens of property, cars more often represent escape and freedom from all ties. They have taken their place in a long American tradition that celebrates physical movement as sign of real liberation.

Several scholars[2] have seen in the car an extension of the frontier, and the frontier's influence on the American mind continuing in the car. The memory of the frontier gives us the myth of the man always able to move on. We remember many stories of men, such as Daniel Boone, who moved further and further into the wilderness as the frontier became too crowded—when the smoke of another chimney became visible, or when there were three other settlers within a hundred miles. And we still hear stories of men driving endlessly over our highways, moving on as soon as they seem in danger of being tied down.

What is more, the frontier has been celebrated as the part of our country's history that formed a distinctively *American* character. Frederick Jackson Turner, who charted the influence of the frontier on American institutions, also considered its impact on the American character:

To the frontier the American intellect owes its striking characteristics. That coarseness and strength combined with acuteness and
inquisitiveness; that practical, inventive turn of mind, quick to
find expedients; that masterful grasp of material things, lacking in
the artistic but powerful to effect great ends; that restless, nervous
energy; that dominant individualism, working for good and for
evil, and withal that buoyancy and exuberance which comes with
freedom—these are the traits of the frontier, or traits called out
elsewhere because of the existence of the frontier.[3]

These qualities, even the negative ones, are certainly the ones
Americans like to think they possess. Whether or not they in fact
grow out of the experience of the frontier, they are associated with
our frontier past to this day. Americans still sometimes ascribe their
virtues to the pioneer spirit and their faults to the cowboy's rough-
ness and violence.

Turner sees the frontier as the scene of what many, including
many literary critics, believe makes Americans American: our liberation from the past. Despite—or because of—its hardships, the
frontier offered a place where it was possible to begin something
completely fresh and new:

At the frontier, the bonds of custom are broken and unrestraint is
triumphant. There is not *tabula rasa*. The stubborn American
environment is there with its imperious summons to accept its
conditions; the inherited ways of doing things are also there; and
yet, in spite of environment, and in spite of custom, each frontier
did indeed furnish a new field of opportunity, a gate of escape
from the bondage of the past, and freshness, and confidence, and
scorn of older society, impatience of its restraints and its ideas, and
indifference to its lessons, have accompanied the frontier. (P. 38)

The frontier's influence continues in the automobile. Even if the
frontier is closed, Americans move as much or more than they ever
did, and that mobility is still "a gate of escape from the bondage of
the past." As Turner himself seems to recognize, movement has in
some sense become our tradition: "Movement has been . . . the
dominant fact [of American life], and, unless this training has no
effect upon a people, the American energy will continually demand
a wider field for its exercise" (p. 37). The *idea* of movement, of the
American always pressing on to some new frontier, has survived,
even if the great tracts of free land have disappeared.

Americans have always seen liberation in movement. From the earliest days of the country, moving has, at the very least, held out the hope of liberation from poverty. But migration has also offered the promise of several other kinds of freedom. Migration has attracted many who, for one reason or another, could not live with the societies in which they found themselves. To some extent the frontier served as a dumping ground for misfits from societies further East. Some of the colonies were settled by transported convicts or by those who had so little hope of finding work in England that they indentured themselves as servants in order to escape to America; and it is not without reason that the Western frontier is remembered for its outlaws as much as for its cowboys and Indians. But migration also meant freedom to those with better motives than the fugitive's: as we are taught from childhood, some of our ancestors came to this country to escape religious or political persecution; others came to escape conscription or economic oppression in Europe.

Besides the misfits and these the ideal immigrants—the Pilgrim fathers, "the huddled masses yearning to breathe free"—there were others heading toward the frontier seeking a less lofty kind of freedom.

> For this lesser but still considerable number, the flight to America was inspired rather by the desire to escape from one's own errors and failures, from debts one couldn't pay, from a reputation too bad to live down, from an atmosphere that seemed poisoned and hopeless, from obligations one was unwilling to meet. By crossing the Atlantic one might escape one's neighbors—and even oneself. In Virginia, past mistakes would be forgiven—and with a second move, even a New England Puritan might be able to leave behind a sense of Original Sin.[4]

It is significant that Pierson sees movement as a way of escaping a sense of Original Sin. As I will show later in the chapter, this is perfectly in keeping with the American tradition. God and guilt belong in this long list of things the "moving American" is running from.

Movement, for all these varied reasons, did not stop when the frontier was closed. Movement is still a real possibility; what is more, the myth created by the frontier and the different kinds of mobility that succeeded it lives on in many forms in American culture.

The myth the frontier created lives on especially in our automobiles. Our mobility tempts us to believe we are completely free, not bound by memories or obligations. It is always possible to move somewhere new, to start completely fresh. There may be a goal for the traveler, but often the destination hardly matters—there may be none. The call of the open road is to movement pure and simple, not to any place down the highway.

This dream of endless travel has always been a primarily masculine myth. Often our mountain men are completely alone before nature; they may bring wives and families, but these are merely incidental to the frontiersmen's journey into the wild. Women often are one of the things left behind on the journey into the wilderness. In Cooper's novels, the frontiersmen are celibate: those who marry go back East. In much the same way, the automobile has been a primarily masculine interest. There may be a woman in the right-hand seat, but in popular culture men are the drivers. Men are supposed to know about cars, women are supposed be be ignorant about them. Men are supposed to be masters of the art of driving, while women know little of it. It is mostly men who attend car shows and make automobiles their obsessions; they are the heirs of the American tradition of men setting out for new territories, leaving the encumbrances of women and society behind.[5]

O'Connor began writing as interest in the automobile was reaching its height. The wartime shortage of cars and of rationed gasoline gave way to an explosion of interest in cars in the late forties and early fifties. Many servicemen must have wanted the freedom of an automobile after being released from the restrictions of military life—just as O'Connor's Hazel Motes buys an Essex soon after his discharge. But the idea that a car and a highway mean freedom is at least as old as the first mass-produced cars. The years before the war produced images of the Ford as a means of escape: the Joadses' car does not take them to the promised land, but it does at least take them away from the dust bowl.

As her letters show, O'Connor had a keen interest in what we now call popular culture. She often writes about this or that strange thing she has seen in the newspapers, describing ads for Chinese herb doctors, stories about Roy Rogers taking his horse to church or a "saddle preacher" bringing the gospel to rural Florida on a horse named MacArthur, and the wisdom of Dr. Crane, the advice columnist in the Atlanta paper. She could hardly have been unaware of the associations the automobile had in the American mind. What is more, O'Connor welcomed the close analysis of images that were being imposed upon the public by the mass media. She read and admired Marshall McLuhan's book, *The Mechanical Bride: The Folklore of Industrial Man.*[6] In this work McLuhan examines advertisements and other artifacts from popular culture, such as movie posters and comic books, almost as an art critic would examine the work of a master. His purpose is to reveal the ways in which the growing mass media manipulate "the public mind" (p. v). In fact he is revealing some of the myths that pervade our popular culture.

There is a great deal in McLuhan's enterprise that would have attracted O'Connor's sympathy. To begin with, both were Catholics, and so had to some degree the same standpoint from which to criticize the culture around them. What is more, both looked at that culture with as much amusement as indignation. They saw many of the ideas presented in the media as false and dangerous—but they also recognized how funny some of them were. The myths McLuhan found in advertisements could hardly have been surprising to O'Connor, but her admiration for his book reveals her own interest in "the folklore of industrial man." She certainly made use of that folklore in her novels and stories.

McLuhan devotes several chapters of *The Mechanical Bride* to the different ideas, including freedom, that have been associated with the automobile. In the chapter entitled "Freedom—American Style" (pp. 116-18), he analyzes a magazine ad for Quaker State Motor Oil. The advertisement, which must have been published during the war, seems to be trying to appeal to as many American values as possible—in a few short paragraphs it manages to make freedom, patriotism, and love of family all part of buying motor oil. A picture of a family picnic fills most of the page. At the picnic basket a man kneels, smiling at his wife, who offers him, with eyes downcast, a plate heaped with food. A little girl also kneels, holding out her empty plate. In the background, a boy approaches with a portable radio in his hand and a dog at his feet. Beyond this family scene are an empty field and an automobile. The caption is "Freedom . . . American style." The text goes on to explain what that freedom is:

> It's the feeling you have when you get up in the morning and stand at an open window—the way you breathe in God's sunlight and fresh air. It's whistling before breakfast, disagreeing with the bank over your monthly statement, leaving a tip for the waitress if you feel like it.

It's working hard now with the idea of quitting someday. . .
It's looking forward with confidence—even while you willingly
put up with gas rationing—to packing a lunch again and piling
the family in the car for an outing.

From this point the ad continues its appeal to patriotism—"It's
realizing this is a nation on wheels that must be kept rolling—and
that *your* wheels are part of all wheels"—before going on to suggest
that freedom is also using Quaker State. McLuhan's analysis, which
he casts in the form of questions for a discussion group, concentrates
on what a contradictory idea of freedom the advertisement conveys.

What would you say was the income level of this family
group? Estimate this from the car, the Scottie, the portable radio,
and the appearance of the family. If this is "freedom... American
Style," then is it not freedom and not American to have less money
and fewer possessions? Was Henry Thoreau un-American?
What proportion of Americans enjoy this style of freedom?
. . . . . . . . . . . . . . . . . . . . . . . . . . . . . . . . . . . . . . . . . . . . . . . . . . . .
Is there any basic connection between freedom and prosper-
ity?
. . . . . . . . . . . . . . . . . . . . . . . . . . . . . . . . . . . . . . . . . . . . . . . . . . . .
Looking at the standardized equipment of this family and
their standardized pattern of living, discuss how far they can be
said to be free as human beings. . . . does "freedom" mean the right
to be and do exactly as everybody else?
. . . . . . . . . . . . . . . . . . . . . . . . . . . . . . . . . . . . . . . . . . . . . . . . . . . .
And the star-spangled scene of the free man cussing the bank
or gypping the tired waitress who didn't sparkle and zip around
is a curious way of getting at the essence of freedom.

McLuhan, after explicating the contradictory messages of this ad
ends,

The writer of the ad, in short, takes a dim view of the capacities of
his readers, especially when he makes his final gesture of including, as it were, a can of motor oil in every picnic hamper.

But it is evidence of the power of the myth of freedom that
people try to exploit it even when it is not suited to their message.
McLuhan's motor oil ad is equally an illustration of the power of the
ideas of family and patriotism, whose connection with Quaker State
is no more obvious. There is not much liberation in the act of buying

expensive motor oil, but an ad writer selling to Americans must make the purchase seem an expression of the buyer's freedom. "Buy this because you're the American type—always ready to chuck it all and head out. Ready to quit your job and move on, ready to pile the family in the car and go for an outing just as the frontiersmen packed up their wagons and moved west." That the advertiser invokes the dream of escape even when it is not particularly appropriate to the product being sold shows how powerful the myth of freedom is.

The advertiser's appeal to the ideal of freedom—as embodied in a car—has remained common. A commercial for the Mercury Cougar which has been shown on television recently shows all the elements of the myth of freedom, with only an alteration in the gender of the protagonist to show that these are the eighties. A woman in a dress-for-success suit appears at her boss's desk and drops a pile of papers. Then she leaves her press card or security pass on the desk and leaves. A Tina Turner sound-alike begins singing "Proud Mary"—"Left a good job in the city, working for the Man every night and day, but I never lost a minute of sleeping worrying about the way things might have been." The woman gets in her Cougar, and drives out of town. Shots of the car moving through the streets and out onto the highways are intercut with shots of the woman at the wheel, undoing her dress-for-success tie. She arrives at the beach—and the afternoon sun shows that she, like all pioneers, has been heading west. Freed from her yuppie jacket, she assumes a pose of liberation, and then enters a cabin, sits at a typewriter, and taps out, "Chapter One."

Here are all the elements of the old myth—the liberation from the old ties, the movement west, the fresh start. What McLuhan's Quaker State ad makes contradictory by mixing with family and patriotism, appears here in a purer form. The man at the picnic only planned to quit, and he had a family to share his car with. The woman in the Cougar is free of all that. And it is not out of keeping with the myth that she has gone off to write the great American novel (I doubt that any viewer imagines that she is working in any other genre), for as R. W. B. Lewis points out, we like our authors, as well as their works, to fit the pattern of the liberated individual going out to face the unknown. (There is still the paradox of selling freedom along with an expensive product. A new car and the payment book that usually comes as standard equipment would discourage most people from quitting a job to start a book.)

The advertisers are exploiting a myth that is pervasive in American popular culture.   Our movies and television shows are full of versions of the man always moving on, perhaps looking for some unknown thing, never becoming entangled for very long in any society.  The frontiersman reappears in a car or on a motorcycle.  The celebration of truck drivers a few years ago grew out of this tradition.  (It is significant that the truckers became heroes as outlaws, able, with a little help from their good buddies on the CB to outwit the smokies and ignore the double nickel.)  Television has often drawn upon this image of the man-on-the-move in its programs as well as in its commercials:  the fellows on "Route 66" were always moving on, yet not going anywhere but down the highway.

In motion pictures cars have played a larger and larger role.  Many films have shown the adventures of the isolated individual—or small group—traveling the highways.  In recent years a number of movies have appeared in which the main action is the journey of an automobile through a host of dangers.  Many may try to stop it and its occupants, but though its enemies (patrol cars and other vehicles belonging to the authorities and the oppressors) are wrecked, it emerges from chases, jumps and spins unscathed.  This is not a genre that has attracted the praise of film critics, but people who go to the movies enjoy pictures like these, and they are successful.  They are also peculiarly American: not only do they depend on this country's vast expanses of empty highways, but they also grow out of the American dream of escape.  It is difficult to imagine a French or Italian *Cannonball Run.*

Popular songs, perhaps more insistently than any other element in popular culture, have celebrated the automobile and driving—especially driving with "no particular place to go."[7]  An amazing number of the songs played on AM radio stations involve cars in one way or another, so that the driver on the highway is often accompanied by a musical celebration of movement.  The countless car songs that have come out over the last forty years rarely describe driving toward some goal.   Rather, the sheer pleasure of moving is justification enough for traveling down the highway.[8]  To see how this tradition has lived on, one need only listen to Bruce Springsteen's records.  Though the Boss also criticizes the myth the car embodies (he sometimes sings about wrecks and about the good of staying put), he can also present it in all its power.  In a song like "Thunder Road" he even makes the movement a substitute for salvation in a religious sense:

All the redemption I can offer, girl,
Is beneath this dirty hood
With a chance to make it good somehow
Hey what else can we do now?
Except roll down the window and let the wind blow
Back your hair?
Well the night's busting open
These two lanes will take us anywhere . . .[9]

This connection may seem strange, but I do not think it is unusual. It would not have surprised Flannery O'Connor in the least. Hazel Motes shows even more faith in his car as a savior when he says that "Nobody with a good car needs to be justified."[10]

The car has represented freedom not only because it can be driven wherever the driver pleases—because "these two lanes will take us anywhere"—but also because the automobile brought with it a new sexual freedom. Recently some vehicles—vans for instance—have been notorious as venues for sexual encounters. The sexual possibilities of the automobile are certainly a frequent theme of rock 'n' roll songs. But it seems that sexual liberation has been one of the by-products of the automobile almost from its first appearance.[11] At the very least, automobiles contributed to the development of less supervised courtship customs. A car allowed not only the escape from a chaperone—which a simple walk would also do—but also the freedom of privacy in a reserved space.

The danger of some of the possibilities thus created was not lost on Catholic educators, and I am sure O'Connor heard something about them while growing up. I have seen an old high-school apologetics text that described the automobile as "one of the greatest dangers to the chastity of modern youth." Such warnings are now hilarious, probably did little good, and were undoubtedly completely accurate.

O'Connor takes advantage of the sexual element in the myth of the automobile in both her novels. In *Wise Blood*, Hazel Motes wishes to prove his freedom. In part he tries to do this simply by driving his Essex, but while sitting in his car the idea of seducing Sabbath Lily Hawks comes to mind. Sabbath Lily, who is herself out to seduce Motes, makes as much use as she can of Motes's car in pursuing her goal. In *The Violent Bear It Away*, Tarwater is molested by the man who picks him up in a lavender and cream-colored car. Sexual danger, together with sexual liberation is part of the popular meaning of the car O'Connor exploits.

The sexual liberation that cars brought with them is, however, only a secondary reason for their identification with freedom in the American mind. It is much more important that they offer each individual the ability to control his own movements, to choose his own course. Some feeling of power and freedom comes to most people, I think, when they are traveling unimpeded down a highway. Perhaps traffic jams annoy us so much because they remind us of our limitations just when we are beginning to forget them, when we are beginning to feel free. In any case, the association of the automobile with freedom springs from the reality of freedom it offers.

It might be interesting to compare the associations that have grown up around the automobile and the train in popular culture. If I am not mistaken, trains are much more often linked to helplessness and hopelessness than cars are. (There are a lot of wreck stories and songs concerning both cars and trains, but they, I suppose, are about the same.) If the automobile is associated with freedom, with being in control of your destiny, trains are associated with being helpless or fated, with destinies that cannot be changed. The train's whistle is a lonesome one—and the train may not run right.[12] In many blues and country songs, deserted lovers think of the train that takes their loves away from them—"How long, how long, baby, Has that evenin' train been gone?"[13] The train goes where its tracks take it, not where you would like it to, and it lends itself to images of being powerless to change things. Or it appears when a speaker feels determined, not able to change his course of action. In "The House of the Rising Sun," the speaker says, "I've got one foot on the platform, the other's on the train/ I'm goin' back to New Orleans, to wear that ball and chain." She cannot change things; she cannot even decide not to return to "spend her life in sin and misery." Even today, when trains are not such a common part of the life of most people as they once were, they reappear when the image is of a fate that cannot be resisted. Springsteen, for example, chooses the image of a "Downbound Train," rather than one of the cars he grew up with, when his story is of a life that is inexorably falling apart.[14] His choice of image is perfectly fitting: on a train we often feel helpless; it goes where it goes and if something goes wrong we do not know why and can do nothing about it. The associations that have grown up around both the car and the train reflect the social—even the technical—reality of the two forms of transportation. O'Connor exploits these differing associations in *Wise Blood*, where Hazel Motes feels confined on a train, but free in a car.

The images of liberation associated with the car must often, I think, have an influence on a person's image of himself, even on the deepest level. If we are told constantly that we are free and that we can always drive away, we may begin to believe it even in the spiritual realm. The Victorian poet announced defiantly that he was the master of his fate, the captain of his soul.[15] A modern American might say—or at least believe—that he is behind the wheel of his soul, and while he is in the driver's seat he will take his fate down what road he pleases.

The image twentieth-century people have of themselves embraces many contradictory elements, but one of the strongest of them is an atomist individualism, a complete faith in the power of the free and isolated individual. (The French existentialists, I understand, were car lovers; it was by no means inappropriate.) Cars, as we experience them, and even more as we imagine them, embody this image perfectly. In just the same way, they embody the image of the free and unrooted individual that has grown up in American literature over the last two centuries.

## A Literature of Drifters

> Such was that happy Garden-state,
> When Man there walk'd without a Mate:
> After a Place so pure, and sweet,
> What other Help could yet be meet!
> But 'twas beyond a Mortal's share
> To wander solitary there:
> Two Paradises 'twere in one
> To live in Paradise alone.
>     —Andrew Marvell, from "The Garden"

English novels have traditionally described the individual in society. If they chart the wanderings of an outcast, it is only so he can return to Paradise Hall amid rejoicing. Most nineteenth-century English novels end with a marriage—a ceremony which marks both the creation of a new social unit and the entry of the young individual into society's traditional structures. The nineteenth-century American novels that are still read rarely end with this sort of union of two individuals, and of a couple with the society around them. Instead, the American hero usually remains outside, the sole survivor of his ship, the uncivilized boy still ready to light out for the territory. At the end of the American hero's picaresque adventure, there is no return home.

Even after the contrast between English and American novels ceased to be marked by the conventional ending, the differences in their interests remained. English novelists still seem more interested in showing the myriad interrelationships that make up society than do American writers.[16]  American writers still concentrate on the isolated hero. While America has produced authors, such as Howells and James and Fitzgerald, who describe relations between the sexes and between the individual and society, the authors that seem most characteristically American—Melville, Twain, Hemingway—depict, for the post part, isolated males cut off from their communities. The main tradition of American literature, in both fiction and nonfiction, is not concerned with people in societies—not even with people in American society. Our classics are about the man alone.

The scholars who have charted the course of American literature, Leslie Fiedler and R. W. B. Lewis, for example, have recognized the solitary and ever-moving male as the central figure in our tradition. They have sometimes even celebrated this figure as quintessentially American. Americans may have written novels about young men and women finding their places in society, but the real American hero stands alone—or moves on alone.

I am not trying to suggest that O'Connor's work was much influenced by the theorists themselves. I am certain that she was well acquainted with the tradition they describe, and that she plays off against it in her works. And while I cannot prove that O'Connor read much of Lewis and Fiedler, it is hardly possible that she could avoid at least hearing something of them.[17]  She was certainly not put off by the theory, even in its most provocative form. She says in a letter to John Hawkes, "I'm not skittish about Leslie Fiedler. He doubtless knows a good thing when he sees it, even if he does have to wrap it up in Freud."[18]

Fiedler does concentrate on the sexual elements in the tradition of the ever-moving American hero, making the involvement of the white hero with a colored man central. I think it might be truer to see what Fiedler called a "homoerotic" element as another expression of the escapee's rejection of society. But, whether or not the hero is seeking rest in "the arms of a dusky male lover," the American tradition is, as Fiedler sees it, dominated by the man running away, and this figure's prominence is what, for better or worse, most strongly differentiates our literature from the European.

While English and continental novels deal with society and the relations between the sexes, with marriage and adultery, the great American novels do not. Aside from James and some of Hawthorne, America has produced "books that turn from society to nature or nightmare out of a desperate need to avoid the facts of wooing, marriage, and child-bearing."[19] Fiedler sees Rip Van Winkle presiding over the birth of our tradition, finding a long line of flights from women and responsibilities extending from him. Rip, who has the good fortune to sleep until his wife is dead and he has become a stranger in his own land, certainly does achieve some version of the American Dream. But most American heroes make their escapes not in time, but in space. While Rip escapes his wife and community by letting twenty empty years pass over him, his successors make their escapes by traveling, in one way or another, into the wilderness.

> Ever since, the typical male protagonist of our fiction has been a man on the run, harried into the forest and out to sea, down the river or into combat—anywhere to avoid "civilization," which is to say, the confrontation of a man and woman which leads to the fall to sex, marriage, and responsibility. (Fiedler 1982, p. 26)

"Down the highway" could appropriately be added to Fiedler's list of possible escapes. The modes of escape vary over the years, but the story remains the same.

The tradition that Fiedler describes is almost entirely male, both in its writers and their protagonists. As Nina Baym points out, the myth the Americanists, like Fiedler, have declared central to the American tradition effectively excludes women.[20] (It also excludes many kinds of men.)

> The myth narrates a confrontation of the American individual, the pure American self divorced from specific social circumstances, with the promise offered by the idea of America. This promise is the deeply romantic one that in this new land, untrammeled by history and social accident, a person will be able to achieve complete self-definition. Behind this promise is the assurance that individuals come before society, that they exist in some meaningful sense prior to, and apart from, societies in which they happen to find themselves. The myth also holds that, as some-

> thing artificial and secondary to human nature, society exerts an
> unmitigatedly destructive pressure on individuality. To depict it
> at any length would be a waste of artistic time; and there is only
> one way to relate it to the individual—as an adversary. (Baym,
> p. 71)

Women appear in this myth, not as the protagonists who confront the possibilities of the new land, but as hindrances to the male protagonists. "In these stories, the encroaching, constricting, destroying society is represented with particular urgency in the figure of one or more women" (p. 72).[21]

The very mobility demanded of the hero by the American myth did something to exclude women from it. Though she does not consider it as important as the identification of women with society, Baym recognizes that the demand for a hero who is always able to move on excludes women. "In order to represent some kind of believable flight into the wilderness, one must select a protagonist with a certain believable mobility, and mobility has, until recently been a male prerogative in our society" (p. 72). Baym goes on to say that, since most men are not as mobile as the myth requires, "the story is really not much more vicarious, in this regard, for women than for men." But it does mean that the heroes of the American myth will be male, as the frontier was primarily male.

The tradition built on this myth—and the literary theories built on that tradition—exclude a great many American authors. They exclude women authors because women are cast as "entrappers and domesticators" as characters, and as sentimental scribblers as writers. They are not so likely to fill their works with the moving American myth in its classic form.[22] Writers who are interested in how people behave in society and, like British novelists, describe wooing and marriage are left at the fringes of the canon. William Dean Howells in describing the moral dilemmas people face in business and courtship cuts himself off from the mainstream American theory. If only, in *The Rise of Silas Lapham*, he had sent Tom Corey to Mexico alone, after escaping Penelope! And it seems to me this theory leaves little room for religious writers, since the hero must travel through the world completely free, no more responsible to God than to a wife or civilization.

Beyond excluding a great many authors—and, more importantly, a great range of human experience—from the first ranks of American literature, the myth that theorists like Fiedler celebrate presents a very limited masculine ideal. The protagonists in this tradition can only be boys or boyish men. "The mythic America is boyhood,"[23] and our classics are boys' books. The tradition has no place for responsible male adults. This boyishness is certainly a central part of much American literature—and of much American popular culture: the cowboy is eternally boyish. But Americanist critics, even if they see this boyishness as problematical, make it essentially *American*. Our nation has no place for other masculine ideals. Certainly other literatures do have different—and maturer—male ideals to offer. The gentleman in English fiction must learn to act like an adult; in some continental fiction (Manzoni's for instance) a man must learn to mold his behavior to fit Christian precepts. But the American hero—at least as the Americanists present him—is always escaping from adult roles.

R. W. B. Lewis also presents the American hero as an ever-moving male. Lewis describes how this figure, whom he calls the American Adam, enters American fiction, and how he develops in our novels.[24] But Lewis is equally interested in the career the hero has had outside fiction. Like many other Americans, our Adam got his start in theological controversy before moving on to a faster growing field of literature. Even after he makes a new beginning in fiction, the memory of those theological arguments clings to the ever-new American hero.

Once he enters fiction, Lewis's American hero has few positive characteristics. What is most important about him is his freedom from all constraints. He is not tied to the past by memory, to any place by duty or habit, or to any person by a permanent burden of responsibility. He is alone in the world, but his isolation is full of possibilities.

> The evolution of the hero as Adam in the fiction of the New World—an evolution which coincides precisely, as I believe, with the evolution of *the* hero of American fiction generally—begins rightly with Natty Bumppo. I call such a figure the hero in *space*, in two senses of the word. First, the hero seems to take his start outside time, or on the very outer edges of it, so that his location is essentially in space alone; and, second, his initial habitat is space as spaciousness, as the unbounded, the area of total possibility. The Adamic hero is discovered, as an old stage direction might have it, "surrounded, detached in *measureless oceans* of space." (P. 91)

Of course, the space that Natty Bumppo travels through is, most literally, the frontier of woods and prairies. And the frontier has indeed held out to many Americans the dream of complete freedom and endless possibilities.

The frontier is also beyond the influence of society, and Lewis's Hero in Space has little to do with any settled society. Natty Bumppo, for instance, hardly ever comes within a hundred miles of settlements. Lewis sees the isolation of heroes like Cooper's as characteristically American: "The individual in America has usually taken his start outside society; and the action to be imitated may just as well be his strenuous efforts to *stay* out as his tactics for getting inside" (p. 101). Whether it is indeed possible for any individual— even in America—to begin life outside society seems doubtful, but it is certain that many heroes in American fiction, especially the heroes in space Lewis describes, do their best to stay out of it.

In avoiding society, Natty Bumppo and the other heroes Lewis describes must also avoid women. The only part of the plot of *The Deerslayer* that Lewis sees standing out from "the medley of capture and rescues" is the final episode, when "Judith Hutter, a raven-haired charmer of doubtful background, tries to talk Natty round to marrying her, in language he modestly fails to grasp" (p. 104). Both Cooper and Lewis seem to regard Natty's escape from women for the solitary life of the woods and plains a triumph.

> Cooper was wise to . . . leave him alone at the close of *The Deerslayer,* in his spatial world unencumbered by wife and family, and to conclude the entire Leatherstocking series with the hero's birth and young manhood. For according to the vision Cooper shared, the end was paradoxically a fresh beginning, and no trans-forming experience was envisaged or desired beyond it. (P. 105)

The hero must remain free. What is more, he must remain ever new. He must keep all the possibilities before him open by choosing none that would burden him with responsibilities and limit his actions in the future. There are endless fresh beginnings, but no consumma-tion.

Since the hero is always beginning fresh, he has no past, or none that need be recalled. He is instead "the inventor of his own charac-ter and creator of his personal history" (p.111). Since he makes himself, he need not recall his own past. The section of Cooper's works that Lewis examines most closely is the passage in which

Deerslayer becomes Hawkeye. In this scene he is "'witnessing his own birth'—or rebirth as the American Adam: accomplished appropriately in the forest on the edge of a lake, with no parents near at hand, no sponsors at the baptism, springing from nowhere" (pp. 104-5). No parents since he has no past; no sponsors for he is part of no society. American heroes often create new identities (Natty Bumppo has a different name in every novel; Huck Finn has been everyone from a girl to Tom Sawyer by the end of his trip down the river.) They usually have hazy pasts; like Huck Finn, they don't take much stock in dead people.

The vision of being free and new in some vast open space, without parents or sponsors, untroubled by the memory of any dead person, pervades American literature, and extends far beyond romances set on the frontier. It is the image that closes Stevens's "Sunday Morning," and answers the voice that tells "the tomb in Palestine" is nothing more than the grave of Jesus:

> We live in an old chaos of the sun,
> Or old dependency of day and night,
> Or island solitude, unsponsored, free,
> Of that wide water, inescapable.
> Deer walk upon our mountains, and the quail
> Whistle about us their spontaneous cries;
> Sweet berries ripen in the wilderness;
> And, in the isolation of the sky,
> At evening, casual flocks of pigeons make
> Ambiguous undulations as they sink
> Downward to darkness, on extended wings[25]

Freed from the past, from the memory of sin and redemption, we are as free as the beasts that move through the isolation of the wilderness.

If only to avoid society and women and his own past, the hero in space must keep moving. When Cooper writes about a novel about Renaissance Venice, his hero must end unhappily, for

> there was no place for him to escape to. But in those novels where the setting is the untracked American forest, the world always lies all before the hero, and normally, like Huck Finn, he is able to light out again for the "territories."
>
> The principle of survival in his essential character requires him to constantly "jump off" (this was the current phrase)—to

keep, as it were, two jumps ahead of time. (P. 100)

Lewis sees his hero following the trail broken by the real frontiersmen who kept moving ahead of advancing civilization. But though the hero's exploits may be grander than the real pioneer's, the range of his activities is severely limited. Deerslayer—like the other heroes in space—may keep moving like the Daniel Boone who was angry that he had "not been two years at the licks before a damned Yankee came and settled down *within a hundred miles of me!*" (p.100). But he cannot, like Boone, found a settlement, marry, and beget children. To keep his "essential character" he must refuse any offer of marriage, and keep heading toward "freer country to the west."

Constant motion through space, then, is what marks the American Adam as he appears in fiction, but Lewis also finds the ideal of always moving on in other versions of the myth. The idea of moving appears often in Whitman's poems, and Lewis associates it with the childlike newness of his persona.

> Whitman begins . . . as a child, seemingly self-propagated, and he is always going *forth;* one of his pleasantest poems was constructed around that figure. There is only the open road, and Whitman moves forward from the start of it. Homecoming is for the exile, the prodigal son, Adam after the expulsion, not for the new unfallen Adam in the western garden. (P. 50)

Whitman in poems like "Song of the Open Road" does make a traveling speaker sound fresh and all sufficient. Once he is on "the long brown path . . . leading wherever I choose" he is in control of his fate—"I am myself good fortune." Moving down the open road he can make his own world.[26]

Lewis sees the moving hero, in both fiction and poetry, as but one expression of the ideal of the American Adam. This archetypal American hero—or image of the American nation—is completely new and able to choose his course. "The world is all before him," but his choices have not been limited by an earlier decision, as Adam's were when he and Eve "Through Eden took their solitary way." Lewis describes him as "a figure of heroic innocence and vast potentialities, poised at the start of a new history" (p.1). He is innocent because he is outside the web of old commitments and old sins, and has not yet made or committed any of his own. His potentialities always remain just that, for in realizing them he would be likely to lose his innocence. The Adam struggles to remain always on the point of a new beginning, but never to carry the beginning on to an end. He is outside society—either far from it or an outcast—because societies are built of memories and old choices, and he has no part of that inheritance. He has little to do with women. There is no place for an American Eve. The only role for a woman in the American Adam's story is that of Lilith, the shadowy temptress who finally did not matter much. The American Adam stands alone. He seems not even to have to face God, for he is often as not described as self-created, or self-begotten. The figure needs a God to limit his possibilities no more than a father to stain his innocence with an inherited sin. He is

> an individual emancipated from history, happily bereft of ancestry, untouched and undefiled by the usual inheritances of family and race; an individual standing alone, self-reliant and self-propelling, ready to confront whatever awaits him with the aid of his own unique and inherent resources. It was not surprising , in a Bible-reading generation, that the new hero (in praise or disapproval) was most easily identified with Adam before the Fall. (P. 5)

It is as if the voyage to America had erased all human history—and the guilt that went with it—from Adam on.

The real situation of the white settlers in America gave some support to the idea of a new and fresh start. The immigrants were far from their ancestral homes and settling a land that was new, at least, to them. The unfenced green land must have seemed like a garden when it did not appear as a howling wilderness. The image of the American as a new Adam, however, does not seem to have appeared until New England had been under cultivation for quite some time. The earliest settlers, if they needed a biblical model, seem to have seen themselves as God's chosen nation in the wilderness, not as the primal man in the Garden.

Adam is not really a very good image of the American. Perhaps the westward movement of the settlers made it seem like a reversal of the exile of the first men into the lands east of Eden. Americans up to the present have dreamed of a return to Eden—"We've got to get ourselves back to the Garden."[27] But as the Bible presents it, the Fall is not so easily reversible. And Genesis offers a better image for the actions of the American nation on this continent than Adam. Adam found himself alone in the Garden, but the first Americans did not find an empty land. As in the old story, the farmer killed his brother who did not till. It is not surprising that the tradition of the American Cain did not take root—Americans have never wanted to admit that they bear any stain or mark—but the figure of one who was at once the first farmer and the first vagabond would seem perfect for this country.[28]

The image of the American as Adam took its strength, however, not so much from the real American experience as from a theological premise. Man is innocent and needs no savior. Puritanism had emphasized the effects of the Fall, and the need of each soul for the aid of Jesus. "In Adam's Fall we sinned all," the primer reminded New England children. Nineteenth-century writers denied that human nature bore any hereditary taint, and held up the image of Adam before his Fall. Each person began life as free and innocent as Adam did. This theological emphasis explains why so little of Adam's story appears in the American versions of it. For the American Adam's story ends just where the biblical Adam's begins: he finds himself alone and innocent; perhaps, in Whitman's version of the myth, he names the animals. Then he finds new scenes in which he can be alone and innocent, for if the story went on, there would come the woman, and the fall, and the long generations of fathers and sons—of sons implicated in their fathers' deeds.

As Lewis describes it, what the nineteenth-century progressives found most offensive in the Calvinism that had dominated the intellectual life of New England was "the doctrine of inherited guilt; the imputation onto the living individual of the disempowering effects of a sin 'originally' committed by the first man" (p. 28). Man is not originally corrupt or depraved, but innocent. This conception of the nature of man was the impetus for the New England Unitarian and Transcendentalist movements in the early nineteenth century. The rejection of Original Sin was bound up with the denial of the Trinity, for it did away with the function of the Trinity's second person.[29] If each began "his spiritual career with an unsullied conscience, there was no need for expiation ... no need ... of a propitiation of sin" and thus "the reason for the divinity of Jesus evaporated" (p. 31). And a universe in which both man and nature are good hardly requires a God to look after it at all, as Emerson and his disciples discovered. The personal God who threatens punishment and offers salvation evaporates into an Oversoul almost indistinguishable from nature itself.

Emerson's own ideas grew out of a rejection of the doctrine of Original Sin and salvation through the merits of Jesus. A remnant of the dogma of Christ's redemptive sacrifice drove him out of his Unitarian church. He left his pulpit rather than continue the practice of Communion: no savior's body or blood was given up for him. As Horace Bushnell recognized in the nineteenth century, the premise of Emerson's Nature was a rejection of the idea of Original Sin and Redemption: "Redemption itself, considered as a plan to raise man out of thraldom under the corrupted action of nature . . . is a fiction. There is no such thraldom, no such deliverance" (Lewis, p. 70). Some later American writers have followed Emerson's line of reasoning. In "Sunday Morning" the rejection of the idea of a redemptive sacrifice, of "the Dominion of blood and sepulchre" leads to the rejection of the idea of the divinity of Jesus:

> She hears, upon that water without sound,
> A voice that cries, "The tomb in Palestine
> Is not the porch of spirits lingering.
> It is the tomb of Jesus, where he lay."

Like Emerson removing the bread and wine, Wallace Stevens would "dissipate/ The holy hush of ancient sacrifice."

With his belief in original innocence, Emerson could say, "Here's for the plain old Adam, the simple genuine self against the whole world" (Lewis, p. 6). That he can use the idea of the "old Adam" as a positive image shows how much of the traditional Christian view of the nature of man Emerson has rejected. While the "old Adam" had long meant the sinful nature that had to be recognized and struggled against, to Emerson it is the authentic self that is innocent, good, and able to stand against the whole world. He is not the old Adam of St. Paul and Augustine and Jonathan Edwards, but an ever old and ever new Adam, who has the world before him, but nothing behind him.

Lewis describes nineteenth-century American literature as a struggle between groups supporting different views of the Adamic figure. Taking his terms from Emerson, he calls the old Calvinists the party of Memory, and the new believers in innocence the party of Hope. He adds a middle group, which he calls the party of Irony, who doubted man's innocence but did not return to the Calvinist's doctrines of predestination and total depravity. Certainly the conflict of writers with a different view of Man's guilt or innocence has dominated American literature. The Puritans preached the memory of the sin; the Transcendentalists expressed the hope of innocence; reactions to both positions continue to this day. The controversy has shaped American fiction as much as any other part of our culture. Our first novels appeared when the party of Hope was in the ascendancy, and so, as Fiedler says, have the air of being "innocent, unfallen in a disturbing way"[30] But the other view of Man has also manifested itself in our novels. The hope of innocence itself recalls the memory of guilt. As Fielder puts it, the American novelist "lives on the last horizon of an endlessly retreating vision of innocence—on the 'frontier,' which is to say, the margin where the theory of original goodness and the fact of original sin come face to face" (p. 27). Lewis sees the real flowering of our fiction coming when the innocent, Adamic hero must return to confront a fallen world, as in Hawthorne and Melville.

The image of physical motion has appealed to American writers because it expresses the idea of innocence. A man can move on and leave it all behind. By traveling on he can escape from the past, from history, from the sins of the fathers. As the nation itself began afresh thanks to the journey across the Atlantic, and continues to offer fresh starts on the frontier, each man can start afresh. The fresh starts offered by endless movements provide an escape from the burdens of sin—for at the very least the doctrine Original Sin means that no complete fresh start is possible, and that no one can be completely self-reliant. Emerson may have little good to say about travel, but the ideal of self-reliance he holds up implies never-ending movement. He admires the

> sturdy lad from New Hampshire or Vermont, who in turn tries all the professions, who *teams it, farms it, peddles*, keeps a school, preaches, edits a newspaper, goes to Congress, buys a township, and so forth, in successive years, and always, like a cat, falls on his feet.[31]

In fiction the American tradition of innocent male wanderers stretches from Natty Bumppo in the woods and prairies through Huck Finn and Jim floating down the Mississippi on their raft to Hunter Thompson and his attorney driving through Las Vegas in a car with a trunk full of drugs. From *The Deerslayer* and *Huckleberry Finn* to *Fear and Loathing in Las Vegas*[32] American literature has been full of stories about men running away but not going anywhere in particular.

It is often easier to say what these wandering American heroes wish to escape than what they hope to find. Huck Finn wants to escape first the constraining "sivilization" the Widow forces on him—school and clean clothes—and then Pap's brutality. But it is impossible to say where he is going except that he is going away. Jim is of course a different story. He, unlike Huck, knows what he wants to do with his freedom—he envisions living with his wife and children — and he has a plan for his movements: down to Cairo, up the Ohio, into the free states. But Huck from the beginning to the end just wants to go, across the river, into the Territory, away. Even grown-up American heroes share Huck's motivations: Ishmael decides on a whaling voyage because he finds himself in the mood either to travel or to begin knocking people's hats off in the street.

Hunter Thompson and his Samoan attorney—who can both drive the great white whale and annoy strangers in the streets— seem to be trying to escape everything by driving cars and taking drugs. Society is their enemy: it does not oppress them the way the Widow and Pap oppress Huck, but they feel themselves set against it nonetheless. The goal of their movements is hardly clearer than Huck's. Thompson has his magazine assignments—first to report on an off-road motorcycle and dune-buggy race, then to cover a convention on drugs and law enforcement. But these tasks seem only to provide the cash for rented cars and a stockpile of drugs. They float by like Huck's raft, are used and forgotten. The other goal of the journey is "The American Dream," and the phrase is ambiguous enough to cover the entire frightening trip. The Dream has produced the city devoted to hopes of getting rich quick in the western desert, the races of hundreds through the sands, and the lawmen gathered to control the outlaws. But more than that, the American Dream is the Frontier myth of always moving on and finding ever fresh chances. Thompson and his companion fulfill that dream by moving on and on with no final destination.

Huck Finn's only desire at the end of the journey down the river is to keep on moving. Twain's contrived happy ending gives both Huck and Jim their freedom—Jim's from slavery and Huck's from Pap—and all Huck can use freedom for is continued escape. "I reckon I got to light out for the Territory ahead of the rest, because Aunt Sally she's going to adopt me and sivilize me and I can't stand it."[33] Huck's story is a quest without a grail: the movement is its own reward. In *Fear and Loathing* Thompson is constantly lighting out for somewhere or other. There is no new empty land available, but the cars and drugs allow for endless trips and tripping.

The justification for movement seems to be a very simple kind of freedom. In *Huck Finn* the journey down the river sometimes appears perfectly idyllic:

> We said there warn't no home like a raft, after all. Other places do seem so cramped up and smothery, but a raft don't. You feel mighty free and comfortable on a raft. (P. 139)

The best home is one that moves, that leaves you unrestricted. The car in *Fear and Loathing* shares some of the raft's appeal: the rest of the world does seem "cramped up and smothery" beside it. But there is hardly anything idyllic in its drives through the desert. The dream of movement seems to have turned sour, only remaining preferable to staying put. The frontier has been closed for eighty years and there is no real Territory to light out for. Thompson begins his trip in Los Angeles, as far west as you can go. What is left of the frontier myth, of the dream of lighting out for the territory, is the ability to move, an image of the man alone against a strange and often hostile world.

As Huck and Jim float down the Mississippi, they visit a number of river towns and find themselves briefly involved in several societies. In each case, they are lucky to escape quickly, for almost everything they see is corrupt and false. There are slave hunters who will not aid a sick man for fear of contagion, Kentucky gentlemen who take their rifles to church and kill and mutilate even boys in a feud whose cause is long forgotten, a colonel who kills a helpless drunk on the slightest provocation, and then reveals the cowardice of the mob that would avenge him, revivalists easily duped by charlatans, confidence-men who would trick the helpless out of their savings, and men who would tar and feather those thieves. The two on the raft are all right as long as they can keep moving and do not become entangled in any of these stationary scenes of corruption. The moving raft is a place of innocence; the stable shore, the setting for evil. The story seems to go wrong when Huck stops moving: when Tom Sawyer takes control, he refuses to move, delays the escape, and makes Huck and Jim as immobile as the people they have passed.

In *Fear and Loathing* there is a similar opposition between the two in the car and the people they meet as they travel. Thompson and his attorney are by no means innocents, but those they meet are so "decadent and depraved" that they look on them with wonder and revulsion. Everyone in Las Vegas seems to be either evil, false, or contemptibly naive. They are also dangerous. As in *Huck Finn*, the world the travelers move through is hostile; if the secret of either the runaway slave or the cache of drugs is revealed, the journey will end in disaster. Thompson and his attorney have as much in common with the King and the Duke as with Huck and Tom, but all of them share the same fear of the societies they pass through. All are willing to dupe those they encounter when it seems necessary. Huck and Jim may not hate or despise those they pass, as the King and the Duke and Thompson and his attorney do, but they are separated from them just as completely.

I would not want to press my comparison of Huck Finn and Thompson's narrator too far. There is certainly all the moral difference in the world between the two characters. But they are nevertheless still versions of the same American story. Thompson in *Fear and Loathing* seems like a Huck Finn who has grown up and turned mean. He is the outcast little boy lighting out for the Territory dressed up as a journalist. One of the things that makes him finally so unpleasant is that there is still so much of the irresponsible boy in him: his adolescent hostility to authority, his childish confidence in his ability to lie his way out of a scrape, and his thoughtless readiness to move on and leave any mess he has created behind, do not seem innocent in a grown man. The combination of childish recklessness and grown-up talk about guns and drugs is probably what makes *Fear and Loathing* so popular among college students.

Not only is Thompson's hero no longer a boy, he does not have a real evil to run from—Huck and Jim are really escaping slavery—or a real wilderness to escape to—there is no Territory to light out for. The tradition of flight continues, but in the embittered form of dangerous drugs and aimless drives back and forth across the desert. The opposition to society remains, but society seems now guilty as much of bad taste as of moral evil. Thompson seems to merge with another part of the tradition of the ever-moving American hero. Like the King and the Duke, and the ambiguous figure Melville left floating somewhere on the river with them, he plays the Confidence Man—not the innocent refugee from society, but its ruthless enemy.

In their travels, the heroes of *Huck Finn* and *Fear and Loathing* leave behind not only society, but also the entire female sex. Women appear only incidentally. For Huck Finn, women at first represent the social restraints he is trying to escape. The Widow Douglas and Miss Watson are trying to "sivilize" him—they have him wear tight clothing, tell him not to smoke, and teach him a little about religion. None of it seems natural to Huck, and he is glad to get away from them. On the way down the river, Huck runs into a very few women—Mrs. Loftus who gives him pointers on being a girl, Mary Jane, whom he protects from the King and the Duke—but none of them play any great role in his story. The only woman in the last section in the novel is Aunt Sally, who wants to continue the Widow's attempts to civilize Huck.[34] At the beginning and the end of Huck's journey women appear as a restraining force to be escaped. They play a small role in one or two of his adventures, but for the most part female influence means confinement—and Huck's descriptions of the works left behind by Emmeline Grangerford make feminine civilization appear dreary to the point of deadliness.

In *Fear and Loathing*, women play an even smaller role. Not only are Thompson and his attorney unencumbered by even the memory of women, but they move through almost entirely male societies— the cross-country race and the DA's convention. Lucy, the one woman who appears for more than a page or so, is almost faceless. She is first an opportunity for an adventure, and then a threat to be escaped, never more than that. The traveling men pick her up for narcotic and sexual adventures, and move on when those are over. She is just one more entanglement to be escaped—like the Highway Patrol. While Huck Finn wants to escape women, he at least feels some respect for them—Aunt Polly may never have told any stretchers; Mary Jane is a girl with sand—but Thompson's men seem to look on women, even more than on most things, with fear and loathing. Lucy is at first sight disgusting; then she becomes dangerous; and finally, after she has been terrified and humiliated, she is simply forgotten. Escape from her is presented as one of the narrator's minor triumphs. There is not much room for a woman in the tradition of the ever-moving American.

The only real bonds that develop in this tradition are between men who find themselves traveling together. The traveler does not require a companion—Huck joins Jim only by accident and does not seem to plan to take anyone with him when he sets out for the territory—but he often enjoys one. These male comrades often seem to be two against the whole world. While a female companion might involve the traveler in the webs of society—either by trying to domesticate him or by encumbering him with the responsibilities of marriage and family—a male companion presents no such danger. Men running together will not tempt each other to settle down. The two travelers usually come from such radically different societies that they cannot return to any home together, and are made even more outcast by their relationship with each other.

Since Leslie Fiedler's notorious essay "Come Back to the Raft Ag'in, Huck Honey,"[35] it has been impossible to ignore that many of the great works in the American tradition center on the relationships between white and colored men. Cooper's heroes are a white man and an Indian, Dana's companion in California is Hawaiian, Huck's friend Jim is black—and Hunter Thompson drives through the West with a Samoan attorney, a polynesian like Ishmael's Queequeg.[36] Whether "homoerotic" is the best term to describe Jim and Huck or Natty Bumppo and Chingachgook may be questionable, but it is certainly true that these male friendships take precedence over any relationship with women. And these male alliances can exist only outside society—on the frontier, in the whaling fleet, on the raft away from shore. The outcast running from society is separated even more completely from that society by the friends he chooses. If the American hero has a companion, it is one who will keep him running.[37]

Beyond women and society, the heroes of the American tradition are often also trying to escape something else: God. The Lord takes His place with women and social conventions as curbs on the free individual. Huck Finn is running from God in some sense from the first chapter of the novel. Considering the picture of paradise that Miss Watson has given him, it is not surprising that he makes up his mind not to try for it. Huck's moment of greatest strength and goodness comes when he gives up on praying, tears up the letter turning Jim in, and says, "All right, then, I'll *go* to hell" (Twain, p. 244).

Huck triumphs when he defies Miss Watson's God, but Twain's view of the Almighty is not so simple as his character's. Though it would be foolish to suggest Twain was orthodox, I believe he thought God was really better than believers made him out. In *Huck Finn* Twain has Huck talk ignorantly about Providence fairly often. Sometimes it seems that Huck's escapes really are providential. And Twain shows Huck ignoring some hints that God is really on the side of the escaping slave, not that of the master. In chapter one, the

Widow reads to Huck about "Moses and the Bulrushers," and he is

> in a sweat to find out all about him; but by-and-by she let it out that
> Moses had been dead a considerable long time; so then I didn't
> care no more about him; because I don't take no stock in dead
> people. (Twain, p. 12)

If Huck had taken stock in dead folk, and listened to the story of
Moses leading the children of Israel out of bondage, he might not
have needed to choose between betraying his friend and going to
Hell. It seems very significant that Huck is ignoring a story that
reflects his own; if Twain had not wanted us to see that Huck avoids
what might guide him, he could have had Miss Watson read about
Elisha and the bears.

In much of the American tradition, however, the hero's escape
from God is not qualified by any such irony. God is either simply
ignored or positively rejected by the traveling hero. In Hunter
Thompson's *Fear and Loathing*, God is ridiculed along with almost
everything else except drugs and good cars. Thompson keeps a
stream of casual blasphemy flowing through the book—from the
"Holy Jesus! What are these goddamn animals?" that greets his
hallucination in the first paragraph to his farewell "God's Mercy on
you swine" on the last page—but he makes his rejection of God more
explicit than that. In one of the few passages in which Thompson's
narrator reflects on something beyond his bizarre experiences, he
attacks the mystical Timothy Leary wing of the drug culture:

> [A] generation of permanent cripples, failed seekers, who never
> understood the essential old-mystic fallacy of the Acid culture:
> the desperate assumption that somebody—or at least some
> *force*—is tending that Light at the end of the tunnel.
>
> This is the same cruel and paradoxically benevolent bullshit
> that has kept the Catholic Church going for so many centuries. It
> is also the military ethic . . . a blind faith in some higher and wiser
> "authority." The Pope, the General, the Prime Minister. . . all the
> way up to "God." (Thompson, pp. 178-79)

The drug culture Thompson approves is not mystic, and gives no
promise of insight into the order of the universe. Instead it glorifies
escape, violence and power. After attacking the mystical druggies
Thompson expresses his admiration for Sonny Barger of the Hell's
Angels. He seems to prefer to associate the narcotics he relishes, not

with any promised vision of transcendence but with the image of the tough man always able to ride away. As the very name of Barger's gang shows, the man in motion thinks he can defy even God.[38]

*Fear and Loathing in Las Vegas* could be seen as the culmination of the tradition in American writing that I have been describing because it brings all of its elements to their extreme conclusions. The running is purely aimless running, with no hint of a goal. The rejection of society becomes sociopathic. The escape from women becomes misogynist cruelty. The rejection of God becomes unthinking blasphemy and facile nihilism. But even though they have taken on a sour taste, the elements in our tradition from the beginning are all here. And Thompson consciously recalls his precursors: Thompson and his attorney call the second car they rent "The White Whale." Melville's Ishmael, like Huck Finn, stands at the beginning of the tradition—running away from society and women, forming bonds only with another man, carrying on a "quarrel with God."[39]   (It is significant that while Ahab's crew has a goal, the insane quest for the white whale, Thompson really has none. In his car he takes on the role of the hostile force moving aimlessly through the seas, or highways.) The drugged-out pair of cynics in the rented car are the spiritual descendants of the earlier couple in the whaling ship, and even of the two innocents floating down the Mississippi on a raft.

Between Huck Finn and Hunter Thompson, American literature has included many men moving aimlessly through the world, always lighting out for somewhere. The tradition of the free male wanderer has been perhaps the strongest strain in American nonfiction from the beginning. Most of the nonfiction best-sellers of the nineteenth century describe a young man leaving the restrictions of society and going alone into the world, either on a ship to the South Seas (like Melville in *Typee*), or before the mast to California (like Dana), or up the Oregon Trail (like Francis Parkman), or to the wilds of the Yucatan (like John Lloyd Stevens). In this century the behind-the-wheel-meditation has taken the place of more exotic travels. Steinbeck and his dog set out in search of America, which they, perhaps not unreasonably, expect to find somewhere along the highway. Pirsig takes his son and his readers on a tour of Western and Eastern philosophy, but he makes the trip on a motorcycle heading west. Least Heat Moon drives the U.S. highways looking for a break with the past, as much as for anything else—"a man who couldn't make things go right could at least go"—and, as much as the others, he seems to reach his goal.[40] Movement is the basis and most of the justification for these literary travels. The assumption of the genre is that the man who travels the back roads without a destination will discover in the course of his wanderings the truth about himself or the essence of the American character. In some such books, however, the only truth the driver seems to find at the weary end of his travels is that life is as pointless as his aimless journey. These works seem to suggest, in fact, that aimless travel itself is the essence found on "A Journey into America." Jack Burden, in *All the King's Men*, comes to about that conclusion during his long drive west.

It is appropriate that in the twentieth century this tradition, both in fiction and nonfiction, expresses itself in the automobile. As *Fear and Loathing* and Kerouac's *On the Road* show, the car is the perfect vehicle, in every sense, for the myth of the self-propelling male. The driver is not limited by the flow of a river or slowed to the pace of his own footsteps. He can light out instantly and go anywhere. Like the frontier myth in popular culture, the literary myth of the completely free, completely new American finds expression in the automobile.

Cars are prominent in the stories of several early twentieth-century avatars of the American Adam. Jay Gatsby, for instance, attempts to live the myth of the Adamic American in the old East instead of on the frontier. He, like Deerslayer, is self-created; he has found his own name, and created most of his past. He seems hardly a part of the society he moves in. He gives off the air of innocence. What makes his story different is that innocence is already really lost, and he is trying to recapture not so much his own innocence as Daisy's. (When he dresses her all in white, Gatsby seems to be trying to transform the married woman into the virgin he once knew.) The novel is also full of movement—of the aimless movement of the automobiles back and forth between New York and the Eggs. Gatsby's aimless movement in the bright new car serves the same purpose as did the wanderings of earlier Adamic figures. Fitzgerald, however, both admires and knows the futility of the Adamic dream, and so Gatsby is destroyed after his car is wrecked. That an entangling woman precipitates his downfall is perfectly in keeping with the Adamic myth: the disaster comes when he allows a woman to control his fate and drive his car.

The innocent, self-created Adam is forced back into history when his car is wrecked. No longer in control of his destiny, he is killed because of the actions of another. And at the end, his father appears, the figure the self-created American would most want forgotten. *The Great Gatsby* presents touchingly ambiguous images of the dream of innocence and newness and the fact of history. The last paragraphs are a memory of the first explorers coming to the new world, but Nick recognizes that the dream of finding an ever-fresh, green land is an impossible one. And, in a reversal of the usual significance of East and West, he leaves the East of false newness for the stability of the old Midwest, where families have lived in the same house for generations. Gatsby, driving his car back and forth over the grim highway to New York, tried to be ever new and inno-cent, and tragically failed.

Some later American writers have positively asserted Man's innocence and linked it with the car. The main subjects of the beat poets seem to be Man's goodness and the importance of movement. Certainly one of the things Allen Ginsberg inherits from Whitman is a belief in the innocence of all things. He can describe scenes that would have convinced Emerson or Ellery Channing of the fact of total-depravity, and then say that everything is "holy."[41] Automo-biles and the open highway appear often in Ginsberg's poetry—to say nothing of the fiction of his friend Kerouac—and the ability to wander across the country seems to have something to do with the faith in man's holiness.

The automobile not only carries twentieth-century versions of the American Adam; it often sounds like the American Adam itself. Lewis describes his hero as "self-propelling" (p. 5). He is, literally, an *automobile*.[42] His capacity for independent and self-directed movement gives the new Adam his character, for it allows him to make fresh starts, to leave the past behind, and to imagine himself unencumbered by any past crime and responsible to no one. The capacity for independent and self-directed movement has also given the automobile its popularity—and it does free the driver from the limitations of distance and the railway timetable. It was perfectly natural that the image of the hero who displays his freedom and innocence by always moving on should be united with the image of the car that can drive in any direction at any time.

## The Memory of Fall and Defeat

O'Connor, I believe, attacked the myth of the ever-moving, innocent, American hero through the image of the automobile. She certainly numbered herself among the opponents of the tradition from which that image grew—the New England tradition that denies Original Sin and asserts Man's innocence. She instead counted herself the heir of two traditions that opposed it. She was glad to be a Southern writer, in part because Southerners believe in sin and remember the Fall. And as her literary model she chose Hawthorne, who had reminded New England of the sins of the fathers,[43] which it would rather have forgotten.

O'Connor wrote that she felt more kinship with Hawthorne than with any other American (*The Habit of Being,* p. 457). Part of the affinity must have grown out of their writing the same kind of fiction. She often quotes Hawthorne's distinction between the novel and the romance and says that she, like him, wrote the latter. But she also admired Hawthorne for being an opponent of the party of Hope. She recalls frequently that Hawthorne's daughter Rose became Mother Alphonsa in religious life, the founder of a congregation of Dominican nuns who care for cancer patients. O'Connor at times presents the daughter's acts as the fulfillment of the insights of the father, though in a lighter mood she says "My evil imagination tells me this was God's way of rewarding Hawthorne for hating the Transcendentalists" (*The Habit of Being,* p. 145).

O'Connor was consciously an opponent of the party of Hope, the strain in American literature that denies Original Sin and declares Man's innocence, often through the image of the ever-moving male. She has nothing good to say about Emerson, and traces "the vaporization of religion in America" to his decision "that he could no longer celebrate the Lord's supper unless the bread and wine were removed" (*The Habit of Being,* p. 511). She is naturally a disciple of the party of Irony.[44] She admires Hawthorne because in the face of those who proclaimed man's innocence and denied the necessity of salvation, he asserted the reality of sin.[45]

Hawthorne stands almost entirely outside the tradition of the innocent, wandering male. His characters cannot escape the past and create themselves anew, and they are not innocent. *The Scarlet Letter* reaches its climax when Dimmesdale admits his guilt and refuses to run away. Throughout that novel, both Dimmesdale and Hester have the chance to take the road into the wilderness—the road an Adamic American hero would take. Their triumph comes, not with an escape from society and the past into the wilderness, but with a return to the scaffold where the novel opens, a public confession that joins them to their community, and an admission of guilt.

The Americanist theorists have a great deal of trouble making *The Scarlet Letter* fit into their patterns. Hawthorne's novel is filled with characters rarely found in American fiction. The central male character is not a boy but an adult male, capable not just of evil but of guilt and repentance. Even more unusually, the central figure is not a man at all, but a sexually developed woman. Females in American fiction are usually either girls or domesticating mothers, aunts, and aged spinsters. They serve primarily to set off the male hero's quest for newness and innocence. Hester is a mother, but she does not represent domesticity and civilization. She is herself out-cast. The novel's exploration of guilt and innocence centers on her at least as much as on Dimmesdale. She triumphs, not by running from her past and her guilt, but by acknowledging them.

The other American literary tradition O'Connor took part in was the South's, and in it, as in Hawthorne, she would have found little confidence in Man's innocence. Southern writing—at least until after the era of Faulkner and the Fugitives—does not seem to have been particularly hospitable to the ideal of the new Adam. Instead of describing fresh and innocent figures who have no past and travel endlessly onward, ever creating themselves anew, South-ern writers, until recently, have tended to tell the stories of people who have all too much past, who stay in the old place remembering the deeds of generations long dead. Southern writing seems to emphasize the idea of Original Sin in one form or another.

Belief in Original Sin seems strong in Southern culture gener-ally. Southerners are still more likely than Americans elsewhere to believe in the reality of sin and the necessity for salvation through Jesus Christ. The different directions in which Protestantism devel-oped in the North and South point up the contrast. In New England the Calvinist belief in Original Sin evaporated in Unitarianism and its offshoots. In the South, on the other hand, the most powerful Protestant groups have been those that stress the believer's sinful-ness, and the need for Jesus as a personal savior. Nothing could be farther from the Unitarian confidence in the perfectibility of man than the theology of the Baptist and Pentecostal groups that preach that all men are lost unless Christ saves them.

Why Protestantism should have taken such different directions in North and South is a difficult question. Perhaps there are social reasons behind the New England's faith in Man's goodness and the South's belief in his depravity. It may be that Northerners have not been so often confronted by their complicity in an inherited sin. It sometimes appears that New England can forget its early crimes—the Indians for instance, seem to appear in the New England imagination only out West or at the first Thanksgiving; the scenes of their being dispossessed of their lands are quickly passed over—and that it has committed its sins at a sanitized distance whenever possible. Southerners, on the other hand, have had their society's sin always before them.   The reality of slavery, and of the different kinds of oppression that followed, could not be ignored.  The wrong done to the black must, I think, have contributed to the white Southerner's belief in the reality of sin, whether he acknowledged the wrong or not.   And many white Southerners justified their institutions by asserting that the other race was itself evil[46]—morally depraved or Children of Ham.  But whether perceived as the victim or cast in the role of demon, the black must have reminded the white of the reality of evil, and strengthened his belief in sin.

What is more, since the Civil War the South has known defeat, an experience of which, until very recently perhaps, the rest of the country has remained innocent.  O'Connor, when discussing the advantages of the Southern writer, quotes Walker Percy's response when asked why there are so many good Southern writers: "Because we lost the War."[47]  O'Connor goes on to give Percy's comment a theological gloss:

> He didn't mean by that simply that a lost war makes good subject matter.  What he was saying was that we have had our Fall.  We have gone into the modern world with an inburnt knowledge of human limitations and with a sense of mystery which could not have developed in our first state of innocence—as it has not sufficiently developed in the rest of our country.

The war was not only a lost cause, but also a bad cause to begin with, and part of the Southerner's recognition of human limitations may come from having been justly defeated.[48]  Failure in a good cause might not have shaken the belief in the innocence of the inhabitants of the new continent.

In any case, whether it grew out of their region's defeat or their race's position as oppressor, or simply because the theology of the Great Awakening did not fade away in the South as it did in the North, a recognition of the reality of Original Sin is pervasive in Southern writers.  Along with it Southern writers maintain an interest in history, in the way the acts of one generation affect the lives of their descendants, and in the intricate web of society, and the way one person's actions touch the lives of others.  The characters in

Southern fiction are not, in other words, heroes in space: they are not outside time, but caught up in history; they are not found in "Measureless oceans of space," but in some place with a character of its own; they live, not in the "unbounded, the area of total possibility," but in societies, where their actions are limited by any number of things, people, and ideas.

I do not think that many characters in Faulkner's novels, for example, fit the pattern of the American Adam. His characters may wander through the world, but they always seem to have some goal, even if it is a crazy one. They make their journeys in order to find or to build or to bury, not just to escape the entanglements of their old societies. The inhabitants of Yoknapatawpha County have long memories, and they remember the actions of their fathers and grandfathers.

Some of Faulkner's characters do appear as almost Adamic figures—patriarchs who would create their own worlds—but Faulkner shows that they are not in fact new and innocent. Sutpen in *Absalom, Absalom!* seems like a new Mississippi Adam when he appears in Jefferson. He seems to come out of nowhere, and begins creating his own world in Sutpen's Hundred. But Faulkner does not let the Adamic image remain intact. Sutpen is not without his history, and his history is the key to all his acts. He builds his little kingdom in the wilderness because of a slight he endured as a child back in the Tidewater. The memory of being sent to the back door of the mansion by the liveried black servant is the root of most of his actions—seeking his fortune in Haiti and the West, abandoning his first wife and eldest son, always trying to establish his own white line in a great house. He begins life caught in a web of wrong, and never escapes from it.

Sutpen, furthermore, leaves to his descendants a legacy of unexplained wrong that they never escape. None of Faulkner's characters seem to begin in innocence. Most of them are involved in inherited guilt of one kind or another. They also seem burdened by the history of their region, and by an innate corruption, an Original Sin. Some, like Ike McCaslin, may break out of the web of hereditary evils by recognizing them, but none are born free.

R. W. B. Lewis puts Isaac McCaslin in the tradition of the American Adam. He is "the closest equivalent in recent fiction" to Cooper's Deerslayer (*The American Adam*, p. 104). Just as Deerslayer is born anew in the forest when he kills his first Iroquois and becomes Hawkeye, McCaslin feels that "at the age of ten he was witnessing his own birth" when he first goes hunting with the older men.[49] But the contrasts between the two characters begin at this moment of new birth. Deerslayer is reborn as Hawkeye after his first victory. He is christened by his dying adversary and claims his new name as he stands alone and triumphant. McCaslin feels his new birth when he joins the company of older hunters. His experience is also described as an "apprenticeship" and a "novitiate." Deerslayer appears fully developed, like Adam in the garden. McCaslin, like Adam's descendants, must be trained and grow into maturity.

Hawkeye continues to be born afresh in each succeeding novel and is burdened by no inherited guilt or memory of ancestors. In "The Bear," however, Faulkner allows only one character this Adamic freedom from the memory of parents: Old Ben, "the old male bear itself, so long unwifed and childless as to have become its own ungendered progenitor" (p. 210). The humans are all caught up in history and burdened—as Isaac McCaslin sees most clearly—by the deeds of their progenitors. In his discussion with his cousin in the fourth part of "The Bear," Isaac recalls the whole history of the human race from Adam down to his own day. He resolves to give up his land because of the crimes of his ancestors, first in taking the land that was not theirs, and then in polluting it by keeping slaves, by fathering children on those slaves, and by committing incest with those children. Isaac overcomes his family's guilt by admitting it, not by escaping and making himself new.

Isaac McCaslin remembers what R. W. B. Lewis calls the "hopeful legend," that the New World provides "a second, last chance for humanity." But unlike most American heroes, McCaslin does not accept the myth our nation teaches.

> He knows, too, that the legend is false and that the New World began with its portion of historic, sinful inheritance. The knowledge protects him from the danger of innocence; but the memory of lost hope sends him on a lifelong errand of private atonement for everything that had betrayed it. The notion of original innocence tantalizes Isaac's sensibility not less than the accepted fact of original sin. . . . Isaac is a Natty Bumppo re-created by the dark energies of a Hawthorne. (*The American Adam,* p. 197)

The belief in Original Sin is even clearer in Robert Penn Warren than in Faulkner. Warren often recalls the idea of Original Sin, and often attacks the earlier American writers who denied it. He keeps questioning and correcting the party of Hope. Emerson is dead right at 38,000 feet, but on the ground his faith in man's innocence sounds false: human nature is wartier than he admits.[50] In *Brother to Dragons* Warren carries on a long conversation with Thomas Jefferson in the beyond, asking the president to square his faith in Man with the fact of the senseless crime committed by his nephews. He presents the believer in the innocence and perfectibility of man with the wickedness in his own blood. The dialogue in no place and any time calls into question the faith in Man's original goodness that seems particularly American. O'Connor admired this "Tale in Verse and Voices," as well as *All the King's Men*.[51]

The idea of Original Sin dominates *All the King's Men*. "Man is conceived in sin and born in corruption and he passeth from the stink of the didie to the stench of the shroud. There is always something."[52] Willie Stark means that there is always some dark part of a man's past for the blackmailer to find, but the grim phrase that is repeated through the novel means more than that. There is no innocence, and everyone shares some complicity in the evils around him. The past, for good or evil, cannot be escaped. What Jack Burden discovers is the sin of his father. He also discovers his own complicity in evils of his time. The discovery of his real father, of his father's crime, and of the way his own actions have led to the destruction of his friends, is finally liberating. Armed with the knowledge of his own guilt, Jack can right the course of his own life—marrying Anne Stanton, finishing the biography of his ancestor, and tending his dying putative father. Jack's story ends on a note of completion and fulfillment only because he has found and acknowledged the sins of his family and himself. There is indeed always something.

But earlier in the novel Jack Burden wants, not to acknowledge the guilt he is involved in, but to run from it. When he learns that Anne Stanton is having an affair with Stark, he suffers both because his early image of innocence is destroyed and because he realizes that he has, by bringing Anne and Stark together, brought its destruction about. He runs from guilt in a car heading west. In his long drive from Louisiana to Long Beach, California, he recapitulates the journeys of all the other Americans who have lit out for the West when they had a past they wanted to escape or a present they could not endure.

> That was why I had got into my car and headed west, because when you don't like it where you are you always go west. We have

always gone west . . .
        That was why I came to lie on a bed in a hotel in Long Beach,
California, on the last coast amid the grandeurs of nature. For that
is where you come, after you have crossed oceans and eaten stale
biscuits while prisoned forty days and nights in a stormy-tossed
rat-trap, after you have sweated in the greenery and heard the
savage whoop, after you have built cabins and cities and bridged
rivers, after you have lain with women and scattered children like
millet seed in a high wind, after you have composed resonant
documents, made noble speeches, and bathed your arms in blood
to the elbows, after you have shaken with malaria in marshes and
in the icy wind across the high plains. That is where you come, to
lie alone on a bed in a hotel room in Long Beach, California. (pp.
383-84)

The frontier lives on in the drive down the highway.
    But the journey does not have a goal. Its purpose is escape from
the past, with its memories and its guilt. And escape is what Jack
finds, for a time, in his drive. As he drives west, the past unfolds in
his memory. As he drives back, he is no longer remembering the
things which he had remembered coming out.

        For example. But I cannot give you an example. It was not so
    much any one example, any one event, which I recollected which
    was important, but the flow, the texture of the events, for meaning
    is never in the event but in the motion through event. Otherwise
    we could isolate an instant in the event and say that this is the
    event itself. The meaning. But we cannot do that. For it is the
    motion which is important. And I was moving. I was moving
    West at seventy-five miles an hour, through a blur of million-
    dollar landscape and heroic history, and I was moving back
    through time into memory. . .
        To the hum and lull of the car the past unrolled in my head like
    a film. (P. 339)

And once he has driven far enough, the past is gone.
    In the drive and the motion, Burden is seeking something like a
return to childhood innocence. What is more, he does in some sense
find that innocence in his drive west. He has kept the image of Anne
as an innocent child.

        Then, there came the day when that image was taken from me. I
    learned that Anne Stanton had become the mistress of Willie

Stark, that somehow, by an obscure and necessary logic I had handed her over to him. That fact was too horrible to face, for it robbed me of something out of the past by which, unwittingly until that moment, I had been living.

So I fled west from the fact, and in the West, at the end of History, the Last Man on that Last Coast, on my hotel bed, I had discovered the dream. That dream was the dream that all life is but the dark heave of blood and the twitch of nerve. When you flee as far as you can flee, you will always find that dream, which is the dream of our age. (P. 386)

The drive gives him the "bracing and tonic" dream that nothing means anything, that "nothing is your fault or anybody's fault." And having decided that nothing is any more than the Great Twitch, Burden can go back:

For after the dream there is no reason why you should not go back and face the fact which you have fled from (even if the fact seems to be that you have, by digging up the truth about the past, handed over Anne Stanton to Willie Stark), for any place to which you may flee will now be like the place from which you have fled. . . . And you can go back in good spirits, for you will have learned two very great truths. First, that you cannot lose what you have never had. Second, that you are never guilty of a crime which you did not commit. So there is innocence and a new start in the West, after all. (P. 386)

This innocence may be very different from that of the nineteenth-century American Adam, but it is part of the same tradition. And the innocence through nothingness certainly was the dream of the age in 1946, when *All the King's Men* first appeared. The argument for Man's freedom from guilt that Jack intuits on his hotel bed in Long Beach is not so different from the doctrines Sartre was expounding in France.[53]

Warren has Burden awaken from the dream that all is the Great Twitch, and by the end of *All the King's Men* Jack believes that there is always something rather than that there never is anything. Warren, like many Southern writers, retains his belief in Original Sin. But he also uses the car as an image of freedom and escape.

The automobile has probably taken on the role of liberator in the South more than in other sections of the country. It is in the South that Junior Johnson became a folk hero.[54] Johnson's fame rests not only on his skills as a stock-car driver but also on his ability to outdrive the law and escape the revenue agents. It is his car that makes him free. The movies and television shows that center on the narrow escapes of a driver with a good car are usually set in the South. TV's "Dukes of Hazard" even linked the heroes' car with Southern tradition: it was called The General Lee. The South, even more than the empty West, becomes the space through which an outcast can travel—leaving behind a string of wrecked patrol cars— safe as long as he keeps moving. Just as it is hard to imagine a European "Smokey and the Bandit" or "Dukes of Hazard," it is difficult to imagine one set in Oregon or Vermont. These fantasies of invulnerable drivers have little to do with reality, of course, but I think their setting is revealing nevertheless. The dream of always being able to drive away from trouble—or straight through it—has been strong in the South.

The juxtaposition of a continuing belief in Original Sin and the need for a savior with a new confidence in freedom through movement provided O'Connor with a great opportunity. It allowed her to contrast different views of the nature of man through concrete visual images. It allows her to have a man who believes he is completely free and clean of all guilt drive his car past a rock on which have been painted the words: "WOE TO THE WHOREMONGER AND BLASPHEMER WILL HELL SWALLOW YOU UP? Jesus Saves" It would not be hard to find road-side signs like that in real life—or to find drivers who have as much faith in their own freedom and cleanness as does Hazel Motes. It would be harder to locate one whose confidence is mixed with as much doubt, or to whom the question mattered so much.

## "The Life You Save May Be Your Own"

O'Connor makes her fullest use of the automobile and all that is associated with it in *Wise Blood,* but the car and the traditions linked with it are also prominent in some of the short stories. In "Parker's Back," O. E. Parker plays the role of the ever-moving American. He escapes from his mother and from the God preached in the revival tent, and then travels the world without any goal, first on board ship, like Ishmael, then wandering through the country in a beat-up truck. He has not meant to "get himself tied up legally" with a woman (*Complete Stories,* p. 511). But Parker has the good fortune to have his wanderings ended by Sarah Ruth. Sarah Ruth—the domesticating woman—opposes the tradition of endless escape: "One of the things she did not approve of was automobiles" (p. 510). In "The Life You Save May Be Your Own" an automobile is at the center of the action, and the central character, Mr. Shiftlet, has a great deal in common with the heroes of the traditions I have described.

Shiftlet takes his place in the long line of ever-moving males escaping from entanglements contrived by women. When he first appears he is a traveling man—a tramp. He comes out of nowhere. He just appears on the road before Mrs. Lucynell Crater's desolate farmhouse one day. He gives his name and tells Mrs. Crater where he is from, but then he lets on that it may all be a lie:

> A sly look came over his face. "Lady," he said, "nowadays, people'll do anything anyways. I can tell you my name is Tom T. Shiftlet and I come from Tarwater, Tennessee, but you never have seen me before: how you know I ain't lying? How you know my name ain't Aaron Sparks, lady, and I come from Singleberry, Georgia, or how you know it's not George Speeds and I come from Lucy, Alabama, or how you know I ain't Thompson Bright from Toolafalls, Mississippi?" (*Complete Stories*, pp. 147-48)

Like many American heroes, Mr. Shiftlet, or whoever he is, can create himself by choosing a name. He rattles off in a moment as many names as Huck Finn or Natty Bumppo use in the course of their long journeys. Shiftlet also says that he has had a number of jobs in his "varied life":

> He had been a gospel singer, a foreman on the railroad, an assistant in an undertaking parlor, and he had come over the radio for three months with Uncle Roy and his Red Creek Wranglers. He said he had fought and bled in the Arm Service of his country and visited every foreign land. . . . (P. 148)

He is also a carpenter. Shiftlet has, in fact, tried almost as many callings as Emerson's sturdy lad from New Hampshire or Vermont. He can, in the fashion of the American Adam, constantly create himself anew.

Shiftlet, however, is not entirely new and fresh. He carries in his body the evidence that he must have a past. In his left coat sleeve there is only half an arm. He is not Adamic in his newness and perfection, but already maimed by some history. The missing arm points up the contrast between Shiftlet and the Adamic role he plays in much the same way that Ahab's wooden leg shows the difference between the captain and the Adamic Ishmael. Ishmael acknowledges no injury, no past, and no goal, and he bears a name of his own choosing. Ahab, however, is burdened with an evil name he did not give himself, and his wooden leg is a constant reminder of his past, and, at the same time, of the goal of his voyage. Melville and O'Connor both use the missing limb to mark a character who is not new or innocent. Shiftlet's deformity is also an outward sign of his spiritual state: before the story ends it is clear that Shiftlet is more crippled in soul than in body.

When Shiftlet comes down the road, Mrs. Crater is sitting on the porch with her idiot daughter. While he approaches she remains motionless. She only rises when he is actually in her yard. The contrast between motion and stability expresses much of the difference between the old woman and the young man. Mrs. Crater sits. She is fixed to one place, her farm. She has her daughter Lucynell for a companion. She is burdened with the responsibility for both the farm and the daughter. Shiftlet is alone, unencumbered, and moving.

Mrs. Crater sees things she wants in Shiftlet. The farm is run-down and needs attention, and she is willing to trade food and a place to sleep for carpentry work. (While Shiftlet is talking she is wondering "if a one-armed man could put a new roof on her garden house.") But, more importantly, she is "ravenous for a son-in-law" (p. 150). She needs a man who will care for the daughter, as well as tend the farm, and begins dropping hints to Shiftlet about the subject during their first conversation.

Shiftlet is faced with the danger that besets the moving man in our tradition: women who would encumber him with responsibilities and end his travels. Mrs. Crater wants a man who will stay put. "Any man come after her [Lucynell] 'll have to stay around the place" (p. 149).

While Mrs. Crater is sizing up her visitor as a possible son-in-law, Shiftlet also has his eye on something he wants. Almost the first thing he notices is the "square rusted back of an automobile" (p. 146). It is on his mind from the beginning. As Mrs. Crater is introducing herself, he is thinking about what make and year the car in the shed is. While she is telling him that any man who wants her daughter will have to stay around the place, his eye is "focussed on a part of the automobile bumper that glittered in the distance" (p. 149).

Having discovered what each wants from the other, Shiftlet and Mrs. Crater begin bargaining. Mrs. Crater gives Shiftlet a place to stay—the backseat of the car, where he sleeps with his feet out the side window. Shiftlet begins making the repairs Mrs. Crater wants, and teaches Lucynell to say her first word. He then announces that he is going to make the car run, and Mrs. Crater suggests he teach Lucynell another word: "sugarpie." Soon the negotiations become more direct:

> The next day he began to tinker with the automobile and that evening he told her that if she would buy a fan belt, he would be able to make the car run.
> The old woman said she would give him the money. "You see that girl yonder?" she asked, pointing to Lucynell . . . "if it was ever a man wanted to take her away, I would say, 'No man on earth is going to take that sweet girl of mine away from me!' but if he was to say, 'Lady, I don't want to take her away, I want her right here,' I would say, 'Mister, I don't blame you none. I wouldn't pass up a chance to live in a permanent place and get the sweetest girl in the world myself. You ain't no fool,' I would say."
> "How old is she?" Mr. Shiftlet asked casually.
> "Fifteen, sixteen," the old woman said. The girl was nearly thirty but because of her innocence it was impossible to guess.
> "It would be a good idea to paint it too," Mr. Shiftlet remarked. "You don't want it to rust out."
> "We'll see about that later," the old woman said. (P. 151)

He wants the car moving; she wants a man who will live in a permanent place; it is all very clear.

Both Mrs. Crater and Mr. Shiftlet talk a great deal about Lucynell's innocence. Shiftlet asks early on "where you would find an innocent woman today?" Mrs. Crater has the answer—her baby girl whom she wouldn't give up "for a casket of jewels."[55] The American tradition makes a great deal of innocence—the innocence of boys and boyish men. O'Connor shows innocence only in a helpless feebleminded girl. The traveling man is as corrupt and conniving as the stationary woman.

When the bargain is finally complete, Shiftlet gets a painted car and some cash as well. Money has been one of the things on Shiftlet's mind since he arrived—early on he tells Mrs. Crater that "there's some men that some things mean more to them than money"—and

he contrives to get the promise of money for a wedding trip before
he agrees to the marriage. In their final negotiations, Shiftlet and
Mrs. Crater again argue over moving and staying put. Shiftlet says
he cannot marry unless he has the money to take his wife "on a trip
like she was somebody. I mean take her to a hotel and treat her. I
wouldn't marry the Duchesser Windsor. . . unless I could take her to
a hotel and giver something good to eat." To Mrs. Crater, taking a
trip does not make sense: it is having a place to stay that matters:

> Lucynell don't even know what a hotel is. . . . Listen here, Mr.
> Shiftlet, . . . you'd be getting a permanent house and a deep well
> and the most innocent girl in the world. You don't need no money.
> Lemme tell you something: there ain't any place in the world for
> a poor disabled friendless drifting man.

As Shiftlet keeps talking, Mrs. Crater sees what the price will be,

> "Listen, Mr. Shiftlet," she said "my well never goes dry and
> my house is always warm in the winter and there's no mortgage
> on a thing about this place. You can go to the courthouse and see
> for yourself. And yonder under that shed is a fine automobile."
> She laid the bait carefully. "You can have it painted by Saturday.
> I'll pay for the paint."

Once Shiftlet knows he will get the car, the deal is settled. All
that remains is some dickering over how much cash Shiftlet will get
for his trip. Shiftlet gets the offer raised from $15 to $17.50, but that
is as far as Mrs. Crater will go. "That's all I got so it isn't any use you
trying to milk me. You can take a lunch."

While Mrs. Crater talks of the advantages of staying in one place
with a deep well and the most innocent girl in the world, Shiftlet
talks about why a man has to move.

> "Lady, a man is divided into two parts, body and spirit."
> The old woman clapped her gums together.
> "A body and a spirit," he repeated. "The body, lady, is like a
> house: it don't go anywhere; but the spirit, lady, is like an automo-
> bile: always on the move, always . . ." (P. 152)

It is at this point that Mrs. Crater realizes that she will have to throw
in a painted car. "I'm only saying a man's spirit means more to him
than anything else," Shiftlet continues while asking for the money

for his trip. "I got to follow where my spirit says to go." The woman talks about having a place to stay and the man about being able to move.

"A *man* is divided into two parts, body and spirit"; "a *man's* spirit means more to him than anything else." Shiftlet's division between the moving spirit and the unmoving body seems to apply to men only. Women, who stay put, are perhaps less spiritual than the men who move when the spirit says go. If this is Shiftlet's theory, it puts him again into the mainline of the American tradition, in which only men are capable of escaping the traps of society and its responsibilities and finding fresh, new, innocent selves by escaping into the wilderness or down the road.

As Mrs. Crater's farm, with its responsibilities and its deep well, is feminine, the car is masculine and attracts all of Shiftlet's attention. The old car has not moved since the farm has been in the hands of women—"The day my husband died, it quit running." Automobiles, like moving itself, are linked with masculinity. And Shiftlet keeps emphasizing that he is a man: after he reels off the list of names that might be his, he says, "Maybe the best I can tell you is, I'm a man" (p. 148). When he says he can fix anything on the farm he again proclaims, "I'm a man" (p. 149). And when he strikes his deal with Mrs. Crater he explains what a man is like and what a man needs. Shiftlet keeps emphasizing the masculine role he plays, and the car is certainly part of it.

Once the car is painted and all is settled, Shiftlet and Mrs. Crater and Lucynell drive into town for the wedding. The ceremony at the courthouse leaves Shiftlet discontented.

> As they came out of the courthouse, Mr. Shiftlet began twisting his neck in his collar. He looked morose and bitter as if he had been insulted while someone held him. "That didn't satisfy me none." he said. "That was just something a woman in an office did, nothing but paper work and blood tests. What do they know about my blood? If they was to take my heart and cut it out," he said, "they wouldn't know a thing about me. It didn't satisfy me at all."
>
> "It satisfied the law, " the old woman said sharply.
>
> "The law," Mr. Shiftlet said and spit. "It's the law that don't satisfy me." (P. 153)

The law could hardly satisfy him. It means involvement and entanglement with society—anything but the freedom to be always on the move. Shiftlet, like the heroes of the running-male tradition in American literature from Deerslayer on, is opposed to the law. They, like Shiftlet, are all antinomians, and proclaim their doctrine by always moving on, fleeing the law, just as they flee women and home.

Once the unsatisfactory ceremony is complete, and they have stopped at the farm to drop off Mrs. Crater and pick up their lunch, Shiftlet drives away with Lucynell. Shiftlet does not say a word as he leaves, and Mrs. Crater, who is clutching the car as she says her good-byes, only lets go when the car pulls out. Once he is on the road, Shiftlet begins to feel the joy of motion.

> Although the car would go only thirty miles an hour, Mr. Shiftlet imagined a terrific climb and dip and swerve that went entirely to his head so that he forgot his morning bitterness. He had always wanted an automobile but he had never been able to afford one before. He drove very fast because he wanted to make Mobile by nightfall. (P. 154)

For a moment, Shiftlet's spirit is satisfied.

The satisfaction does not last long. He soon becomes "depressed in spite of the car." Shiftlet's new wife seems to be the cause of his depression, for it descends on him after he has "stopped his thoughts long enough to look at Lucynell in the seat beside him." The woman and the responsibility she represents ruin the pleasure of driving. After about a hundred miles, Shiftlet stops at a diner. Lucynell rests her head on the counter and falls asleep as soon as she sits down. Shiftlet tells the boy behind the counter to give her her ham and grits when she wakes up. "'Hitchhiker,' Mr. Shiftlet explained. 'I can't wait. I got to make Tuscaloosa'" (p. 155). He drives off, having avoided the entanglements of women.

Once on the road again, Shiftlet is even more depressed. He decides that he wants company. "There were times when Mr. Shiftlet preferred not to be alone. He felt too that a man with a car had a responsibility to others and he kept his eye out for a hitchhiker." Finally he picks up a boy standing at the side of the road with a suitcase.

Once he has a companion, Shiftlet feels no better.

> The child held the suitcase on his lap and folded his arms on top of it. He turned his head and looked out the window away from Mr. Shiftlet. Mr. Shiftlet felt oppressed. (P. 155)

The hitchhiker is a wandering male like Shiftlet himself, and Shiftlet tortures him with talk about running away from women. In the most sentimental fashion, he talks about mothers—"I got the best old mother in the world so I reckon you only got the second best"—and says "I never rued a day in my life like the one I rued when I left that old mother of mine." By this point the boy's hand is on the door handle. Shiftlet ends, "My mother was an angel of Gawd.... He took her from Heaven and giver to me and I left her."

This talk drives the boy to rage. He jumps out of the car after yelling at Shiftlet, "You go to the devil! ... My old woman is a flea bag and yours is a stinking pole cat!" He does not want to hear about the blessedness of women while he is making his escape from them. Shiftlet, however, seems almost free of the guilt for abandoning a woman with which he torments his passenger. He talks about leaving his old mother, who was "an angel of Gawd," soon after abandoning Lucynell at the diner, and hearing the boy behind the counter say that Lucynell "looks like an angel of Gawd" (p. 154). Thanks to her idiocy, Lucynell is as close to angelic innocence as a person can be; while mothers, like Mrs. Crater, are as involved in sin as the rest of humanity. Shiftlet's sentimental talk about mothers points up the real quality of the act he has committed.

After the boy is gone, Shiftlet drives on. The day has been hot and sultry and a storm has been brewing. As Shiftlet's car moves down the road, the clouds begin to descend.

> Mr. Shiftlet felt that the rottenness of the world was about to engulf him. He raised his arm and let it fall again to his breast. "Oh Lord!" he prayed. "Break forth and wash the slime from this earth!"

As if in answer to his prayer, the storm descends on Shiftlet himself.

> After a few minutes there was a guffawing peal of thunder from behind and fantastic raindrops, like tin-can tops, crashed over the rear of Mr. Shiftlet's car. Very quickly he stepped on the gas and with his stump sticking out the window he raced the galloping shower into Mobile.

Shiftlet seems to be fleeing from the divine wrath he has invoked. That the skies respond to Shiftlet's prayer with guffawing thunder is appropriate: "Why do the heathen rage? . . . He that sitteth in the heavens shall laugh; the Lord shall have them in derision" (Psalm 2:1, 4). Shiftlet flees God, just as he flees women. He tries to escape both by always moving on. That his destination is Mobile can hardly be accidental. His goal is to be always mobile, always moving, and in this he is like many American heroes.

He is also like them in the direction of the journey. Mr. Shiftlet is heading West. Like the frontiersmen, like Natty Bumppo going out to the prairie, like Huck Finn lighting out for the territory, Shiftlet follows the course of the setting sun. "The Life You Save May Be Your Own" opens with Shiftlet watching the sun set over Mrs. Crater's farm. His first words to Mrs. Crater are, "Lady, I'd give a fortune to live where I could see me a sun do that every evening" (p. 146). Mrs Crater assures him that it does it every evening. She means that the sun sets over her three mountains every day; her sunsets take place only on her farm. Shiftlet, however, seems to be attracted by the dream of the golden West. After he has abandoned Lucynell, he drives off into the West, and the sun begins to set directly in front of the automobile.

Shiftlet's goal, finally, is the freedom of the open road, but he hides his true character as much as possible. The real attraction movement has for him only appears clearly once or twice—when he first gets the car moving and when he drives away from Mrs. Crater's farm. For most of the story he dissembles. He presents his air of "composed dissatisfaction as if he understood life thoroughly" (p. 146). He prays at the end though he is running from God. He praises women—in his talk about an innocent women and his old mother— but he is running from them. He plays a number of roles in the story, and plays them convincingly enough to get what he wants. To put it another way, he creates himself anew several times. The figure of the Confidence Man is not altogether separate from the figure of the innocent, moving male—Huck Finn, for instance, is constantly lying and assuming new identities—and Shiftlet joins the two.

One of the roles Shiftlet plays is that of Jesus himself. There is a fair amount of incongruous Christ-imagery in "The Life You Save May Be Your Own." As Shiftlet watches the first sunset, he extends his arms so that "his figure formed a crooked cross" (p. 146). He is a carpenter. And his resurrection of the automobile seems almost miraculous: when he drives the repaired car out of the shed for the first time, he wears "an expression of serious modesty on his face as if he had just raised the dead" (p.151). He is in many ways an Anti-

Christ: he offers what must seem like salvation to Mrs. Crater and Lucynell but brings disaster on them instead.

He is, in fact, almost diabolic. In a letter to John Hawkes, O'Connor wrote that Meeks in *The Violent Bear it Away* is "like Mr. Shiftlet of the Devil because nothing in him resists the Devil" (*The Habit of Being*, p. 367). "The Life You Save May Be Your Own" is a story of grace resisted. In Mrs. Crater and Lucynell, Shiftlet is presented with an opportunity for a real sacrifice, an opportunity to love unlovable people. Shiftlet refuses it in order to remain free and mobile. In escaping from female entanglements, he is not preserving his innocence, but rejecting a chance to redeem his sinful self. The roadside sign he passes warns him to "Drive Carefully. The life you save may be your own" (p. 155). Shiftlet is trying to save only his own life— while he is given the chance to at least improve Lucynell's or Mrs. Crater's. But "He that loveth his life shall lose it; and he that hateth his life in this world shall keep it unto life eternal" (John 12:25). The wickedest and most abandoned characters in O'Connor's stories are those, like Mr. Shiftlet and the Bible salesman in "Good Country People," who keep moving and never have to face God.

Hazel Motes commits crimes greater than Mr. Shiftlet's, but he in the end seems more like a saint than a devil, for he has the good fortune to see his car wrecked. In *Wise Blood*, as in many O'Connor stories, the offer of grace comes when the hero is stopped in his tracks and can run from God no longer. For Hazel Motes that offer comes when he loses his car and with it the ability to assert his innocence and freedom by always moving on.

# 3

## "Nobody with a Good Car Needs to Be Justified"

To take an example from my own book, *Wise Blood*, the hero's rat-colored automobile is his pulpit and his coffin as well as something he thinks of as a means of escape. He is mistaken in thinking that it is a means of escape, of course, and does not really escape his predicament until the car is destroyed by the patrolman. The car is a kind of death-in-life symbol, as his blindness is a life-in-death symbol.

—"The Nature and Aim of Fiction"

Caravaggio's *Conversion of Saint Paul* is dominated by the saint's horse.[1] The blinded Saul lies in the foreground, his emblematic sword by his side, while his mount, which is being restrained by a servant, towers above him, filling most of the canvas. Caravaggio presents the story as most of us remember it: the enemy of Christ struck down from his horse by a light from heaven as he goes to attack the Church in a new city. Many people are surprised to learn that there is no horse in the biblical account of Saul's conversion. In Acts Luke says that Saul is struck down on the road to Damascus, but Luke never mentions whether Saul is knocked from a horse, a camel, or simply from his feet. Most early paintings show the conversion of a pedestrian. The horse only entered Paul's story in the Middle Ages, and then because it could carry a good deal of symbolic baggage along with the last of the apostles.

Before the horse became a usual part of depicting the conversion of Saint Paul, it had become the symbol of Pride. The fall to which Pride leads was usually depicted as a fall from a high horse. In representations of the Seven Deadly Sins, the emblem of Pride became a knight falling from his mount. Representations of the conversion

107

of Saint Paul like Caravaggio's grow out of a tradition that fused the conversion on the road to Damascus with the emblem of the sin of Pride. In the fusion of the two images, both Paul's story and the idea of Pride are interpreted. Paul's life is shown to be the story of a proud man humbled by God; Pride is revealed as the quality that makes one God's enemy. When the horse of Pride takes its place in the story of Saint Paul, the combined image carries more meaning than either the story or the emblem does separately.

In *Wise Blood*, Flannery O'Connor also manipulates the story of St. Paul, and her method is much like that of the medieval artists who made the horse an expected part of any conversion of Saul. She combines the biblical story of the enemy of Christ struck down on the road to Damascus with an image from contemporary culture, an image laden with meaning. *Wise Blood* owes much of its power to the fusion of the story of St. Paul, as acted out by Hazel Motes, with the automobile. There is overwhelming evidence in the manuscripts of *Wise Blood* that O'Connor consciously used the automobile and the Paul story to shape the final version of her novel.[2]

Motes's rat-colored Essex carries as many associations as the knight's horse did in the Middle Ages, but it conveys the image, not of the deadly sin of Pride, but of the modern idea of perfect freedom. In *Wise Blood* O'Connor takes advantage of all the significance that movement has acquired in the American tradition. The automobile becomes the embodiment of the idea of complete freedom, freedom from the past and from responsibilities, freedom even from the taint of Original Sin and the need for a savior. When the car in *Wise Blood* becomes a parallel to the horse in Paul's story, this extreme idea of personal freedom—which is finally not so different from Pride—is used to show what makes a man God's enemy and what he must lose before he can become one of His disciples.

The automobile also carries echoes of the philosophical movement that celebrates each individual's perfect freedom in the face of an indifferent universe. Existentialism was agitating the intellectual world as O'Connor wrote *Wise Blood*, and she attacks it through Hazel Motes and his Essex. Motes often sounds like a backwoods existentialist in his preaching, and he is always proclaiming his absolute freedom: his car can take him anywhere he wants to go.

What is more important, the car takes its place in the long American tradition that links freedom and innocence, and denies the reality of Original Sin through the image of constant motion and endless fresh starts. The two things that Hazel Motes constantly asserts are his innocence and his freedom. He keeps saying that he is clean and that his car will take him anywhere he wants to go. His attacks on the central doctrines of the Christian Church have the same source. He has been taught from childhood that he is not clean or innocent, but that he has been redeemed, washed in the blood of the Lamb. Motes hates the idea of having his freedom restricted by dependence on a savior, and so he protests that he is clean, that he needs no Redeemer, that his Essex will take him anywhere. He begins preaching to deny the same doctrines: there was no Fall, and therefore no Redemption. No one depends on Jesus. What Motes finally denies is the Incarnation: he wants a Jesus who is all Man with no God in him. And, in this, his Church Without Christ follows in the path of earlier American churches that have moved from denying Original Sin to rejecting the divinity of Jesus.[3]

In attacking these doctrines Motes takes on the role of Saul, the Church's persecutor. As the novel progresses, the story of St. Paul, which first appears with Asa Hawks, the blind preacher, becomes more and more closely associated with the car. Motes does not begin his attacks on the Church of Christ in earnest until he has bought the Essex and can climb on its hood to preach blasphemy as the way to salvation. The car is his weapon when he kills Solace Layfield because Layfield, like Saint Stephen, believes in Jesus. Finally, Motes drives off to start the Church Without Christ in a new city, taking on the roles of both the American hero ever moving off to begin afresh somewhere else and of Saint Paul going to persecute the Church in Damascus.

The complete fusion of automobile and the story of Saint Paul comes when a highway patrolman pulls Motes over. The patrolman, who does not give any reason for stopping Motes beyond, "I just don't like your face," asks him to drive his Essex to the top of a hill. He then has Motes turn his car to face the embankment, tells him to get out, and pushes it over. After Motes sees his Essex lying on its roof with its wheels spinning, he walks home and blinds himself with lime. The founder of the Church Without Christ, who has often eloquently preached that he is clean and needs no Redemption, becomes an almost silent man practicing extreme penances "to get clean."

The story of Saint Paul tells of Jesus stopping one of his enemies dead in his tracks, but stopping him only to save him. The ideas that have become associated with the automobile deny both the possibility of being stopped and the need for a savior. By bringing the two together, O'Connor attacks the philosophies, from the American tradition of innocent male wanderers to existentialism, that deny Original Sin and the sinner's need for a savior. In both her fusion of the Saint Paul story with the automobile and in the strange subplots about con-men and mummies, O'Connor celebrates the doctrines of the Redemption and the Incarnation—the doctrines Saul of Tarsus, before his conversion, would have denied.

## Oedipus, Teiresias, and Saul

Hazel Motes's career is constantly reminiscent of Saint Paul's, but it is true that O'Connor had another blinded figure in mind while writing *Wise Blood*. As she says in one of her letters, "Hazel Motes is not an Oedipus figure, but there are the obvious resemblances." She goes on to trace this influence exactly:

> At the time I was writing the last of the book, I was living in Connecticut with the Robert Fitzgeralds. Robert Fitzgerald translated the Theban cycle with Dudley Fitts, and their translation of the *Oedipus Rex* had just come out and I was much taken with it.... Anyway, all I can say is, I did a lot of thinking about Oedipus. (To Ben Griffith, February 13, 1954, *The Habit of Being*, p. 68)

Both Motes and Oedipus put out their eyes, and both do so after realizing that they are not clean. Both protest that they bear no stain until the knowledge of their guilt comes on them all at once. And both come to some kind of insight after destroying their vision. By the time Motes dies, he seems to have achieved as much peace and resignation as Oedipus finds at Colonus. But there is all the difference in the world between the sins that drive the two characters to blind themselves. Oedipus's sin is one he himself has committed. He has become a parricide and an incestuous husband unknowingly, and the murder and the marriage take place long before the punishment comes. But he blinds himself to atone for his own actions.[4] In *Wise Blood*, Original Sin takes the place of Oedipus's early and unwitting fault. When Motes is accused of "Fornication and blasphemy and what else?" he reacts angrily, just as Oedipus responds angrily to what Teiresias tells him of his sin. But Motes does not deny the charges. Since coming to Taulkinham he has indeed begun to practice fornication and blasphemy. But to him they are beside the point. "They ain't nothing but words . . . If I was in sin I was in it before I ever committed any. There's no change come in me" (p. 53). It is the sin he was in before he ever committed any that Motes first wants to deny and finally to be cleansed of.

Asa Hawks, the street-corner preacher who accuses Motes of fornication and blasphemy, also has his obvious resemblances with a character from the Oedipus story. The blind preacher recalls Teiresias, the blind prophet. Like Teiresias, he can perceive the sin in the proud man who claims to be sinless, and enrages him by saying so. O'Connor would have known Teiresias not only from Sophocles, but also from "The Waste Land." Hawks, playing Teiresias to Motes's Oedipus, perceives the scene; his story, not his words, foretells the rest.[5] And there is something of the sordid and passionless sexuality that swirls around Teiresias in "The Waste Land" in the fornication Motes seeks out in Taulkinham.

Although Motes and Hawks are in some ways versions of Oedipus and Teiresias, it is more significant that both are versions of Saul of Tarsus. Over and over again their words and actions recall the enemy of Christ who was violently stopped on the road, blinded, and converted. But it is only up to the moment when he is struck down on the road to Damascus that Paul's career is echoed in the lives of Hawks and Motes. They call to mind the Saul who was present at the martyrdom of Saint Stephen, "consenting to his death" (Acts 7:59; KJV 8:1), who "made havoc of the church" (Acts 8:3) after Stephen's death, and whom the Lord stopped as he went to persecute the church in another city.

> And Saul, as yet breathing out threatenings and slaughter against the disciples of the Lord, went to the high priest, and asked of him letters to Damascus, to the synagogues: that if he found any men and women of this way, he might bring them bound to Jerusalem. And as he went on his journey, it came to pass that he drew nigh to Damascus; and suddenly a light from heaven shined round about him. And falling on the ground, he heard a voice saying to him: Saul, Saul, why persecutest thou me? Who said: Who art thou, Lord? And he: I am Jesus whom thou persecutest. It is hard for thee to kick against the goad. And he trembling and astonished, said: Lord, what wilt thou have me do? And the Lord said to him: Arise, and go into the city, and there it shall be told thee what thou must do. Now the men who went in company with him, stood amazed, hearing indeed a voice, but seeing no man. And Saul arose from the ground and when his eyes were opened, he saw nothing. (Acts 9:1-8)

And all that Motes does recalls what Luke reports the Lord saying to Paul after he is struck down: "Saul, Saul, why persecutest thou me? It is hard for you to kick against the goad" (also Acts 26:14). Motes, who like Paul persecutes Christ by attacking His church, is always kicking against the goad.

But no scales fall from Motes's eyes after he has been blinded (Acts 9:18), and he never becomes a preacher for Christ, another apostle. Indeed, there are few references in *Wise Blood* to the converted Paul, the apostle to the gentiles and writer of epistles. Some Pauline doctrines, however, are important to the novel. The idea of justification by faith keeps coming up. Motes denies that he needs to be justified, but seems to think that he had been saved by his faith in his own freedom—or in his beat-up car.

The first version of Paul in *Wise Blood* is Asa Hawks, the seedy evangelist Motes encounters while walking downtown during his second night in Taulkinham. Hawks recalls Paul in several ways. He is a preacher, and like Paul in Athens (Acts 17:17), he preaches in the marketplace, which in Taulkinham takes the form of a street-corner vendor's potato-peeler stand. But Hawks is hardly an ardent preacher like Paul. He calls himself "a blind retired preacher," and while he begs to support himself, this mendicant does not seem to be inspired by any ideal of apostolic poverty. "If you won't repent, give up a nickel. . . . Help a blind unemployed preacher. Wouldn't you rather have me beg than preach?" (p. 40). But, however reluctantly or insincerely, he does preach, and his preaching is powerful enough to sting Hazel Motes into preaching his own blasphemous doctrines in the streets of Taulkinham.

Beyond his preaching, Hawks's main similarity to Paul is his blindness. Hawks identifies his blindness with Paul's several times. When Motes asks him, "If Jesus cured blind men, howcome you don't get him to cure you?" Hawks replies, "He blinded Paul" (p. 111). Hawks says nothing about the scales falling from Paul's eyes after his baptism.

But Jesus did not blind Hawks; he kept him from blinding himself. Hawks shows Motes a newspaper clipping with the headline, "Evangelist Promises to Blind Self." The article reports that Asa Hawks, an evangelist of the Free Church of Christ, has promised to blind himself to justify his belief that Jesus Christ has redeemed him. The clipping tells when the blinding is to take place—the date is about ten years before the action of the novel—and it shows a picture of Hawks as a younger man, without the scars left by the lime he streaked toward his eyes, and without the dark glasses he wears when Motes meets him. Sabbath Lily, Hawks's daughter, explains, "He did it with lime. And hundreds was converted. Anybody who blinded himself for justification ought to be able to save you" (p. 113). (Sabbath Lily, like Mrs. Flood at the end of *Wise Blood*, seems to believe that the blind can lead the blind.)

Motes does not learn for some time that Hawks did not, in fact, blind himself. After he leaves, Hawks complains that "That bastard got away with my clipping" (p. 113), and Sabbath Lily asks if he does not still have his other clipping, the one that says, "EVANGELIST'S NERVE FAILS." Then O'Connor describes what happened at the revival meeting ten years before.

Hawks had actually intended to blind himself. In order to work himself up to it he had preached for two hours on the Blindness of Paul. Then he saw himself struck, like Paul on the road to Damascus, with a "Divine flash of lightning." He felt enough courage to go though with it, put his hands in the lime, and streaked it on his face.

> He had been possessed of as many devils as were necessary to do it, but at that instant they disappeared and he saw himself standing there as he was. He fancied Jesus, Who had expelled them, standing there too, beckoning to him; . . . (P. 114)

Jesus stops Hawks from doing this crazy thing and makes him see himself as he is. When Motes does do it, he is also seeing himself as he is: he is recognizing that he is in fact not sinless and self-sufficient. His act, taken in its own terms, is an acceptance of the truths he has been trying to avoid. After Hawks sees Jesus beckoning to him, he runs out of the tent and into the alley and disappears. He is stopped from doing what he had planned to do in order to show his faith in Jesus, but he does not follow the Jesus who beckons him. It is an offer of grace refused. In Motes's self-blinding and extreme penances, strange as they are, there is a call answered, and an offer of grace accepted.

Though Hawks appears to be a blind preacher, he can actually see. He is thus a false version of Oedipus, Teiresias, and Saul. He is an Oedipus who has not put out his eyes, a Teiresias who is not blind, and a Paul who has not been blinded by Jesus—a Paul whose vision Jesus has preserved. But he is also a true version of all three. He has at least tried to blind himself, like Oedipus, and he does fulfill the roles of the blind prophet and the blinded apostle. Like Teiresias,

Hawks perceives the sin of the confident man who will later blind himself. Like Paul he proclaims Jesus in the marketplace and calls sinners to repentance. Hawks brings no fervor to his mission. If he still believes that "Jesus is a fact," it is not a fact that pleases him much. But despite the hypocrisy that must be obvious to everyone but Hazel Motes, Hawks brings the words of the gospel to the streets of Taulkinham. And the message is not one Motes can ignore.

Motes is fascinated by Hawks from the moment he first sees him. When the blind preacher and his child appear at the peeler stand, Motes stares at them with such complete attention that he is deaf to the questions the pitchman directs at him. What catches Motes's attention are the two characteristics that link Hawks to Paul: his preaching and his blindness. When looking over the peeler stand at Hawks, Motes sees a "tall cadaverous man with a black suit and a black hat on" (p. 39). Like Motes himself, Hawks *looks* like a preacher. Beneath the brim of the preacher's hat, Motes sees the dark glasses and the cheeks streaked with scars. Hawks's blindness and his calling soon become the mysteries that Motes desires to penetrate. When he first stands face to face with Hawks, Motes leans toward him "as if he were trying to see through the dark glasses" (p. 49). There is something he does not understand in Hawks, something wrong about him both as a blind man and as a preacher. By the time Motes realizes that the Hawks is really neither, he has come close to assuming both roles himself.

At the peeler stand Hawks does not preach or call for repentance. Instead he begs, asking his hearers if they would not, after all, rather have him beg than preach. But in the tracts his daughter passes out there is enough gospel to upset Motes. Motes does not read beyond the words "Jesus Calls You" on the cover (p. 41). It is not a call he wants to hear. Motes methodically tears the tract to pieces and lets the remains flutter to the ground. Hawks's daughter, Sabbath Lily, watches him destroy the pamphlet, and says "I seen you" before moving away.

Sabbath Lily gives Motes a pretext for following Hawks. Motes has no real interest in the girl, but since he claims he does not care about Jesus he cannot admit that he follows Hawks because Hawks is a preacher. In following Hawks Motes answers, in a strange way, the call made by the pamphlet, but he cannot admit it. When he sees Hawks walking away, Motes is divided over whether to follow him. "Haze could see the blind man moving down the street some distance away. He stood staring after him, jerking his hands in and out of his pockets as if he were trying to move forward and backward at the same time" (p. 43). His reaction to this preacher is not very different from the way he stood as a child "with his dirty hands clenching and unclenching at his sides" when his preaching grandfather told him that Jesus had died to redeem him (p. 22). He follows the preacher, but buys a peeler to give Sabbath Lily, so it will seem that he is just responding to the "fast eye" she gave him.

When Motes catches up with Hawks and his daughter, the preacher's first words are, "I can smell the sin on your breath" (p. 49). Like Teiresias before Oedipus, Hawks perceives the sin that the proud man would deny. He asks Motes why he has followed him, and is not deceived by Motes's pretense that he has followed Sabbath Lily. (He has his daughter accept Motes's potato-peeler all the same.) Hawks tells Sabbath Lily why Motes has really run after them: "He followed me...Nobody would follow you. I can hear the urge for Jesus in his voice" (p. 50). Ignoring the chatter of Sabbath Lily and Enoch Emery, Hawks and Motes sit on the steps of an auditorium and taunt each other with the name of Jesus. Motes is more wounded by the Hawks's threats of salvation than the preacher is by Motes's curses.

Hawks reminds Motes of the things he wants to escape in Taulkinham. He talks about sin and salvation—the ideas that Motes thinks he has left in Eastrod, Tennessee. "Listen boy... you can't run away from Jesus. Jesus is a fact." But Motes thinks he can run from Jesus. He claims that he has already traveled far enough to escape Him: "I come a long way... since I would believe anything. I come halfway around the world."

Hawks can tell that Motes has not traveled far enough to be free of Jesus:

> "You ain't come so far that you could keep from following me," the blind man said. He reached out suddenly and his hands covered Haze's face. For a second Haze didn't move or make any sound. Then he knocked the hands off.
>
> "Quit it," he said in a faint voice. "You don't know anything about me."
>
> . . . . . . . . . . . . . . . . . . . . . . . . . . . . . . . . . . . . . . . . . . . . . . . . . .
>
> "Some preacher has left his mark on you," the blind man said with a kind of snicker. "Did you follow me to take it off or give you another one?" (P. 51)

In this laying on of hands, as much the act of a prophet as of a blind man, Hawks reaches the heart of Motes's predicament. Motes will not accept Jesus and he cannot ignore Him. He has indeed been marked by a preacher, by the grandfather who planted in him the conviction that if he needed to be saved, Jesus would save him. Motes follows Hawks in part because he does desire that salvation, and in part because he wants to prove that he does not need it.

Hawks reminds him that he does need it. By demanding that Motes repent his sins, Hawks threatens him with the Redemption he wants to avoid:

> "Repent! Go to the head of the stairs and renounce your sins and distribute these tracts to the people!" and he thrust a stack of pamphlets into Haze's hand.
>
> Haze jerked his arm away but he only pulled the blind man nearer. "Listen," he said, "I'm as clean as you are."
>
> "Fornication and blasphemy and what else?" the blind man said.
>
> "They ain't nothing but words," Haze said. "If I was in sin I was in it before I ever committed any. There's no change come in me. . . . I don't believe in sin" . . .
>
> "Jesus loves you," the blind man said in a flat mocking voice, "Jesus loves you, Jesus loves you . . ."
>
> "Nothing matters but that Jesus don't exist, . . ." (Pp. 53-54)

The accusation Hawks makes is true. Although all his life up to his arrival in Taulkinham, Motes has been as pure as possible, he has indeed just begun practicing fornication with Mrs. Leora Watts, and has made a point of committing blasphemy. But the sins he has committed are not what trouble Hazel Motes. It is Original Sin, the sin he was in before he ever committed any, that he first wants to deny and then to be cleansed of. What is horrible in the idea of sin is the forgiveness and Redemption that may follow it. Hawks's final taunt—"Jesus loves you"—stings Motes most sharply. He wants to be free, and not to owe his Redemption to a loving savior.

After Hawks orders him to help pass out tracts, Motes himself begins preaching to the crowd leaving the auditorium. His sermon is an attack on Christ, and from this point on he assumes the role of the unconverted Saul, attacking the Church of Christ. The doctrines he denies are sin and Redemption.

> Sweet Jesus Christ Crucified. . . . I want to tell you people something. Maybe you think you're not clean because you don't be-

lieve. Well you are clean, let me tell you that. Every one of you people are clean and let me tell you why if you think it's because of Jesus Christ Crucified you're wrong. I don't say he wasn't crucified but I say it wasn't for you. Listenhere, I'm a preacher myself and I preach the truth. . . . Don't I know what exists and what don't? . . . Don't I have eyes in my head? Am I a blind man? Listenhere . . . I'm going to preach a new church—the church of truth without Jesus Christ Crucified. It won't cost you nothing to join my church. It's not started yet but it's going to be. (P. 55)

Motes announces a Church in which there is no salvation because there is no taint of sin.

In response to Motes's attack on Jesus Christ Crucified, Hawks laughs and shouts out his name so that Motes will be able to find him when he follows him again. And Motes will follow Hawks. Motes tells everyone he meets that he is clean and that he does not believe in sin, but he tries especially hard to prove it to Hawks, perhaps because Hawks can see it is not true. Until he realizes that Hawks is not the blind preacher he appears to be, Motes keeps trying either to show the blind preacher that he does not believe in sin or—a motive Motes will not admit—to get him to try and save him. Before he seeks out Hawks again, however, Motes starts his church in earnest, preaching from the top of a rat-colored Essex.

## "Nobody with a Good Car Needs to Be Justified"

On the morning after he meets Hawks, Motes wakes up realizing that he is going to buy a car. He leaves the bed of Mrs. Leora Watts, the prostitute with whom he has been staying since his arrival in the city, and goes out to find a used-car lot that looks like it will have a car he can buy with fifty dollars. He stops at a place with the sign SLADE'S FOR THE LATEST (p. 68). Motes has only fifty dollars, but the car he finally buys only costs him forty, plus a little extra for five gallons of gasoline. (Motes does not seem to realize that he has not been given the full amount.)

Motes has never had a car before. He does not have a driver's license, and has hardly ever driven. But once he gets the car it becomes the most important thing in his life. From the time he leaves Slade's up to the moment the patrolman pushes the Essex over the embankment, Motes is either in his car, or preaching from its nose, or talking about it. Motes constantly praises his car. He keeps saying that his Essex is a good car, despite all evidence that it is really a heap. The car becomes his home—much more than Leora Watts's room or the boardinghouse he moves into. While Slade watches him trying to get the car started, Motes tells him, "I wanted this car mostly to be a house for me. . . . I ain't got any place to be" (p. 73). With the car Motes gets a place to be that is not any single place. Instead of a home that remains forever where it is, accumulating more and more memories as time goes by, Motes gets a home that will give him endless fresh starts and take him away from any past he has created.

After buying the Essex, and getting it going (he has to be reminded to take the brake off when he leaves the lot), Motes drives out into the country. He has trouble getting the car moving in town, but once he passes over a viaduct and gets onto the highway, he begins to go very fast. He is soon stopped by a herd of pigs crossing the road. Once he gets going again, he finds himself stuck behind a slow moving pickup truck with a bed piled with furniture and a crate of chickens. Motes does not want to slow down, and pounds on his horn to get the truck to speed up, but his horn will not work and the pickup truck does not go any faster.

This first shows how little Motes can really make his car do. He has trouble getting it moving and slowing it down. (For a while it stops entirely every time he tries to reduce speed.) He cannot make the horn work. He cannot even get a truckful of wet barred-rock chickens to make way for him. But what happens as the pickup slows down even further is even more significant: Motes is for the first time stopped on the road out of the city:

> The road turned and went down hill and a high embankment appeared on one side with pines standing on it, facing a gray boulder that jutted out of the opposite gulley wall. White letters on the boulder said, WOE TO THE BLASPHEMER AND WHOREMONGER! WILL HELL SWALLOW YOU UP? The pickup truck slowed even more as if it were reading the sign and Haze pounded his empty horn. He beat on it and beat on it but it didn't make any sound. The pickup truck went on, bumping the glum barred-rock chickens over the edge of the next hill. Haze's car was stopped and his eyes were turned toward the two words at the bottom of the sign. They said in smaller letters, "Jesus Saves." (P. 75)

This interruption of Motes's drive foreshadows the final destruction of his car. (He is now at the bottom of an embankment;

when the end comes he will be at the top.) He is stopped in his tracks by an accusation much like Hawks's: the roadside sign and the blind preacher accuse him of the same sins. But what causes Motes to stop and stare is not the rebuke in capital letters; it is the promise in fine print. The idea that Jesus saves, not the threat of Hell or the charge of fornication and blasphemy, is what bothers Motes.

While Motes stares at the sign, a large oil truck is stopped behind him, and the driver, after blowing his horn for a while, comes to ask Motes why he is parked in the middle of the road. Motes tells him he is reading the sign, and goes on to say, "There's no person a whoremonger, who wasn't something worse first. . . . That's not the sin, nor blasphemy. The sin came before them" (p. 76). As he did when answering Hawks's charge of fornication and blasphemy, Motes with his own words brings up Original Sin, the "sin he was in before he committed any." The sign says that Jesus saves; if Motes is stained with Original Sin, Jesus may save him.

This reminder of the promise of salvation sends Motes back into town. He wants to learn where he can find Hawks, so that he can prove to him that he does not believe in Jesus. While stopped in front of the sign, he says, "I don't have to run from anything because I don't believe in anything," and he is going to find Hawks so he can prove both. It turns out, however, that he has to run as long as he claims not to believe in anything. He stops running when he stops preaching that there is "no truth behind all truths."

It takes Motes a while to find Hawks again. He first goes to the park and tries to get his address from Enoch Emery, but though the boy with wise blood shows him quite a bit at the zoo and the Frosty Bottle and the MVSEVM, he cannot give Motes the address. Motes is so enraged by Enoch's inability to tell him where to find Hawks that he leaves the boy stunned and bleeding on the ground. That evening he drives around Taulkinham until he finds Hawks and his daughter, and he follows them home.

He does not, however, confront Hawks immediately. Before going to see the blind preacher again he starts his own church. Motes parks his car in front of a movie theater, climbs up on the hood of the Essex, and launches the Church Without Christ's first sermon with the words, "Where has the blood you think you been redeemed by touched you?" (p. 104). This question does not bring much response: some moviegoers stare at Motes; three boys come out of the lobby to look at him, but the question does not seem to matter to any of them; a little man calls Motes a "wise guy." It seems that only Motes thinks

Redemption is a subject worth talking about. He repeats the question, and once again he gets no answer.

Motes then turns to attacking Christ's Church, once more taking on the role of Saul, the Church's persecutor.

> "What church you belong to, you boy there?" Haze asked, pointing at the tallest boy in the red satin lumber jacket.
>
> The boy giggled.
>
> "You then," he said impatiently, pointing at the next one. "What church you belong to?"
>
> "Church of Christ," the boy said in a falsetto to hide the truth.
>
> "Church of Christ!" Haze repeated. Well I preach the Church Without Christ. I'm a member and a preacher to that church where the blind don't see and the lame don't walk and what's dead stays that way. Ask me about that church and I'll tell you it's the church that the blood of Jesus don't foul with Redemption. (P. 105)

The doctrine Motes attacks is the Redemption. The last thing he wants is a savior. It seems that to Motes it is better to be blind or lame or dead than to see or walk or live and owe it to Jesus. It is the idea of owing anything to Jesus that Motes cannot bear.

Even this powerful denial of basic Christian doctrines does not catch the moviegoers' attention. "He's a preacher," one of the women said. "Let's go." The questions that are terribly alive for Motes—the ideas that preoccupy him because he so much wants them not to be true—do not even enter his audience's minds. Motes cannot just let the question of Jesus as Savior go: he has to fight it.[6]

As the few people who have gathered to hear him begin to leave, Motes attacks the whole salvation history the church teaches.

> "Listen, you people, I'm going to take the truth with me wherever I go," Haze called. "I'm going to preach it to whoever'll listen at whatever place. I'm going to preach there was no Fall because there was nothing to fall from and no Redemption because there was no Fall and no Judgment because there wasn't the first two. Nothing matters but that Jesus was a liar."

Motes's denial ranges from the Fall at the beginning of history to the Last Judgment on Doomsday. What he is really attacking is the idea of Original Sin. If there was no Fall, then Adam's descendants are not stained with a hereditary guilt, and they need no redeemer to save them. Motes always clearly sees that the doctrines of Original

Sin and of Jesus' redemptive sacrifice are inseparable, and his preaching is always an attack on both.

After Motes has repeated his sermon to three groups of movie-goers, the woman in the theater's ticket booth tells him to leave.

> She stuck her mouth to a hole in the glass and shouted, "Listen, if you don't have a church to do it in, you don't have to do it in front of this show."
>
> "My church is the Church Without Christ, lady," he said. "If there's no Christ, there's no reason to have a set place to do it in." (Pp. 105-6)

Motes's Church is more appropriately preached from the hood of a car. A set place implies continuity and memory of the past. Catholic churches are dedicated to the memory of something—of St. Rose of Lima or of the Immaculate Conception or of Christ the King. And any Church is a reminder of a story stretching into the past and onward into the future—back to the Fall and the crucifixion, and onward to judgment and glory. Motes denies that continuity. His church promises only fresh starts and freedom from the burden of Adam's sin or Jesus' sacrifice. Nothing could be more fitting than that he drives his pulpit through the streets of Taulkinham and finds a new congregation outside every movie theater.

On the night he founds his church, Motes preaches in front of three movie theaters. The next day, he goes back to the house Hawks is staying in and rents a room. Then he goes to see Hawks. When he announces that he has moved into the boardinghouse, he still claims that he is only returning Sabbath Lily's "fast eye," but what he is really attracted by is still the mystery of Hawks's blindness. "He wasn't looking at the girl; he was staring at the black glasses and the curious scars that started somewhere behind them and ran down the blind man's cheeks" (p. 108).

Hawks does not welcome him. He seems to have used up what little evangelical energy he had in calling Motes to repent at the peeler-stand. Now he looks at Motes with a "sour and unfriendly" look, and does not say a word to him. Motes tries to jolt him into paying attention to him by telling him that he has started his own church, "The Church Without Christ." But the news does not break through Hawks's indifference.

> "You can't let me alone, can you?" Hawks said. His voice was flat, nothing like it had been the other time. "I didn't ask you to

come here and I ain't asking you to hang around," he said.

Haze had expected a secret welcome. He waited, trying to think of something to say. "What kind of a preacher are you?" he heard himself murmur, "not to see if you can save my soul?" (P. 108)

Hawks closes the door in his face. Motes has come to see Hawks with two contradictory purposes, and has been frustrated in both. He has wanted both to prove that he does not care about Jesus and Redemption and to be saved—to have the preacher either take the mark off him or give him a new one. Hawks, however, will neither be shocked by the blasphemy of Motes's church nor try to save him. His impassive response to Motes's provocations drives Motes to make both purposes clearer than they were when he came. He leaves after finding himself speaking the wish for salvation that he has denied so earnestly, and once he is back out in the car he begins thinking of new ways to show Hawks that he does not believe in Jesus.

As Motes assumes the role of a preacher, Hawks gives it up. Motes appears at Hawks's door in the boardinghouse having already started his church and preached in the streets of the city. Hawks, however, no longer shows even flashes of a real mission. Just as Motes begins to take on the role of Saul, attacking Christ in his street-corner sermons, it is revealed that Hawks has been a false version of Paul. When his visitor has gone, Hawks takes off his dark glasses, goes to the window, and watches him drive away. His sight is revealed for the first time. He is neither a preacher nor a blind man, but Motes is on the road to being both.

While Hawks is watching Motes drive off from one crack in the window shade, Sabbath Lily is looking at him from another. Once he is gone, father and daughter discuss their visitor. Hawks has not been pleased by Motes's continued interest in him. He calls him a "Goddam Jesus-hog." Motes would not want to think he was a glutton for Jesus, but Hawks can see that he is—and he does not like it. Sabbath Lily reminds him that he was once not so different from Motes. "Well, look what you used to be. . . . Look what you tried to do. You got over it and so will he." Hawks still complains that Motes makes him nervous, and in fact what bothers him may be the reminder of what he used to be, and of how he responded when Jesus beckoned him. He may also be threatened by Motes's wish to penetrate the mystery behind his dark glasses. When Motes next visits him, he barely has time to get the glasses back on before the younger man comes through the door.

Sabbath Lily is attracted to Motes's eyes. "They don't look like they see what he's looking at but they keep on looking." Motes of course is looking for something beyond Sabbath Lily and Taulkin-ham—something he does not find until after he is stopped on the road out of town. But Sabbath Lily wants him all the same, and she persuades her father to assist her.

> "Listen here," she said, sitting down on the cot with him, "you help me to get him and then you go away and do what you please and I can live with him."
> "He don't even know you exist," Hawks said.
> "Even if he don't," she said, "that's all right. That's howcome I can get him easy. I want him and you ought to help and then you could go on off like you want to." (P. 109)

Hawks thinks about this for a moment, and finally responds, "Well, that might be fine . . . That might be the oil on Aaron's beard." While the psalmist thought that the oil for the prophet's beard was brothers dwelling together in unity (Psalm 133:1-2), for Hawks it is going off alone. Motes might revise the Psalm in the same way. But Sabbath Lily plans to stop Motes from traveling, and she knows what will get his attention. She tells her father how to manage their campaign. "Tell him about how you blinded yourself for Jesus and show him that clipping you got."

When Motes goes out to his Essex he is unaware that he is the subject of any other person's plans. He is still thinking about how to prove to Hawks that he does not believe in sin.

> Haze had gone out in his car to think and he had decided that he would seduce Hawks's child. He thought that when the blind preacher saw his daughter ruined, he would realize that he was in earnest when he said he preached The Church Without Christ.

What is more, things have not been going well for Motes with Mrs. Leora Watts, and he wants to move on.

> He felt that he should have a woman, not for the sake of the pleasure in her, but to prove he didn't believe in sin since he practiced what was called it. (P. 110)

But he has found his stay with Leora Watts humiliating. Now Motes wants someone to teach something to, and, because Sabbath Lily is so homely, he assumes she must be innocent. Motes is planning another fornication on principle.

It is appropriate that Motes makes these plans while driving in his Essex. Whenever he is in the car he feels free—free especially from the burden of sin. What he plans during the ride is another proof that he is in control of his fate and does not believe in sin.

Motes goes back to Hawks's room late in the afternoon. He pushes his way in and asks a question he has prepared in advance: "If Jesus cured blind men, howcome you don't get Him to cure you?" Then Hawks tells him that He blinded Paul, and, for the last time, calls on Motes to repent.

> The fake blind man leaned forward and smiled. "You still have a chance to save yourself if you repent," he said. "I can't save you but you can save yourself."
> "That's what I've already done," Haze said. "Without repenting. I preach how I done it every night on the . . . "

Motes is about to tell how he has saved himself—how he has discovered that he needs no savior to redeem him—when Hawks hands him the article describing his plans to blind himself. "This is how I got the scars," he tells Motes.

Motes reads the article three times and begins looking for a way to escape: "he took his hat off and put it on again and got up and stood looking around the room as if he were trying to remember where the door was." Sabbath Lily explains what her father did— suggesting also that some of his power must have passed on to her.

> "He did it with lime," the child said, "and there was hundreds converted. Anybody that blinded himself for justification ought to be able to save you—or even somebody of his blood" she added, inspired. (P. 113)

Motes remembers why he does not need to be saved, and replies "Nobody with a good car needs to be justified" before hurrying out of the room.[7] The story of the preacher putting out his eyes after preaching on the blindness of Paul has upset him—he can only murmur his confession of faith in his car—and he has forgotten to leave the message that he came to bring. He has to go back to hand Sabbath Lily the note he has written before rushing out to his car.

While Sabbath Lily reads the note—"Babe, I never saw anybody

THAT LOOKED AS GOOD AS YOU BEFORE IS WHY I CAME HERE"—and taunts her father with reminders of the clipping he has not shown his visitor, Motes goes off to strengthen his faith in what protects him from the need for a savior. He drives immediately to the nearest garage and orders some work done on his Essex.

Motes wants the horn fixed, the leaks in the gas tank patched, the windshield wipers tightened, and the starter made to work more smoothly. As the mechanic inspects the car, Motes asks how long it will take to put the car in perfect order. He is told that it cannot be done, but his faith in his car is not shaken.

> "This is a good car," Haze said. "I knew when I first saw it that it was the car for me, and since I've had it, I've always had a place to be that I can get away in."
>
> "Was you going some place in this?" the man asked.
>
> "To another garage," Haze said, and he got in the Essex and drove off. At the other garage he went to, there was a man who said he could put the car in the best shape overnight, because it was such a good car to begin with, so well put together and with such good materials in it, and because, he added, he was the best mechanic in town, working in the best-equipped shop. Haze left it with him, certain that it was in honest hands. (P. 115)

Motes wants a place to be he can get away in, a home that will not build up a past, a refuge that always offers another fresh start. No leaky gas tank will make him give up his faith in his getaway.

Motes's protestations of faith in his car become more and more strident as it becomes obvious that the Essex will not take him very far. He can show some reservations about the car before he buys it from Slade, but once it is his own he admits hardly a doubt about it. The car becomes the embodiment of the freedom he believes in— freedom from the dead past of Eastrod, Tennessee, and from frightening lessons about sin and Redemption he learned from his mother and grandfather, freedom from lasting entanglements with women, and, most of all freedom from the Jesus who might save him. While he is in the driver's seat he can control his fate, and start fresh whenever he pleases. As the novel progresses, more and more happens to show that Motes is not in control of his destiny and that his car will not take him where he wants to go. But all the evidence to the contrary only makes him proclaim confidence in his freedom and his car more loudly.

## Can a Bastard Be Saved?

The day after Motes gets his car back from the best mechanic in town he takes it for a drive in the country. He wants to see how it works on the open road. But he is denied the pleasure of traveling down the highway alone. When he is about a mile out of town he hears a throat clearing behind him, and when he turns around he finds Sabbath Lily rising from the floor to take a seat on the two-by-four that serves as a back seat. Sabbath Lily, who has prepared herself for the ride with Motes—"She had a bunch of dandelions in her hair and a wide red mouth on her pale face" (p. 117)—tells Motes she has been in the car all the time, "and you never known it."

Motes is not pleased by the surprise. It takes him a moment to remember that he plans to ruin the preacher's daughter.

> "What do you want to hide in my car for?" he said angrily. "I got business before me. I don't have time for foolishness." Then he checked his ugly tone and stretched his mouth a little, remembering that he was going to seduce her. "Yeah sure," he said. "glad to see you."

As Sabbath Lily climbs into the front seat and prosecutes her campaign, Motes stiffly plays along with her flirtation, but his heart is not in it. "He had not wanted any company. His sense of pleasure in the car and in the afternoon was gone" (p. 118). The feeling of freedom the car and the open road give him evaporates when this female climbs into his front seat.

Sabbath Lily does not engage Motes's interest until she begins talking about her father. Sabbath Lily tells him that her father and mother were not married when she was born. Motes cannot understand.

> "A bastard?" he murmured. He couldn't see how a preacher who had blinded himself for Jesus could have a bastard. He turned his head and looked at her with interest for the first time.

Sabbath Lily continues by telling him that she is a real bastard, and that a bastard shall not enter the kingdom of heaven. But Sabbath Lily's salvation is not Motes's concern. While Sabbath continues her story, Motes, who has almost run his Essex into a ditch while staring at her, slowly forms the sentence, "How could you be a bastard when he blinded him . . ." (p. 119).

But the girl does not answer Motes's question. Instead she tells him about the letters she has sent to the advice column in the newspaper. She has asked Mary Brittle, evidently the Ann Landers of Taulkinham, whether, considering that she is a bastard and will not enter the kingdom of heaven, she should neck.[8] "I shall not enter the kingdom of heaven anyway, so I don't see what difference it makes." Motes is still thinking of the blinded father, and does not notice the suggestion in Sabbath Lily's story. After reporting Mary Brittle's reply—

> [Y]our real problem is one of adjustment to the modern world. Perhaps you ought to re-examine your religious values to see if they meet your needs in Life. A religious experience can be a beautiful addition to living if you put it in the proper perspective and do not let it warp[9] you. (P. 119)

—Sabbath Lily begins scratching Motes's ankle with the toe of her sneaker and describes the next letter she sent to the advice column.

> I says, "Dear Mary, What I really want to know is should I go the whole hog or not? That's my real problem. I'm adjusted okay to the modern world." (P. 120)

Neither Sabbath Lily's story nor her toe gets Motes's attention. He is still trying to understand how a man who blinded himself for Jesus could have fathered a bastard.

> "Your daddy blinded himself," Haze repeated.
> "He wasn't always as good as he is now," she said. "She never answered my second letter." (P. 120)

While Sabbath Lily chatters on, Motes confronts the idea of her father's conversion. The girl persuades him to stop the car and take a walk, but he is thinking only of what could have transformed Hawks. Motes tries to puzzle out the mystery, and gets very little help from Sabbath Lily. What he wonders about is how complete the preacher's transformation was. Did he not believe in his youth and then come to? Was he a very evil-seeming man before his conversion, or was he just partway evil-seeming? It seems that Motes is trying to discover just how much unbelief he will need to protect him from coming to believe in Jesus. He finally imagines that Hawks before his conversion was disturbingly like himself: "I suppose before he came to believe he didn't believe at all" (p. 121).

By this point Sabbath Lily has led him off into the fields, but Motes, despite his plans for seduction, is not in the mood for pastoral dalliance.

> He saw that sitting under a tree with her might help him to seduce her, but he was in no hurry to get on with it, considering her innocence. He felt it was too hard a job to be done in an afternoon. She sat down under a large pine and patted the ground close beside her for him to sit on, but he sat about five feet away from her on a rock. He rested his chin on his knees and looked straight ahead. (P. 121)

Sabbath Lily knows what subject will get her new beau's attention. "I can save you," she tells him, "I've got a church in my heart where Jesus is King." The name of Jesus and the idea of salvation start Motes talking.

> I believe in a new kind of jesus . . . one that can't waste his blood redeeming people with it, because he's all man and ain't got any God in him. My church is the Church Without Christ!

Sabbath Lily asks if a bastard can be saved in Motes's church. The question gives Motes some trouble. He answers first, "There's no such thing as a bastard in the Church Without Christ. . . . Everything is all one. A bastard wouldn't be any different from anybody else" (p. 122). But as soon as Sabbath Lily says, "That's good," what he has just said begins to bother Motes. He may have given her the idea that his church promises her salvation.

While Sabbath Lily opens her collar and lies on the ground asking him to admire her white feet, Motes is still worrying about the salvation he may have promised. "The thing in his mind said that the truth didn't contradict itself and that a bastard couldn't be saved in the Church Without Christ." Motes's church offers no salvation. It promises only freedom from the Jesus who might save. A "jesus" who is all man with no God in him will save neither the bastard nor anybody else. Everything is all one and no one need fear that he will in the end owe his salvation to a redeemer. The "new jesus" will not save you, but he will leave you free.

Sabbath Lily has not followed Motes in his meditation on the soteriology of the Church Without Christ. After Motes finally lies down a few feet away from her, Sabbath Lily crawls over to him, and with some playful words, lifts his hat and lowers her face over his until their noses almost touch. Motes shouts at her to get away from him and jumps up violently. Whether or not he is going to shock the preacher by seducing his child, he certainly does not want to be seduced by her. Motes's first thought is of his getaway.

> Haze put his hat back on and stood up, shaken. He wanted to get back in the Essex. He realized suddenly that it was parked on a country road, unlocked, and that the first person passing would drive off in it. (P. 123)

Sabbath Lily tries to resume the flirtation, but Motes hurries back to the car.

Motes feels his freedom threatened by this entanglement with a female, and immediately imagines that the embodiment of his freedom may be stolen. It is not very likely that anyone would bother to steal a car like Motes's beat-up Essex, but Motes often fears that someone will drive it off. His car and his freedom are precious to Motes and he dreads losing them.

Once Motes gets back in the driver's seat he finds he cannot get the car started. A panic overcomes him as he pounds the starter. He cannot make his car take him away, and he cannot discover what the problem is.

> There were two instruments on the dashboard with needles that pointed dizzily in first one direction and then another, but they worked on a private system, independent of the whole car. He couldn't tell if he was out of gas or not. (P. 124)

The starter that only makes "a noise like water lost somewhere in the pipes" and the instruments that tell him nothing—like the silent horn he discovered on his last drive out of town—remind Motes of how little control he really has over his destiny. But Motes soon finds a reason for his inability to drive away: the woman. When Sabbath Lily catches up with him he turns to her fiercely and asks, "What did you do to my car?" Before she can answer, he walks off.

With Sabbath Lily following at a safe distance, Motes heads for a gas station they passed a half-mile back. Once there he finds a one-armed man who drives him and the girl back to the Essex in a pickup truck. While they are moving Motes talks about his Church—"he explained its principles and said there was no such thing as a bastard in it"—but the man does not comment. After they reach the car, the man puts a can of gas into the tank, and Motes tries to start it. Nothing happens, and the man looks under the hood. He looks at the engine for a long time, and finally closes the hood without touching anything. Motes becomes upset and allows a trace of doubt to enter his questions about the car. "'What's wrong in there?' Haze asked in an agitated voice. 'It's a good car, ain't it?'" (p. 125).

The man sits down on the ground and slides himself under the car. He stays under the Essex for some time, but when Motes kneels down to see what he is doing he finds that once again the man is not doing anything. "He was just lying there, looking up, as if he were contemplating." He finally gets out from under the car without having fixed anything or having said what the problem is.

Motes reacts to this silent assessment of his Essex in just the same way he responds to the mechanic who says that his car cannot be fixed: he proclaims, despite all the evidence, that the Essex is a good car, and that it will do whatever he wants it to:

> "Listenhere," Haze said, "that's a good car. You just give me a push, that's all. That car'll get me anywhere I want to go."

The man still says nothing, but gets back in his truck and gives Motes the push he wants. When the Essex finally begins to "belch and gasp and jiggle," Motes's faith is vindicated. He motions for the truck to pull alongside, feeling the triumph of his mobility.

> "Ha!" he said. "I told you, didn't I. This car'll get me anywhere I want to go. It may stop here and there but it won't stop perma-nent. What do I owe you?" (P. 126)

The man replies, "Nothing." It is almost the first word he has spo-ken. Motes asks if he owes anything for the gas, and the man again says "Nothing . . . Not a thing."

Motes does not particularly want to accept a favor—to owe anything to anybody—but he drives on, after saying "All right, I thank you." He then tells Sabbath Lily, "I don't need no favors from him." When he begins to praise the car again, he shows some hos-tility to the man who has helped him.

> It ain't been built by a bunch of foreigners or niggers or one-arm men. . . . It was built by people with their eyes open that knew where they were at. (P. 127)

Motes, who more than anything else, does not want to owe salvation to Jesus, does not want even to owe his mobility to another man. On the road back the car and the truck draw alongside each other again:

> while the two cars paused side by side, Haze and the slate-eyed man looked at each other out of their two windows. "I told you this car would get me anywhere I wanted to go," Haze said sourly.
>
> "Some things," the man said, " 'll get some folks somewheres," and he turned the truck up the highway.

Motes is once again confident that he is in control of his destiny—the car will take him anywhere he wants to go. But as the one-armed man's remark foretells, the car finally does take him somewhere, but not where he wants to go. He reaches his destination only when he loses the car.

During his drive in the country, Motes is confronted by all the things he wants to escape. He is reminded of the true condition of his car, which he has been trying to ignore. He finds himself becoming involved with a woman, and Sabbath Lily begins to make it clear that she will be more than just a way for Motes to prove he does not believe in sin. And finally Motes is confronted with the fact that he cannot escape whenever he pleases, and that he sometimes needs help to get where he is going. At this point Motes can still ignore all these reminders, but the next time he takes the road out of the city all his illusions will be stripped from him.

Motes's drive is presided over by a changing image of another thing he is trying to escape. When Motes gets out on the open road, he drives out under a deep blue sky, "with only one cloud in it, a large blinding white one with curls and a beard," like an old man (p. 117). At the end of the chapter, as he drives on, proclaiming that his car will take him anywhere he wants to go, the cloud appears again: "The blinding white cloud had turned into a bird with long thin wings and was disappearing in the opposite direction" (p. 127). O'Connor mentions the blinding cloud once in the middle of the chapter (p. 120), while Motes is trying to understand Hawks's conversion. A cloud that is transformed from the usual image of God the Father to that of the Holy Spirit, must be a reminder of the God Motes is trying to escape. The cloud also takes its place in the pattern of Pauline imagery in *Wise Blood*. The image of God in heaven is blinding, and the second of the trinity of references to it comes when Motes is thinking of Hawks's blindness. Motes is not finally blinded by a light from heaven, but the blinding light is in the heavens over him, even if others do its work on the road out of Taulkinham.

As Motes drives away from the cloud that has become the dove of the Holy Spirit, he retains the illusion that he is in control of his destiny. Once he returns to the city he continues to nurture the idea that a man with a good car is free and needs no savior, but more and more happens to show that he is not really in the driver's seat.

## Heresy in the Church Without Christ

Back in town, Motes finds over and over again that things will not go as he wants them to. Hawks will neither try to save him nor show any shock at his blasphemous new church. Motes keeps knocking on his door two or three times a day, but Hawks will not see him. The retired preacher only finds Motes infuriating. He does not want Motes coming around to stare at his face, and, though he is often drunk, he does not want to be found that way. But Motes still cannot understand "why the preacher didn't welcome him and act like a preacher should when he sees what he believes is a lost soul" (p. 145). Motes keeps trying to get into Hawks's room. He wants to see what is behind the old man's black glasses.

Whenever Motes knocks on Hawks's door, Sabbath Lily comes out and her father bolts the door behind her. Motes has abandoned his plan for proving that he does not believe in sin by ruining Sabbath Lily. The girl is not playing the part Motes has assigned her in this demonstration, and she quickly becomes a threat to Motes's freedom instead of a means of proving it. The sexual adventure Motes wants as a proof of his freedom and his disbelief in sin is one in which he, the man, is in control. When the girl takes the sexual initiative, he is threatened. The woman becomes an entanglement he must avoid. "He abandoned the notion of seducing her and tried to protect himself" (p. 145). When Sabbath Lily appears in his room one night after he has gone to bed, Motes sees the girl with a woman's nightgown hanging from her shoulders as real danger. While she grins at him, he picks up a chair, raises it like a club, and chases her out of the room. Motes defends his freedom with all the fervor Thomas Aquinas showed in defending his chastity.

Motes cannot even escape from Sabbath Lily in his Essex. "She followed him out to his car and climbed in and spoiled his rides" (p. 145). Motes only really enjoys his car when he is alone in it and it seems as if the Essex can take him anywhere he pleases. With Sabbath Lily in the other seat, Motes feels trapped even when driving. The pleasure of the open road disappears as soon as he has to share it with someone. Motes's desire for control in his sexual adventure is linked with his pleasure in steering his automobile: Motes first gets the idea of seducing Sabbath Lily while driving alone in his car; he abandons it when she starts climbing into the car of her own accord. The man behind the wheel wants to dominate in sexual matters as much as in anything else.

Motes had planned to ruin Sabbath Lily in order to show Hawks that "he was in earnest when he said he preached The Church Without Christ" (p. 110). But Motes's preaching is not progressing much better than his seduction.

> Nothing was working the way Haze had expected it to. He had spent every evening preaching, but the membership of the Church Without Christ was still only one person: himself. He had wanted to have a large following quickly to impress the blind man with his powers, but no one had followed him. (P. 146)

One of his sermons on the "new jesus" his church needs has sent Enoch Emery off to bring it to him in the form of a shriveled mummy, but Enoch is not the disciple Motes wants (pp. 141-42).

When Motes first thinks he has found a real follower, it turns out that his new disciple believes in all the doctrines Motes denies. Motes's proselyte is a sixteen-year-old boy who wants Motes as a "person of experience" to accompany him to a whorehouse he knows of, since this will be his first visit.

> But it was all a mistake because after they had gone and got out again and Haze had asked him to be a member of the Church Without Christ, or more than that, a disciple, an apostle, the boy said he was sorry but he couldn't be a member of that church because he was a Lapsed Catholic. He said that what they had just done was a mortal sin, and that should they die unrepentant of it they would suffer eternal punishment and never see God. Haze had not enjoyed the whorehouse anywhere near as much as the boy had and he had wasted half his evening. He shouted that there was no such thing as sin or judgment, but the boy only shook his head and asked him if he would like to go again the next night.

It is bad enough that the boy believes in sin, which Motes's doctrine denies; it is even worse that he casts doubt on Motes's practice. Motes thinks he can show he does not believe in sin by practicing what it is called. The boy shows that one can practice sin and still believe in it.

Motes keeps longing for a real convert—"If Haze had believed in praying, he would have prayed for a disciple, but as it was all he could do was worry about it"—but when the disciple arrives, he, too, recalls the doctrines Motes wants to abandon. What is more, Motes's meeting with his would-be apostle shows again that he can not make anything work as he wants it to—not the church of which he is the one and only member, not even the car which is his church's pulpit.

Two nights after his wasted evening with the Lapsed Catholic boy, Motes is again preaching from atop the Essex to the crowds outside the movie theaters. He parks his pulpit in front of four different theaters, and "every time he looked up, he saw the same big face smiling at him" (p. 147). The man who shows such interest in Motes seems a bit like a preacher and a bit like something out of show biz:

> He wore a black suit with a silver stripe in it and a wide-brimmed white hat pushed onto the back of his head. . . . He looked like an ex-preacher turned cowboy, or an ex-cowboy turned mortician. He was not handsome, but under his smile, there was an honest look that fitted into his face like a set of false teeth. (P. 147–48)

The man winks at Motes every time he looks at him.

After the last movie has let out, there are only three people, besides the man in the white hat, listening to Motes preach. They are not paying much attention to Motes, and he asks them what they are listening for.

> "Do you people care anything about the truth?" he asked. "The only way to truth is through blasphemy, but do you care? Are you going to pay any attention to what I've been saying or are you just going to walk off like everybody else?"

As if in answer to Motes's question, one of the moviegoers, who has been looking at Motes "as if he were in a booth at the fair" gets ready to leave, and the others follow her. Motes is not surprised by their leaving: "Go ahead and go . . . but remember that the truth don't lurk around every street corner."

But as they are leaving the man in the white hat calls them back and begins witnessing to the power of the prophet on top of the car. Much to Motes's surprise, he begins to talk about how his life has been changed in the two months since he met the prophet. While Motes stands motionless and confused on the hood of the Essex, the man keeps talking, giving each person in his growing audience a special look of admiration and affection. He introduces himself as Onnie Jay Holy and admits that he, too, is a preacher. "I'm a preacher and I don't mind who knows it but I wouldn't have you believe nothing you can't feel in your own hearts." With Motes still standing amazed on top of his car, Holy begins his sermon.

Onnie Jay Holy's sermon is not at all like the harsh and paradoxical sermons Motes himself preaches. Instead it is smooth and sweet.

> "Why, friends," ... "not to have a friend in the world is just about the most miserable and lonesome thing that can happen to a man or woman! And that's the way it was with me. I was ready to hang myself or to despair completely. Not even my own dear old mother loved me, and it wasn't because I wasn't sweet inside, it was because I never known how to make the natural sweetness inside me show. Every person that comes onto this earth," he said, stretching out his arms, "is born sweet and full of love. A little child loves ever'body, friends, and its nature is sweetness—until something happens. Something happens, friends, I don't need to tell people like you that can think for theirselves. As that little child gets bigger, its sweetness don't show so much, cares and troubles come to perplext it, and all its sweetness is driven inside it. Then it gets miserable and lonesome and sick, friends. ... It may want to take its own life or yours or mine, or to despair completely. ... That was the way it was with me, friends. I know what of I speak ... "

Holy goes on like this, and then says,

> "Then I met the Prophet here," ... "That was two months ago, folks, that I heard how he was out to help me, how he was preaching the Church of Christ Without Christ, the church that was going to get a new jesus to help me bring my sweet nature into the open where ever'body could enjoy it." (Pp. 150–51)

Holy keeps witnessing, asking everyone to listen to him and the prophet and "join our church, the Holy Church of Christ Without

Christ, the new church with the new jesus." He is not deterred when Motes begins to object.

> Haze leaned forward. "This man is not true," he said. "I never saw him before tonight. I wasn't preaching this church two months ago and the name of it ain't the Holy Church of Christ Without Christ! (P. 152)

Motes is not at all pleased to hear Holy's sweetened version of his doctrines, even if they have drawn a crowd. Onnie Jay Holy's idea of Original Sweetness (it sounds like a saccharine Wordsworth[10]) is, I suppose, the opposite of Original Sin, the doctrine that so bothers Motes. But Original Sweetness is not the doctrine of Motes's church. And Motes does not promise a new jesus who will help bring your sweet nature into the open. All his new jesus will do is show you that he can do nothing for you, and that you do not have to fear his saving you.

The different names the two evangelists give the churches they preach show the difference between them. Onnie Jay Holy's "Holy Church of Christ Without Christ" promises easy consolation. The new jesus will bring out everyone's inner sweetness and no one will have to face any hard truth: "You don't have to believe nothing you don't understand and approve of. If you don't understand it, it ain't true, and that's all there is to it" (p. 152). This church will bring the consolations of Christianity without any of the trouble of having to follow Jesus, or of believing in mysteries through faith.

Motes's own Church Without Christ, on the other hand, promises no consolation. There can be none because there is no one to bring it. That no jesus will redeem you is all that this church promises—and that assurance of his freedom is all Motes wants. And Motes maintains that what he preaches is true regardless of the believer's understanding or approval of it. He answers his new colleague by saying, "Blasphemy is the way to the truth . . . and there's no other way whether you understand it or not!" (p. 152).

Even though Motes keeps saying that this new apostle is a liar and that he has never seen him before, Holy goes right on preaching. He gives the other reasons for trusting the new church: it is based on the Bible—

> on your own personal interpitation of the Bible, friends. You can sit at home and interpit your own Bible however you feel in your

heart it ought to be interpited. That's right . . . just the way Jesus would have done it.

And, what is more, "This church is up-to-date! When you're in this church you can know that there's nothing or nobody ahead of you, nobody knows nothing you don't know . . ." (p. 153). In these claims Holy is developing Motes's doctrine of a perfectly free self who owes nothing to any redeemer, starts fresh outside of any tradition, and travels without the burden of a past. But, as in the name of his church, Holy keeps bringing bits of the old story back in. Where Motes denies the whole stretch of history from Genesis to Revelation, Holy just says that you can interpret it as you please.

Onnie Jay Holy's sermon goes over with the crowd outside the movie theater much better than any of Motes's have. He is soon ready to start enrolling members and taking up a collection, and nothing Motes says can stop him.

> "Listen!" Haze shouted. "It don't cost you any money to know the truth! You can't know it for money!"
> "You hear what the prophet says, friends," Onnie Jay Holy said. "A dollar is not too much to pay . . ."

As he sees his church succumbing to simony, Motes decides that he has had enough and tries to get away. The trouble is that he cannot control his car any more than he can control his church.

> The Essex had a tendency to develop a tic by nightfall. It would go forward about six inches and then back about four; it did that now a succession of times rapidly; otherwise Haze would have shot off in it and been gone. (P. 154)

Motes's car slides twenty feet and then begins bucking again. This less than graceful departure gives Holy just time to dismiss the congregation until the next night and run after the prophet.

After the Essex has slid and bucked a little farther, Holy catches up with it and climbs in. Now that it is too late to take Motes away, the car begins to run smoothly, and Holy begins to ask about the new jesus and tell Motes about the preaching business. When the outraged Motes tells Holy, "You ain't true," the new convert gives him his credentials. He is a real preacher: he has been on the radio. "Didn't you ever listen to it—called Soulsease, a quarter hour of Mood, Melody, and Mentality" (p. 156). Motes's idea of preaching has never included much ease, and he stops the car, tells the radio evangelist to get out, and finally pushes him out onto the pavement. He tries to drive away, but the car is dead.

Because of the persistence of his new disciple and the reluctance of his Essex to start, Motes has to go on listening to Holy's questions about the "new jesus." To Holy, a new jesus sounds like a hot property, and Motes's rebuffs do not deter him. Motes keeps trying to start the car for his getaway, but when he presses the starter all he gets is "a noise somewhere underneath him that sounded like a person gargling without water" (p. 156). Holy gives him suggestions about both cars and the religion-business.

> "Maybe it's flooded," Onnie Jay said. "While we're waiting, you and me can talk about the Holy Church of Christ Without Christ."
>
> "My church is the Church Without Christ," Haze said. "I've seen all of you I want to."
>
> "It don't make any difference how many Christs you add to the name if you don't add none to the meaning, friend," Onnie Jay said in a hurt tone. "You ought to listen to me because I'm not just an amateur. I'm an artist-type. If you want to get anywheres in religion, you got to keep it sweet. You got good idears but what you need is an artist-type to work with you." (P. 157)

Motes does not want the help of an artist-type, or of anyone else, and he tries harder and harder to get the car started. The car remains inert and Motes finally gets out and tries to push it to the curb. To get the Essex out of the middle of the street, he has to accept the help of Holy, but he does so unwillingly. Motes would rather run his car and his church without assistance.

Once they get the car into a parking space, Motes gets inside and begins to pull down the window shades. The only way he can escape from Holy now is to go to sleep. He cannot just walk home and leave the Essex where it is because he is afraid someone will steal it. Just as he worried about someone driving off in his car while Sabbath Lily flirted with him in the country, Motes imagines car thieves while Holy asks about the new jesus. Both women and a theology that brings Christ back into his church make Motes worry that his freedom will be taken from him.

While Motes arranges his pallet in the back of the car, Holy leans through the front door and makes his final offer. He is willing to pay a little something to see the new jesus. Motes tells him that he will

not find the new jesus incarnate. "There's no such thing or person
... It wasn't nothing but a way to say a thing ... No such thing exists!"
Holy is shocked. He has thought that he has his hands on something
real. "That's the trouble with you innerleckchuls ... you don't never
have nothing to show for what you're saying." Nothing, of course,
is just what Motes wants to show. Nothing is preferable to a savior.

Motes tells Holy to get his head out of his car, but the other man
is angry now. "My name is Hoover Shoats ... I known when I first
seen you that you wasn't nothing but a crackpot" (p. 159). Motes
slams the door, missing Shoats's head but smashing his thumb.
While Shoats howls outside, Motes lies down on his army blanket.
Once he has finished shouting, the radio-preacher returns to the car
and leaves Motes with some threats.

> "You watch out, friend. I'm going to run you out of business. I can
> get my own new jesus and I can get Prophets for peanuts, you
> hear? ... "
> Haze didn't answer.
> "Yeah and I'll be out there doing my own preaching tomor-
> row night. What you need is a little competition ..."

Motes scares Hoover Shoats away with a blast from his horn, which
now seems to be the only part of the car that will work, and after a
few more threats Shoats leaves Motes alone.

Motes spends about an hour in the stalled car and has a bad
dream. When he wakes up, the car starts without any trouble, and
he drives home. Once he gets there, he goes to Hawks's room instead
of his own, and picks the lock.

> Haze squatted down by him and struck a match close to his face
> and he opened his eyes. The two sets of eyes looked at each other
> as long as the match lasted; Haze's expression seemed to open
> onto a deeper blankness and reflect something and then close
> again.
> "Now you can get out," Hawks said in a short thick voice,
> now you can leave me alone ..." (P. 162)

Motes has attained one of his goals. He has seen what is behind
the preacher's glasses. The revelation he finds there is only of an
emptiness more complete than what he has himself been preaching.
The preacher is not going to try to save him, and he will not be
shocked by any blasphemy of Motes's. Motes takes the promise and

the threat of salvation seriously, and it appalls him to find that other people do not.

The night after he discovers that Hawks is not the modern-day St. Paul he took him for, Motes returns to his moving pulpit in the streets of Taulkinham. He climbs on top of his car again and preaches the most weighty of his sermons, a sermon that presents a vision of comforting emptiness even more complete than the denials of the Redemption he has preached before.

> "I preach there are all kinds of truth, your truth and some-body else's, but behind all of them, there's only one truth and that is that there's no truth. . . . No truth behind all truths is what I and this church preach! Where you come from is gone, where you thought you were going to never was there, and where you are is no good unless you can get away from it. Where is there a place for you to be? No place.
>
> "Nothing outside you can give you any place . . . You needn't to look at the sky because it's not going to open up and show no place behind it. You needn't to search for any hole in the ground to look through into somewhere else. You can't go neither for-wards nor backwards into your daddy's time nor your children's if you have them. In yourself right now is all the place you've got. If there was any Fall, look there, if there was any Redemption, look there, and if you expect any Judgment, look there, because they all three will have to be in your time and your body and where in your time and your body can they be?
>
> "Where in your time and your body has Jesus redeemed you? . . . Show me where because I don't see the place. If there was a place where Jesus had redeemed you that would be the place for you to be, but which of you can find it?" (Pp. 165–66)

In this last of his public sermons, Motes unites all the doctrines that make up his church's theology. Each person is perfectly alone and free. No Heaven above and no Hell below. No Fall before and no Judgment after. History is meaningless since there is no place for us in either our parents' time or our children's. And in our own lives the past is gone and the future is false and the present only an opportunity for escape. And no Redeemer enters time to give our lives meaning. Once he has denied all truths, and cut all ties between the self and any other being in time or space or eternity, all that Motes leaves is movement itself. There is no place for you to be; no place is any good unless you can get away from it.

Few people stop to listen to Motes, but he is ready if any of them suggest a place where Jesus may have redeemed them.

> "Who is that that says it's your conscience?" he cried, looking
> around with a constricted face as if he could smell the particular
> person who thought that. "Your conscience is a trick . . . it don't
> exist though you may think it does, and if you think if does, you
> had best get it out in the open and hunt it down and kill it, because
> it's no more than your face in the mirror is or your shadow behind
> you." (P. 166)

While Motes is combating this potential heresy, he is so ab-
sorbed in his preaching that he does not notice that a "high rat-
colored car," much like his own pulpit, has been circling the block.
When it pulls into a parking space two cars away from Motes's
Essex, Hoover Shoats gets out, along with a man dressed just like
Motes himself.

When Motes turns and sees his double standing on top of the
other car, his attention is riveted by this image of himself. "He was
so struck with how gaunt and thin he looked in the illusion that he
stopped preaching. He had never pictured himself that way before."
When Hoover Shoats begins strumming a guitar and introducing
his True Prophet, Motes climbs down and comes to join the crowd
around the other preacher. The new prophet utters a few words on
Hoover Shoats's signal. His sermon is short, but it brings back the
salvation and Redemption Motes has been running from:

> The unredeemed are redeeming theirselves and the new jesus is
> at hand! Watch for this miracle! Help yourself to salvation in the
> Holy Church of Christ Without Christ!

Motes soon leaves the new prophet's congregation, after telling a
woman who asks if he and the preacher on top of the car are twins,
"If you don't hunt it down and kill it, it'll hunt you down and kill
you" (p. 168). The woman is perplexed and Motes drives home.

What he finds there does not please him much more than what
he leaves outside the movie-theater. Sabbath Lily is waiting for him
in his room. Her father packed up and moved out after Motes had
looked into his eyes and now she has no one but Motes. Motes barely
notices her presence. This time he does not chase her away with a
chair. She tells him that since he has run her father off, she will have
to stay with him.

> "Are you going to hit me or not?" she asked. "If you are, go
> ahead and do it right now because I'm not going. I ain't got any
> place to go." He didn't look as if he were going to hit anything; he
> looked as if he were going to sit there until he died.

Motes has just been preaching that no one has any place and that
getting away is all that matters. Sabbath Lily, however, just wants
a place to stay. Since her home cannot be with her father, it will have
to be with Motes.

Before Motes notices the heterodoxy of Sabbath Lily's desires,
she puts her proposition in a form Motes can accept.

> "Listen," she said, with a quick change of tone, "from the minute
> I set eyes on you I said to myself, that's what I got to have, just give
> me some of him! I said look at those pee-can eyes and go crazy,
> girl! That innocent look don't hide a thing, he's just pure filthy
> right down to the guts, like me. The only difference is I like being
> that way and he don't. Yes sir!" she said. "I like being that way,
> and I can teach you how to like it. Don't you want to learn how to
> like it?" (P. 169)

In this form Sabbath Lily seems to be offering Motes another chance
to prove he does not believe in sin by practicing what it is called.
"'Yeah,' he said with no change in his stony expression, 'I want to.'"
Motes had planned to seduce Sabbath Lily in part because he wanted
someone he could teach something to (p. 110), but now the teacher
is the girl. Sabbath Lily, who is trying to find a home, completes the
seduction that Motes had planned to prove his freedom.

When Motes wakes up the next morning he is once again thinking of his freedom. His night with Sabbath Lily has not converted
him to domesticity. He jumps up and puts on his clothes, driven by
a new plan.

> He had one thought in mind and it had come to him, like his
> decision to buy a car, out of his sleep and without any indication
> of it beforehand: he was going to move immediately to some other
> city and preach the Church Without Christ where they had never
> heard of it. He would get another room and another woman and
> make a new start with nothing on his mind. (Pp. 185–86)

Like the decision to buy the car in the first place, this plan comes to
Motes after he has spent the night with a woman. The sexual in-

volvement, first with Leora Watts and now with Sabbath Lily, makes Motes long for escape, for freedom. Motes's new plan for escape is bound up with his car:

> The entire possibility of this came from the advantage of having a car—of having something that moved fast, in privacy, to the place you wanted to be. He looked out the window at the Essex. It sat high and square in the pouring rain. He didn't notice the rain, only the car; if asked he would not have been able to say that it was raining. He was charged with energy. . . (P. 186)

During the night Motes has become ill. One of the things he shares with Hoover Shoats's new prophet is a racking cough, and while Sabbath Lily has been staying with him it has developed into what seems like "a complete consumption in his chest." But now that he can see his escape standing in the rain ready to take him away, he feels better.

But before he can act on the plan that has filled him with energy, Motes is confronted with two images that remind him of the impossibility of really making "a new start with nothing on his mind." Before he can get out of his room he sees in the flesh both the Redeemer he is fleeing and his involvement in long generations of history. Neither history nor Redemption will allow a completely fresh start.

While he is packing his few belongings into his duffel bag, Motes happens to pick up the case that holds his mother's eyeglasses. He tries on the glasses, which do not suit his eyes, and in the blurred image in the mirror he sees both himself and his mother. With his eyes hidden by the glasses, he sees in his face "a look of deflected sharpness, as if they were hiding some dishonest plan that would show in his naked eyes" (p. 187). What is more, he sees his mother's face in his. Since "where you come from is gone," Motes does not want this reminder of the generations from which he springs, and he begins to take his mother's glasses off, but before he can remove them, the door on which the mirror hangs opens, and he is presented with an even more frightening maternal image.

Two faces appear in the blur, and a voice says, "Call me Momma now." It is Sabbath Lily cradling the mummy that Enoch Emery has just brought for Motes. While Motes looks at them in shock, Sabbath Lily says to the shrunken man, "Ask your daddy yonder where he was running off to—sick as he is? . . . Ask him isn't he going to take you and me with him?" Motes is presented with just the sort of entanglement with a woman he wants to avoid. One that will encumber him on his travels, involve him in history—one generation passing something on to another—and make endless fresh starts impossible. The shrunken image of procreation terrifies him.

But the mummy is more Sabbath Lily's child. Enoch has shown it to Motes once before, while it was still in its case at the museum. And Enoch has reminded him of the mummy during one of his sermons. Motes has been talking about the new jesus his church needs—"one that's all man, without blood to waste" redeeming sinners. He calls for someone to show the new jesus to him.

> "Show me where the new jesus is, . . . and I'll set him up in the Church Without Christ and then you'll see the truth. Then you'll know once and for all that you haven't been redeemed."
> . . . . . . . . . . . . . . . . . . . . . . . . . . . . . . . . . . . . . . . . . . . . . . . . . . . .
> "Look at me! . . . and you look at a peaceful man! Peaceful because my blood has set me free. Take counsel from your blood and come into the Church Without Christ and maybe somebody will bring us a new jesus and we'll all be saved by the sight of him!" (P. 141)

In answer to this figural attack on the Incarnation, Motes gets a very literal reply from Enoch Emery. "Listenhere, I got him! I mean I can get him! You know! Him! Him I shown you to. You seen him yourself!"

When he sees Enoch's new jesus in his room, Motes is confronted with a jesus who is, if not flesh and blood, at least flesh. And the idea of Christ incarnate is just what he most wants to deny. He wants a jesus who is "nothing but a way to say a thing"—just a way of saying that there is no Jesus to limit your freedom by redeeming you. As when Hoover Shoats asked to meet the new jesus, the Church Without Christ is again confronted with the heresy of the Incarnation. Motes responds to this reminder of both history and Redemption violently. Once he has recovered from the shock of his vision, Motes grabs the mummy, smashes its stuffings out against the wall, and then throws the shriveled skin out into the rain.

Sabbath Lily is furious that her new toy has been destroyed. What is more, she can see a great deal about Motes. Like her father, she can see even the parts of Motes that he wants to get rid of. And in her rage she tells Motes what she sees.

> "I knew when I first seen you you were mean and evil. . . . I seen you wouldn't let nobody have nothing. I seen you were mean enough to slam a baby against a wall. I seen you wouldn't never have no fun or let anybody else because you didn't want nothing but Jesus!" (P. 188)

With an angry gesture, Motes tries to defend himself against the charge of wanting Jesus.

> "I don't want nothing but the truth!" he shouted, "and what you see is the truth and I've seen it!"
> "Preacher talk," she said. "Where were you going to run off to?"
> "I've seen the only truth there is!" he shouted.
> "Where were you going to run off to?"
> "To some other city," he said in a loud hoarse voice, "to preach the truth. The Church Without Christ! And I got a car to get there in, I got . . ." (Pp. 188-89)

Motes's profession of faith in his church and his car is cut off by a cough. Despite all he says about the truth, that a bloodless, unredeeming jesus is the only truth there is—Sabbath Lily can still see both the urge for Jesus in Motes, and that he is going to keep running from Him.

## The Stoning of Stephen and the Road to Damascus

Before he leaves for a new city, Motes settles his quarrel with the schismatic Holy Church of Christ Without Christ. That night Hoover Shoats and his hired prophet witness again in front of the movie theaters. The man in the glare-blue suit and the white hat stands on top of the car and delivers his short cheerful sermon every time Shoats raises two fingers. The prophet is still dressed up like Motes, but, beyond his clothes and his persistent cough, he has little is common with his original. "His name was Solace Layfield; he had consumption and a wife and six children and being a Prophet was as much work as he wanted to do" (p. 201). This prophet has not escaped the entanglements of wife and family, as Motes just has. And it soon becomes apparent that he is not, like Motes, a rigidly righteous man who commits sins on principle to show he does not believe in them. He is an ordinary sinner who believes in sin. And, as his name suggests, he is not out to prove that there is no Redeemer. Before long he will ask for the solace of Jesus' forgiveness.

Once again, Hoover Shoats and his prophet attract bigger crowds than Motes ever has, and the prophet of the Holy Church of Christ Without Christ does not notice Motes watching his preaching from half a block away. In the course of the evening, Shoats collects more than fifteen dollars to further his mission, and he devotes three dollars to the support of the prophet. Solace Layfield also gets the use of the car from which he preaches. The car does not take Layfield very far.

After the last movie has let out and Hoover Shoats has paid him, Layfield takes his mentor home and drives off towards the outskirts of town. Motes has followed him, and when the two high rat-colored cars are alone on a dark lonesome road, he rams the other prophet's car, and both come to a stop. While Layfield gets out and asks what he wants, Motes silently backs up his Essex, grinds the motor, and knocks the other car into a ditch.

When Layfield comes to the window of Motes's Essex looking for some explanation, Motes's first response is an attack on Layfield's car: "What you keep a thing like that on the road for?" He does not respond to Layfield's defense of the car, and turns his attention from the false prophet's pulpit to his vestments. He tells him to take off his hat. Finally Motes tells his double why he has attacked him.

> "You ain't true," Haze said. "What do you get up on top of a car and say you don't believe in what you do believe in for?"
> (P. 203)

That Layfield believes in Jesus, despite his preaching of a church without Christ, enrages Motes. While Layfield tries to defend himself—"A man has to look out for hisself"—Motes repeats his fatal accusation: "You ain't true. . . . You believe in Jesus."

Layfield does not see what Jesus has to do with his car in the ditch, and Motes again turns his attack to the false prophet's preaching clothes.

> "Take off that hat and that suit," Haze said.
> "Listenere," the man said, "I ain't trying to mock you. He bought me thisyer suit. I thrown my othern away."

This justification does not satisfy Motes. He knocks the white hat off

Layfield's head, and as Layfield tries to escape, he tells him to take the suit off as well.

Solace Layfield runs out into the center of the road, and Motes starts the Essex and follows him. He keeps telling him to take off the suit. Layfield tears off his coat and shirt. He unbuckles his belt and runs out of his trousers. He is trying to take off his shoes when Motes runs him over with the Essex. Motes stops the car, backs up over Layfield's body again, and then gets out to tell him why he has done it.

> "Two things I can't stand . . . —a man that ain't true and one that mocks what is. You shouldn't ever have tampered with me if you didn't want what you got."

What Motes cannot stand is a man who believes in Jesus but says he does not.

But Motes now has to see something he does not want to see. After being knocked from his car on this lonely road, Layfield undergoes something like a conversion, much as Motes soon will when he loses his car. While he lies naked and bleeding in the road, Layfield begins to make his final confession, and, Motes, unwillingly, has to hear it.

> The man was trying to say something but he was only wheezing. Haze squatted down by his face to listen. "Give my mother a lot of trouble," he said through a kind of bubbling in his throat. "Never giver no rest. Stole theter car. Never told the truth to my daddy or give Henry what, never give him . . ."
> "You shut up," Haze said, leaning his head closer to hear the confession.
> "Told where his still was and got five dollars for it," the man gasped.
> "You shut up now," Haze said.

While Layfield is confessing his sins, there is enough of the preacher still in Motes to make him lean close to hear Layfield, even though he orders him to be quiet. When Layfield begins to call on Jesus, however, Motes will not listen any longer.

> "Jesus . . . " the man said.
> "Shut up like I told you to now," Haze said.
> "Jesus hep me," the man wheezed.
> Haze gave him a hard slap on the back and he was quiet.

After delivering this final blow, Motes again leans down to hear if Layfield will say any more, but the new prophet is no longer breathing. Motes checks to see that no damage has been done to his Essex, wipes some blood off the bumper with a rag, and drives back to town.

After Motes has killed Solace Layfield because he believes in Jesus—not just "consenting to his death," like Saul with St. Stephen, but actually doing the deed—Motes starts off to preach against Christ in another town. The next morning, after a night in his car— "not sleeping but thinking about the life he was going to begin, preaching the Church Without Christ in the new city"—he drives to a gas station to get his car ready for the trip. His faith in his car is as strong as ever.

At the station Motes tells the boy tending the pumps to fill the gas tank, check the oil and water, and test the tires. The boy, who seems incredulous that Motes is planning a trip in this car, goes about his tasks while Motes talks about his car and his church.

> He said nobody with a good car needed to worry about anything, and he asked the boy if he understood that. The boy said yes he did, that that was his opinion too. Haze introduced himself and said that he was a preacher for the Church Without Christ and that he preached every night from the nose of this car here.

While the boy is working on the car, Motes gives him a summary of his church's doctrines.

> He said it was not right to believe anything you couldn't see or hold in your hands or test with your teeth. He said he had only a few days ago believed in blasphemy as the way to salvation, but that you couldn't even believe in that because then you were believing in something to blaspheme. As for the Jesus who was reported to have been born at Bethlehem and Crucified on Calvary for man's sins, Haze said, He was too foul a notion for a sane person to carry in his head, and he picked up the boy's water bucket and bammed it on the concrete pavement to emphasize what he was saying. He began to curse and blaspheme Jesus in a quiet intense way but with such conviction that the boy paused from his work to listen. (Pp. 206–7)

What the boy tells Motes, however, might shake a faith less ardent than Motes's. The boy reports that there are leaks in the radiator and the gas tank and that one of the tires will not last more than twenty miles. Motes, however, will not be shaken. He has the boy fill the radiator even if it will not hold water. He proclaims his faith in his car in words that recall Paul's conversion on the road to Damascus.

> "Listen," Haze said, "this car is just beginning its life. A lightning bolt couldn't stop it!" (P. 207)

Motes drives off, leaving behind a trail of water and oil on the road. He gets out onto the highway, and drives very fast through a countryside made up of

> shacks and filling stations and road camps and 666 signs . . . and deserted barns with CCC snuff ads peeling across them, even a sign that said, "Jesus Died for YOU," which he saw and deliberately did not read.

This time he does not let the sign proclaiming his Redemption stop him. But he soon gets the feeling he is not really going anywhere.

Motes's car is not stopped by a lightning bolt, but before he has gone five miles Motes hears a siren and is overtaken by a black patrol car. The patrolman who signals for Motes to pull over appears very friendly. He has "a red pleasant face and eyes the color of fresh ice" (p. 208). At first sight he does not seem very threatening.

Motes has had one other encounter with the law. While following Hawks through Taulkinham that first night, Motes crosses a street against a red light, and a policeman blows his whistle, stops Motes, and gives him a humiliating dressing down, making him look like an ignorant country man in front of the city people. Unlike the patrolman on the highway, the city policeman looks hostile and unpleasant. He has "a thin face and oval-shaped yellow eyes" (p. 45). But he berates Motes for a crime he has actually committed— jaywalking. Later on Motes is never punished for what he has actually done. The murder of Solace Layfield, for example, seems to have no consequences. The patrolman who stops him now, and the policemen who bash his head in with a billy club at the end of the novel, do what they do without much reference to guilt or innocence. It seems an illustration of the idea that under the law all are condemned.[11]

Before the highway patrolman can say anything to him, Motes begins to try to justify himself—despite his good car.

> "I wasn't speeding," Haze said.
>
> "No," the patrolman agreed, "you wasn't."
>
> "I was on the right side of the road."
>
> "Yes you was, that's right," the cop said.
>
> "What you want with me?"
>
> "I just don't like your face," the patrolman said. "Where's your license?"
>
> "I don't like your face either," Haze said, "and I don't have a license."
>
> "Well," the patrolman said in a kindly voice, "I don't reckon *you* need one." (P. 208)

There is not much to like in Motes's face. After the patrolman has done what he will do, that face will be much altered.

The patrolman tells Motes to drive to the top of the next hill. "I want you to see the view from up there, puttiest view you ever did see." Once they are at the top of the hill, the patrolman has Motes turn to face the embankment, telling him that he will be able to see better that way. Then he has him get out—"I think you could see better if you was out."

What Motes sees when he gets out is the patrolman pushing the Essex over a thirty-foot embankment. The car lands on its roof, the three wheels that stay on spin uselessly in the air, and the motor and bits and pieces are scattered over the field. The patrolman explains, "Them that don't have a car, don't need a license" (p. 209), and Motes stares for some time at the view that has been presented to him. He sees more than his wrecked car. A great emptiness opens before him.

> His face seemed to reflect the entire distance across the clearing and on beyond, the entire distance that extended from his eyes to the blank gray sky that went on, depth after depth, into space. His knees bent under him and he sat down on the edge of the embankment with his feet hanging over.

What Motes does not see in all that empty space is any way of escape.

The patrolman appears concerned about Motes. Unlike the other policemen Motes encounters, this one, who is for the most part polite and kindly in his speech, offers Motes help. He offers Motes a ride.

> The patrolman stood staring at him. "Could I give you a lift

to where you was going?" he asked.

After a minute he came a little closer and said, "Where was you going?"

He leaned on down with his hands on his knees and said in an anxious voice, "Was you going anywheres?"

"No," Haze said.

The patrolman squatted down and put his hand on Haze's shoulder, "You hadn't planned to go anywheres?" he asked anxiously.

Haze shook his head. His face didn't change and he didn't turn it toward the patrolman. It seemed to be concentrated on space. (Pp. 209-10)

Motes has been traveling without a destination. He has no goal—he only wants to be able always to get away, always to make a new start. Now that he has lost the vessel of his freedom—the car that allows him the run from his past and from involvement with women, the pulpit from which he attacks the Redeemer—Motes will no longer be without a destination. When he is next stopped by the police, he is going somewhere. His last words are, "I want to go on where I'm going" (p. 230).

The patrolman takes a last look at Motes. He says, "Well, I'll be seeing you," and drives off. His inexplicable destruction of the Essex transforms Motes as completely as the light from heaven transformed Saul. As is usual in O'Connor, the act of violence reveals an offer of grace. Motes will not stop running from God because of the promise of His love—he has pointedly not read the sign reminding him of it on the way out of town—any more than Saul will accept Jesus because of Stephen's preaching. For both Saul and Motes, salvation only comes when their progress is violently arrested. It is being struck down that allows Paul to accept Jesus' love; it is his arrest by the oddly kind highway patrolman that allows Motes to accept Jesus' love in his own strange way.[12]

Once the patrolman is gone, Motes gets up and begins the long walk back into town. Before returning to the boardinghouse, he buys a tin bucket and a bag of quicklime. Once there, he mixes the lime with water at an outdoor spigot, and starts up to his room. As he passes her, Motes's landlady asks, "What you going to do with that, Mr. Motes?" and Motes replies, "Blind myself." Then as Mrs. Flood wonders why anyone would want to do such a thing, Motes goes upstairs and completes his identification with Saint Paul. He blinds himself in the way Hawks had planned to. He does not need to preach for two hours on the blindness of Paul to work himself up to it. Since the loss of his car, he has already assumed the Apostle's role.

## Iconography and Automobiles

With the wreck that leads to Motes's blindness and conversion, the fusion of the automobile and the story of Paul becomes complete. The automobile is most prominent in Motes's story when he is most like Paul—when he preaches against Jesus from it, like Paul attacking the Church; when he kills Solace Layfield with it, like Paul consenting to the death of Saint Stephen; when he drives off in it to start the Church Without Christ in a new city, like Paul going to persecute the Church in Damascus; and finally when the loss of his car on the road to the new city leads to his blindness and conversion. By making the automobile so prominent in a story like Paul's, O'Connor makes a powerful attack on the ideas the car embodies.

In fusing the image of the automobile with the story of Paul's conversion, O'Connor's strategy is much like that of the medieval artists who made the horse an expected part of any representation of the road to Damascus. While Acts says simply that Saul was struck down, the medieval artists and Flannery O'Connor show their versions of the apostle struck down *from* something. They give a physical embodiment to the qualities or ideas that make Saul Christ's enemy. They do not choose these symbols of what a convert must lose before he can follow Christ arbitrarily. Each employs an image that has already, to a greater or lesser extent, come to stand for the things they wish to represent. And in each case the symbolic use of horse or automobile grows out of real social conditions.

There is no illustration of Paul's conversion showing a horse before the fourteenth century.[13] The horse only became common in representations of the conversion of Saint Paul after a mounted knight falling from his horse had become the usual emblem of the sin of Pride. Since Paul was represented holding a sword, he already looked something like a knight, and the two images were easily combined. (The sword was Paul's attribute because it was the instrument of his martyrdom, but it made him look like a knight even if it was originally meant only to remind the viewer of how the saint was beheaded.) Once the images of the sin and of the conversion are fused, Paul's conversion is interpreted as the humbling of a proud man, and Pride is shown as what keeps a man from God and makes him Christ's enemy. The fusion of the two images says more than either does alone.

The emblem of Pride as a falling rider, which had its origins in the mounted female figure in Prudentius, developed as it did because it reflected real social conditions. As Lester Little points out,[14] a mounted knight became the image of Pride because the upper class—those most likely to be tempted to Pride—were, in fact, mounted knights.

> All earthly power was vested in . . . a knightly ruling class, whose obligations included the protection of those who prayed and those who worked. The greatest potential abuse in this society was an unrestrained attack by the powerful against the weak. Warnings against the sin of Pride appear to be a device for checking such an abuse. (P. 34)

Little goes on to say that "No one need deny the original and continuing influence of Prudentius . . . in order to perceive representations of Pride as depictions of feudal knights."

The link between the story of Saint Paul, the sin of Pride, and the social fact of a mounted ruling class can clearly be seen in the mystery play *The Conversion of Saint Paul*[15] from the Digby manuscript. Saul enters all but announcing that he is the embodiment of Pride. With his first words he declares that he is the most dreaded man alive, finely dressed, most famous, and unequaled in all things: "My pere on live I trow is nott found" (p. 666). Just as the emblem of Pride is merged with the conversion of Paul in medieval visual art, the morality play type of Pride is merged with the character of Paul in the play about his conversion. Paul is also clearly a member of the mounted ruling class. The stage direction in the manuscript describes him dressed, "in the best wise like an aunterous knith." After Saul has been introduced and his asking the chief priests for letters to the synagogues of Damascus has been depicted at some length (cf. Acts 9:2), a good deal of attention is directed to Saul's horse. There is a scene showing the ostler preparing the horse in the stable, and both he and one of Saul's knights praise their master's palfrey in much the way Motes praises his car.

> Here is a palfrey,
> There can no man a better bestride.

He will conducte owr lorde and g[u]ide
Thorow the world; he is sure and abyll.
To bere a gentillman he [is] esy and prophetabyll. (P. 669)

Saul rides the horse off stage out of Jerusalem and reappears on the road to Damascus. Then a light shines on him from heaven, and at the moment of his conversion, "Saule faulith down of his horse" (p. 671). Saul is then cared for by Ananias, and the scales fall from his eyes when the Holy Spirit descends upon him. Then, after he has been baptized, Saul withdraws. When he reappears, he is not dressed as a knight and no longer vaunts his glory and his power. Instead, he is wearing "a disciplis wede" (p. 681) and he preaches a sermon. His subject is the sin of Pride. Though he mentions all the deadly sins, it is Pride to which he devotes the most attention, for "Of all vices and folly, Pride is the roote" (p. 282).

O'Connor's use of the car is not so simple as the use of the horse in the Digby *Saint Paul*. While the horse is a relatively simple emblem of Pride, Motes's Essex represents a more complicated set of ideas. O'Connor exploits the accidental iconography that has grown up around the automobile in secular American culture, while the author of the Digby play employed an emblem that was native to Christian iconography. The medieval writer drew on the imagery developed by his allies; O'Connor takes for her own use an image created by the tradition she opposes. But all the same, the automobile and the horse interact with the biblical story in much the same way. The absolute freedom Motes's Essex embodies—which finally is not so different from Pride—is shown as what makes a modern man Christ's enemy, and what he must lose before becoming His disciple. As in the Digby play, the Paul figure's sermons make the meaning of the emblem clearer, though Motes does all his preaching before his conversion.

Just as the medieval artists' use of the horse as an emblem of Pride grew out of the social reality of a mounted ruling class, O'Connor's use of the automobile reflects social realities. The automobile does allow the driver to drive where he pleases, to control his destiny as long as his car will work and no obstacle impedes his progress. While the car is running well and the highway is empty, we do indeed feel free—just as a mounted knight could imagine himself the "Most dowtyd man . . . living upon the ground" (Digby *Saint Paul*, p. 666) as long as he was riding his high horse.

As the horse was only one manifestation of the feudal ruling class's power, the car is only one vehicle of the modern American's mobility. But each fittingly stands for social conditions greater than itself. The horse was an apt sign for the knight's station because it at once made visible the hierarchical opposition between high and low—between those mounted and those on foot—and made manifest the qualities that kept the knight in his station: wealth and prowess in battle. In the same way, the automobile can stand for the many kinds of physical mobility in American culture because it allows the most seemingly unfettered travel. The driver chooses his own course and follows no schedules. In the car he can be anonymous, and while the tank is full he can feel that he needs no assistance. The car is the purest sign of the migration that in reality also takes place in planes and trains and rented vans, on foot and in other people's vehicles.

The car in real life takes its place in the long tradition of American migration. Americans move down the highways now just as earlier generations headed out to the frontier, and the car is their most important means of travel. More importantly, the car comes to stand for the myth that has grown out of movement in America. The tradition of movement has given us the image of a hero, always male, who is Adamic in his innocence and newness; who can always travel onward, assume a new identity, and make a fresh start; who is burdened by no history or inheritance; who constantly escapes the constraints imposed upon him by society and by domesticating women; who can run even from God; and who needs no Redemption because he is not tainted by Original Sin. This is the myth O'Connor embodies in the automobile. She attacks it with all the fervor the medieval artist devoted to denouncing sinful Pride.

Hazel Motes does his best to play the role of the ever-moving American hero. He denies his past: once he is in Taulkinham he will not admit he comes from Eastrod, Tennessee. He travels without any particular goal. He believes, as he tells Mrs. Hitchcock on the train, that "you might as well go one place as another" (p. 14). He uses women only to prove his own freedom, and when he feels trapped by a domesticating female, he lights out for freedom in the best American tradition. He is always trying to escape God, and he vehemently denies both the stain of Original Sin and the need for a redeemer. Motes is clean: he does not need to be washed in the blood of the Lamb. In Motes's story all the qualities of the Adamic hero are bound up with the car. As he realizes after his night with Sabbath Lily, the car makes possible the new beginnings and the escapes from women. Thanks to the car Motes can leave Hawks's child, drive off somewhere, and "make a new start with nothing on his mind" (p. 186). Thanks to the car he can also deny his need for Redemption. "Nobody with a good car needs to be justified."

Motes finally cannot be the Adamic hero, endlessly moving on to make fresh starts, because his car is wrecked and his travels end. Instead of going on to make the fresh start in a new city, he returns to Taulkinham to finish a different sort of story. And even while he is playing the role of the ever-moving American, Motes carries a burden that does not encumber our true Adamic heroes. He remembers. Motes cannot really escape any of the things he flees, because they haunt him wherever he goes. He cannot forget his old home, or his mother and his grandfather, or, worst of all, the Jesus the grandfather preached, the Jesus who died to redeem him and would never let him go. Motes also, like Mr. Shiftlet in "The Life You Save May Be Your Own," carries in his body a reminder that he has a past. He has been wounded in the army. And though the shrapnel has been removed, "they never showed it to him and he felt it was still in there, rusted, and poisoning him" (p. 24). Like Shiftlet's missing arm, Motes's wound marks a man who cannot be Adamic because he all too clearly has been involved in history.

In his preaching, Motes attacks what he cannot stop remembering. His targets are the same doctrines denied by the literary tradition of the innocent, ever-moving hero: the Incarnation and Redemption through Christ's sacrifice on the cross, Original Sin and the burden of history. Just as Motes cannot forget the salvation his grandfather promises, our literary culture has been unable to entirely forget the theology the Puritans planted on this continent. Motes participates in the long tradition in which movement reveals a theological position. Our literature is full of men traveling the world alone, never stopping to become fathers, always escaping to start fresh somewhere else, because these solitary wanderers embody a rejection of the Puritan theology of sin and Redemption. In their freedom from any significant past, their ability to always start fresh, and their self-reliance, these boyish traveling men stand in opposition to the Puritan belief that a meaningful history stretches back to Adam, that no one born into the human family can really start fresh and ignore the burden of his ancestors' sins, and that each soul needs to be saved by Jesus Christ. The ever-moving male becomes the icon of original innocence in the American tradition—the icon O'Connor smashes on the road out of Taulkinham.

From atop his Essex, Motes preaches the theology of the ever-moving hero. He proclaims that each man starts afresh because he is not part of any history. Motes denies both the history on the grand scale stretching from the beginning to the promised end—"There was no Fall because there was nothing to fall from and no Redemption because there was no Fall and no Judgment because there wasn't the first two"—and history in each life—"Where you come from is gone, where you thought you were going never was there, and where you are is no good unless you can get away from it." All that is left is the solitary man, moving ever onward toward no goal and making himself anew.

The parts of the history of salvation that Motes most vehemently rejects are the Fall and the Incarnation, for those two events are the basis of the doctrines he most abhors. The Fall leaves man stained with Original Sin; the Incarnation brings a savior to wash the stain away. The threat of a savior is what troubles Motes. He does not fear being one of the lost; he dreads being one of the saved. He wants freedom, not salvation. He would rather be alone in an empty universe than owe his salvation to a loving God. He preaches a church that promises only that God will leave you alone—a church where "the blind don't see and the lame don't walk and what's dead stays that way"—because he wants nothing more than that. The idea of being saved by Jesus—of relying entirely on Him instead of on his own sovereign self—terrifies Motes, terrifies him as blindness, lameness, and death do not.

Motes calls his Church Without Christ "peaceful and satisfied" because it does not present the awful prospect of salvation. It is not troubled by any hopes that will not be satisfied until the end of time. It does not ask its members to take up their crosses and follow Christ down a road that may lead to a violent death. It promises to leave each person just as he is. Motes asks those who have stopped to listen to him if they would not really prefer that to Redemption.

> If you had been redeemed . . . you would care about Redemption but you don't. Look inside yourselves and see if you hadn't rather it wasn't if it was. There's no peace for the redeemed . . . and I preach peace, I preach the Church Without Christ, the church peaceful and satisfied! (P. 140)

What Motes sees clearly in Redemption is the cost of discipleship. As Christ tells his disciples (Luke 14), following him may be a terrible burden. Many of O'Connor's characters take that burden seriously, especially the ones who do not much want to take it up. The Misfit in "A Good Man Is Hard to Find" realizes that accepting a Christ who raised the dead would require an awful change in the believer's life.

> If He did what He said, then it's nothing for you to do but throw away everything and follow Him, and if He didn't then it's nothing for you to do but enjoy the few minutes you got left the best way you can—by killing somebody or burning down his house or doing some other meanness to him. (*Complete Stories,* p. 132)

Motes also sees that "if He did what He said," there is nothing to do but follow him, and therefore he preaches that He did not do it. "Nothing matters but that Jesus was a liar" (*Wise Blood*, p. 105). What he most wants to be a lie, is the promise of Redemption.

But even though Motes hates the very idea of Redemption, he cannot ignore it. It bedevils him from the first moment we see him. In the first pages of the novel, we see Motes answering the meaningless small-talk of his neighbor on the train to Taulkinham with the words, "I reckon you think you been redeemed" (p. 14). The comment disconcerts Mrs. Wally Bea Hitchcock no end; all she can do in reply is say that life is an inspiration and escape to the dining car. Once Motes himself gets a seat in the dining car, he sits silently, not even speaking to order his meal, until he says to the women at the table, "If you've been redeemed . . . I wouldn't want to be." One of the women laughs.

> "Do you think I believe in Jesus?" he said, leaning toward her and speaking almost as if he were breathless. "Well I wouldn't even if He existed. Even if He was on this train."
> "Who said you had to?" she asked in a poisonous Eastern voice. (P. 16)

The promise of Redemption is not something that Motes can, like many modern people, ignore. Redemption is not a serious question to Mrs. Hitchcock, the nominal Christian, or to the modern young woman in the dining car. To Motes it always is.

In his sermons from atop the Essex, Motes tries to convince himself that Redemption does not matter. He argues for his rejection of the Redemption from most people's indifference to it. He asks the people who have gathered around him outside a movie theater whether it matters to them.

> If Jesus had redeemed you, what difference would it make to you? You wouldn't do nothing about it. Your faces wouldn't move, neither this way nor that, and if it was three crosses there and Him hung on the middle one, that one wouldn't mean no more to you and me than the other two. (P. 140)

But the fervor with which Motes attacks the Redemption shows how much difference it makes to him.

Motes calls for a jesus who could not make a difference. He calls for a jesus who would not be any different from the two thieves. Or who would be different from them only in appearance—one who "don't look like any other man so you'll look at him" (pp. 140–41). The "new jesus" would be the opposite of the Jesus who threatens with Redemption, who looked like other men but nevertheless was also God Incarnate. Motes wants a jesus who is "all man, without blood to waste" redeeming people. He denies the Incarnation because it is the basis of the Redemption. Jesus' blood can redeem because He is God as well as man. Motes wants a Jesus who is all man and can save no one.

When asking for a jesus who has no blood to waste—and thereby inadvertently sending Enoch off to steal the mummy from the museum—Motes asks his congregation to rely on their own blood.

> "Look at me!" Hazel Motes cried, with a tare in his throat, "and you look at a peaceful man! Peaceful because my blood has set me free." "Take counsel from your blood and come into the Church Without Christ. . ." (P. 141)

But his listeners' blood may counsel them to walk in ways Motes does not like. Enoch's wise blood tells him to bring Motes the mummy, the mummy that reminds Motes both of the Incarnation and of the ties between the generations—just the things he is trying to escape. Motes's reliance on himself—on his own blood—is supposed to have set him free from the memory of Redemption and the burden of history, but it cannot, anymore than it can make him a peaceful man, or his preaching can make him forget the Jesus who shed his blood to redeem him.

In attacking the Incarnation, Motes always concentrates on Christ's blood. He does not say much about the flesh the Word became; he constantly attacks the blood shed on the cross. For Christ's blood, even more than his body, is the medium of salvation. At the last supper, Christ tells his disciples after giving them the cup, "For this is my blood of the new testament, which shall be shed for many unto remission of sins" (Matt. 26:28)[16] The church thinks of Christ's blood as washing the believer's sins away. In Revelations John sees a great multitude clothed in white robes—"they who are come out of great tribulation, and have washed their robes, and have made them white in the blood of the Lamb" (Rev. 7:14). The old revival hymn asked, "Are you washed in the blood of the Lamb?" Jesus's precious blood brings forgiveness and Redemption.

Which are just the things Hazel Motes thinks he can do without. He wants a jesus who cannot waste his blood redeeming people. Motes hates the idea of being cleansed of his sins. He offers a church "that the blood of Jesus don't foul with Redemption" (p. 105). Motes will not have his freedom polluted with any Divine forgiveness.

Just as he will not admit an incarnate God who would shed His blood to save His people, Motes also rejects the idea of a stain for that blood to wash away. If he is already clean, he will not have to suffer being washed in the blood of the Lamb. To ward off the threat of Redemption, Motes says he does not believe in sin, especially Original Sin. Motes goes out of his way to sin in Taulkinham to show that he does not believe in sin. From his moving pulpit he preaches that "conscience is a trick . . . you had best get it out in the open and hunt it down and kill it" (p. 166). But actual sins and the conscience that allows people to recognize them are only secondary targets for Motes. He is much more concerned with denying the Fall, and the stain of Original Sin it left. Actual sins often serve only to remind him of the original stain.

Even when Motes claims to be clean, the memory of Original Sin creeps back into his mind. During his first confrontation with Hawks, he tells the preacher, "Listen, . . . I'm as clean as you are" (p. 53). When Hawks names the sins he has indeed committed, Motes does not try to deny the charges. Even if sin is sin, the offenses he has actually committed are secondary. What matters is the sin that came before. "If I was in sin I was in it before I ever committed any." When Motes says he is clean, he means he is not stained by the sin fallen human beings are in before they commit any.

When Motes begins preaching, his first sermon tells all who will listen that they are as clean and unstained as he is.

> Maybe you think you're not clean because you don't believe. Well you are clean, let me tell you that. Every one of you people are clean and let me tell you why if you think it's because of Jesus Christ Crucified you're wrong. (P. 55)

Motes preaches a doctrine of original innocence. Because there is no Original Sin all can be free of Jesus.

Motes, however, cannot forget about Original Sin. He keeps insisting that he is clean because he cannot forget the doctrines that say that man is stained with sin and needs Jesus to wash his sins away. Part of what fascinates him in Hawks is the preacher's recognition that he is not clean. What is more, Motes keeps running across reminders of Original Sin. The sign painted on the boulder that stops his first drive does not awaken Motes's guilt over his fornications and blasphemies; it reminds him of Original Sin.

> "There's no person a whoremonger, who wasn't something worse first," Haze said. "That's not the sin, nor blasphemy. The sin came before them." (p. 76)

The memory of the sin that came before them sends Motes back to town to find Hawks so he can prove he does not believe in sin at all.

To get Hawks's address, Motes goes to see Enoch in the park, and there he keeps proclaiming his innocence and denying Jesus. When Enoch takes him to the Frosty Bottle, the woman behind the counter asks Motes why a "nice quiet boy" like him is with someone like Enoch. (The jokes Enoch has directed at the waitress have made him thoroughly obnoxious to her.)

> I can see, you got a clean nose, well keep it clean, don't go messin' with a son of a bitch like that yonder. I always know a clean boy when I see one. (P. 90)

She goes on talking about the difference between a clean boy and a pus–marked bastard like Enoch. But "clean" means more to Motes than the waitress can know. Motes is soon on his feet and leaning over the counter. He says, "I AM clean," and then repeats it: "I AM clean . . . If Jesus existed, I wouldn't be clean." If there is a Redeemer,

Motes knows he cannot be clean, for then there would have to be the stain for the blood of the Lamb to wash away. To avoid the sin, he has to deny the Redeemer; to avoid the Redeemer he has to deny the sin. Motes's oracular remark about cleanness and Jesus outrages the waitress. She wants to hear none of his crazy talk. But Motes is not finished proclaiming his cleanness.

Enoch soon takes Motes past a row of animal cages, and while he rushes on he finds that Motes has stopped to stare at the eye of a hoot owl that looks out at him from the darkness. While Enoch tries to hurry him on, Motes tells the owl just what he has told the woman at the Frosty Bottle: "I AM clean" (p. 95). The bird's eye, like the blind preacher's eyes behind his dark glasses, fascinates Motes. It is as if the owl, like Hawks, can see that he is not sinless. When he takes his eyes off the owl, Motes demands the preacher's address from Enoch. He wants to find him and prove that he is clean—that he is not stained by Original Sin.

The idea of Original Sin imposes on Motes both the burden of the past and the promise of Redemption. Both would limit his freedom. He can keep up his protestations of cleanness only so long as he has the embodiment of his freedom: his rat-colored Essex. Once it is gone he can no longer escape from either sin or Redemption. After the car is wrecked, he comes back to town and begins to perform extreme penances because, as he tells Mrs. Flood, "I'm not clean" (p. 224). Only the automobile allows Motes to believe that he is sinless and self-sufficient.

## Existentialism and Angst

Beyond the American tradition of the ever-moving male hero, Motes's Essex comes to embody the existentialist ideas that were gaining popularity as O'Connor wrote *Wise Blood*. The doctrines of that movement are finally not so different from the theology implicit in the American tradition of the Adamic traveler. Both emphasize the absolute freedom of the individual alone in the universe. Enough residual Deism lingers about the American tradition to make the freedom boyish innocence and the empty space welcoming—the empty world beckons as the virgin territory of an undiscovered wilderness. The existentialists often make the empty universe terrifying and the necessity for choice dreadful. Hazel Motes differs from the earlier American heroes who light out to make new starts unencumbered by women, their own pasts, and the memory of Redemption, in that he travels with less joy and more anxiety. He is even afflicted with the common complaint of the existentialist hero: in the first chapter of *Wise Blood* we see Motes suffering from nausea.

As Robert Fitzgerald points out in his introduction to *Everything that Rises Must Converge*, O'Connor began her career when intellectual life was dominated by an atheist existentialism that had almost nothing in common with O'Connor's Catholic worldview.

> A catchword when Flannery O'Connor began to write was the German *angst*, and it seemed that Auden had hit it off in one of his titles as the "Age of Anxiety." The last word in attitudes was the Existentialist one, resting on the perception that beyond any immediate situation there is possibly nothing—nothing beyond, nothing behind, nada. Now, our country family in 1949 and 1950 [when O'Connor was living with the Fitzgeralds and working on *Wise Blood*] believed on excellent grounds that beyond the immediate there was practically everything . . . the past, the future, and the Creator thereof.[17]

In Hazel Motes, O'Connor created a Tennessee countryman who wants to hold the fashionable belief in nothingness, but finds a Redeemer forced on him whether he wants Him or not.

The nihilism that Motes preaches from his Essex is as bleak as anything in Sartre or Camus:

> No truth behind all truth is what I and this church preach! Where you come from is gone, where you thought you were going to never was there, and where you are is no good unless you can get away from it. (P. 165)

All that is left is freedom—the freedom embodied in endless movement. The freedom that Motes wants—and the freedom that existentialists describe—is absolute. Motes wants more than the freedom offered by Christianity, the freedom to either accept grace or resist it, to do God's will or oppose it, to work out the plan of Providence as God's friend or as His tool. For Sartre, freedom must be absolute. "Man cannot be sometimes slave and sometimes free; he is wholly and forever free or he is not free at all."[18]

For the existentialist, the individual's perception of his absolute freedom in an empty universe gives rise to the feeling of anxiety, anguish, *angst*. The burden of his freedom, of having to choose and thereby exchange his infinite possibilities for finitude, is a dreadful one. Since God is absent, the individual is left with the terrifying responsibility of creating all the value in the world.

> The existentialist frankly states that man is in anguish. His meaning is as follows—When a man commits himself to anything, fully realizing that he is choosing what he will be, but thereby at the same time a legislator deciding for the whole of mankind—in such a moment a man cannot escape from the sense of complete and profound responsibility.[19]

The individual's responsibility is total, since the existentialist allows no mixture of free choice and historical limitations. The agent is responsible for his whole world. He may make history, but the past has not formed him. "If man makes history, it is because man himself is not made by history."[20] But this awesome responsibility is not the only cause of anxiety. It is also dreadful to recognize that Being is radically contingent—that there is no good reason for there being something instead of nothing—and to know that life is finally meaningless and absurd. The perception of emptiness is also supposed to be liberating. Sartre describes his philosophy as not despairing, but hopeful.

Hazel Motes is constantly burdened by anxiety. From the first moment we see him he is uncomfortable, discontented, unhappy with the world. It seems that the only scraps of pleasure he finds are the few moments when he is driving his car alone over an empty highway. He teaches the same perfect freedom as the French existentialists—in the doctrines of the Church Without Christ, as in Sartre, no values that come from outside the individual are real. If he preaches less about responsibility than freedom, it is because freedom is what he wants. What he dreads even more than freedom and emptiness is the possibility that someone has taken the burden of his sins on Himself. For Motes, as for Sartre, a feeling of nausea rises from the thought of things uncontrolled by the individual's free choice. In Sartre, nausea arises from the perception of the in-itself—the preexisting things out of which man constructs his world of choices. Motes feels his nausea when he is remembering the things beyond his control: his past and the Redeemer who wants to save him.

O'Connor shows her hero suffering anxiety, but Motes is not free in the existentialist sense. He is not alone in the universe, and he does not create it through his choices. Grace intervenes—in strange and violent ways—to remake Motes's world. What is more, the world Motes inhabits is not meaningless; rather it is shaped into Providential patterns. Beneath the actions of the freaks, charlatans, and idiots of Taulkinham, there is a story as old as Saul of Tarsus. Motes is not alone in the universe, no matter how much he would like to be. Motes seeks the perfect freedom the existentialists offered, but he finally exercises freedom of another kind. After he loses his car, he finds liberation in no longer pretending to be perfectly free and the creator of his world. Once he accepts that he is part of a world larger than himself, he no longer has to run.

## Premature Burial and the Promise of Redemption

Motes constantly tries to prove his freedom: to escape from his past, from the memory of Original Sin, and—most of all—from the promise of Redemption. But each attempt at escape only shows how little control over his own fate Motes really has. Every means of escape Motes chooses either comes to seem terribly confining itself or brings back the memories he is fleeing.

From the first moment we see him, Motes feels trapped and is looking for a way to escape. In the first line of *Wise Blood* we see Motes leaning forward in his seat on the train to Taulkinham, "looking one minute at the window as if he might want to jump out of it and the next down the aisle at the other end of the car" (p. 9). The train that is taking him away from the dead world of Eastrod, Tennessee, continues to constrict Motes terribly. Everywhere he turns he feels trapped and enclosed. He blocks the aisles. He cannot get into the dining car when he wants to, and, because of the crowd behind him, he cannot get out of line when he wants to get away. Once he has eaten his meal, he cannot get the steward to come and total his bill so he can get out. When he finally escapes from the table where the city women have been staring at him, he cannot get to his berth without bumping into Mrs. Hitchcock in the corridor and embarrassing himself as he clumsily tries to get out of her way. Everywhere he turns on the train that takes him away from his past, Motes meets with some frustration. What is more, even while he travels away from Eastrod, he carries it with him. When he looks out the window, he does not find an escape; in the space he travels through he sees only his past. "Eastrod filled his head and then went out beyond and filled the space that stretched from the train across the empty darkening fields" (p. 12). The landscape of his past is much like what he travels through on his last drive out of Taulkinham: both are marked by peeling CCC snuff posters (pp. 13, 207).

Something familiar about the porter on the train causes Motes to think he recognizes a link with his old home. He keeps calling the porter Parrum, and saying that he is sure he is from one of the black families in Eastrod. Motes insists he knows the porter, even though the man denies it and says he is from Chicago. For the first time Motes hears the message that where you come from is gone:

> "I remember you. Your father was a nigger named Cash Parrum. You can't go back there neither, nor anybody else, not if they wanted to."
> "I'm from Chicago," the porter said in an irritated voice. "My name is not Parrum."
> "Cash is dead," Haze said. "He got cholera from a pig."
> The porter's mouth jerked down and he said, "My father was a railroad man." (Pp. 18-19)

Wherever the porter comes from, Motes sees in him a reminder of the town to which he cannot return.

Motes suffers even more strongly from memories of his past and feelings of confinement when he gets into his upper berth. He has the porter open his berth hoping to "lie there and look out the window and watch how the country went by a train at night" (p. 17). But when he gets into it he finds that there is no window, and as he lies still trying not to increase the nausea left by his meal in the dining car, it seems that the berth is swallowing him up. "He lay down and noticed that the curved top looked as if it were not quite closed; it looked as if it were closing" (p. 19). The train is carrying Motes away from Eastrod, but he cannot see its movement and is himself immobile. Soon in his half-sleep Motes imagines that he is lying in his coffin.

While Motes imagines being shut up alive in his coffin, he remembers the funerals of his family, and how he expected his relatives to stop the coffin lid from closing down on them. Much of what we learn about Motes's past—and about the other things he is escaping—comes from his memories and fantasies about caskets closing on people who might rise and keep them open. This theme of premature burial, which is echoed several times later in *Wise Blood*, can hardly fail to call to mind Poe's story "The Premature Burial."[21] In one of her letters O'Connor recognizes that her reading as a young-ster of the book she recalls as *The Humerous Tales of E. A. Poe* may have been an influence on her, but adds that "This is an influence I would rather not think about" (*The Habit of Being*, p. 98).

The Poe influence does seem worth thinking about, though, for Poe's hero in "The Premature Burial" also finds himself thinking that his berth is his coffin. Poe's narrator is on a boat, not a train, but as with Hazel Motes in the sleeping car, a mode of transportation becomes a tomb—what might take you anywhere becomes the one place from which you cannot escape. Poe's narrator claims that he really is afflicted by a catalepsy that might lead to his being buried prematurely, and he describes the preparations he has made to in-sure that if he is laid in the family vault alive, he will be able to summon help if he revives. But he also recognizes that his condition is accompanied by "an idiosyncrasy in my ordinary *sleep*" (p. 674; Poe's italics). Like Motes awaking from his dream on the train, Poe's narrator says he cannot "gain, at once, thorough possession" of his senses, and "remained, for some minutes, in much bewilderment and perplexity." His dreams in ordinary sleep are also affected, and become morbid. He imagines a dreadful apparition showing him the coffins of all those who have been buried—many are not yet dead and many others have died only after struggling to escape their tombs.

In his berth on the train Motes is also finally terrified by his dream of being shut up in his mother's coffin, but most of what comes to Motes in his dreams and reveries is no more morbid or fanciful than his waking life. While Poe's narrator is terrified by fancies that are as much the cause of his condition as its result, Motes is reminded of the facts he wants to ignore: his home, his family, and Jesus's promise of salvation. Poe's narrator's moment of terror in his berth leads him to cast his fancies aside and become a new man. Motes's moment of fear leads him to call for the help he denies needing, and from just the places he would not want to get it.

Though it probably has its roots in Poe, the premature burial motif becomes part of O'Connor's attack on existentialism. In being haunted by images of imprisonment, as much as in constantly as-serting his freedom, Motes recalls writers like Sartre and Camus. *Angst*, the catchword of the movement, comes from a root meaning narrowness, and there is little more narrow than a grave. The asso-ciation of the concept of dread or anxiety with enclosure or imprisonment is common in existentialist writers: Sartre's most famous play, *No Exit,* is set in a narrow room in Hell; Camus's *The Stranger* ends in a prison. These writers paradoxically assert that there is freedom even in these places and that the seemingly free everyday world is really more imprisoning, but the dread of confinement is there nonetheless. His anxiety and nausea in the coffin-like berth on the train, as much as his sermons on Nothingness, show Motes a Tennessee existentialist.

Motes's half-waking fantasy that his berth is like a coffin gives way to the memory of his grandfather's vigil.

> The first coffin he had seen with someone in it was his grandfather's. They had left it propped open with a stick of kindling the night it had sat in the house with the old man in it, and Haze had watched from a distance, thinking: he ain't going to let them shut it on him; when the time comes, his elbow is going to shoot into the crack. His grandfather was a circuit preacher, a waspish old man who had ridden over three counties with Jesus hidden in his head like a stinger. When it was time to bury him, they shut the top of his box down and he didn't make a move. (Pp. 19–20)

What Motes remembers of this vigil leads, after some other memories, to recollections of the grandfather's preaching, and the images of the old man dead and lying in a box and alive and preaching from the top of a Ford unite several of Motes's concerns. He is surprised and frightened by the idea that the old man stays dead. He does not expect him to and does not want to himself. After remembering the old man's vigil, Motes thinks of his younger brothers in their scaled-down caskets. When they closed the lid on the older of the two,

> Haze ran and opened it up again. They said it was because he was heartbroken to part with his brother, but it was not; it was because he had thought, what if he had been in it and they had shut it on him. (P. 20)

Yet the adult Motes does not want to face the alternative to staying dead and remaining nailed in a box forever that his grandfather offers, for that is being saved by Jesus, and Motes does not want to owe his salvation to anyone. He fears being closed up in his coffin, but preaches a church where Jesus does not save—where "what's dead stays that way." The same ambivalence recurs in Taulkinham when Motes dreams that his way of escape has become his coffin—he both knows that no one can get him out and wonders why a preacher does not come and try.

After recalling the burials of his brothers and grandfather, Motes lapses into a dream about his father's funeral.

> He saw him humped over on his hands and knees in his coffin, being carried that way to the graveyard. "If I keep my can in the air," he heard the old man say, "nobody can shut nothing on me," but when they got his box to the hole, they let it drop down with a thud and his father flattened out like anybody else. (P. 20)

The father's comic appearance in Motes's dream shows his jocular attitude toward the questions that will obsess his son. Motes imagines that even when he is dead, death is only a matter for joking to his father. But the father's jokes always lead Motes to think that things really are more serious than that. Motes's later memories of his father, in chapter three, show the father's jokes making the boy confront something terrifyingly serious.

After a jolt from the train wakes him from the dream in which his father is put into the ground like everybody else, the half-awake Motes remembers Eastrod. When his father died, there had been twenty-five people there. By the time Motes himself was drafted, there were only ten, but Motes did not notice the decline. His only wish was to stay there unmolested. When the army called, he considered shooting himself in the foot, since he was going to be a preacher like his grandfather, and "a preacher can always do without a foot." The thought of his lost vocation leads Motes to remember his grandfather's preaching. The old man is the preacher who has left a mark on Motes that he cannot remove. What drives Motes through most of *Wise Blood* is the desire to escape what his grandfather promises.

The grandfather's theme is Redemption. He presents the promise of salvation in all its terrifying power.

> His grandfather had traveled three counties in a Ford automobile. Every fourth Saturday he had driven into Eastrod as if he were just in time to save them all from Hell, and he was shouting before he had the car door open. People gathered around his Ford because he seemed to dare them to. He would climb up on the nose of it and preach from there and sometimes he would climb onto the top of it and shout down at them. They were like stones! he would shout. But Jesus had died to redeem them! Jesus was so soul-

> hungry that He had died, one death for all, but He would have
> died every soul's death for one! Did they understand that ? Did
> they understand that for each stone soul, He would have died ten
> million deaths, had His arms and legs stretched on the cross and
> nailed ten million times for one of them?

The old man applies his doctrines particularly to the young Motes.

> Did they know that even for that boy there, for that mean sinful
> unthinking boy standing there with his dirty hands clenching and
> unclenching at his sides, Jesus would die ten million deaths before
> He would let him lose his soul? He would chase him over the
> waters of sin! Did they doubt Jesus could walk on the waters of
> sin? That boy had been redeemed and Jesus wasn't going to leave
> him ever. Jesus would never let him forget he was redeemed.
> What did the sinner think there was to be gained? Jesus would
> have him in the end! (Pp. 21–22)

When Motes founds his own church and makes the nose of a car his
pulpit, he tries to deny all that his grandfather preaches. But even as
he attacks Jesus and the very idea of Redemption, he shows he
cannot forget that he is redeemed.

Even as a child Motes wants to escape from Jesus. He develops
"a deep black wordless conviction . . . that the way to avoid Jesus was
to avoid sin" (p. 22). He wants to stay in Eastrod because there he
will be able to do the accustomed thing, avoid temptation, and—
even if he becomes a preacher—not have to bother much with Jesus.
"Where he wanted to stay was in Eastrod with his two eyes open,
and his hands always handling the familiar thing, his feet on the
known track, and his tongue not too loose." (It turns out that Motes
can do none of these things.) As a boy he decides to avoid sin for the
same reason that he later says he does not believe in sin— especially
the sin he was in before he committed any, and could not avoid. Sin
would prepare the way for forgiveness and Redemption, and Redemption is terrifying.

Some time after his grandfather has preached that Jesus will
"chase him over the waters" and he has decided to avoid Jesus by
avoiding sin, Motes forms an image of what being redeemed and
depending on Jesus would be like.

> Later he saw Jesus move from tree to tree in the back of his mind,
> a wild ragged figure motioning him to turn around and come off

into the dark where he was not sure of his footing, where he might be walking on the water and not know it and then suddenly know it and drown. (P. 22)

Here O'Connor recalls not Paul, but Peter. The story of the other great apostle's walking on the water, however, illuminates Motes's reasons for attacking Jesus and his Church.

In Matthew's Gospel, Christ sends his disciples out to sea after feeding the multitudes with the loaves and fishes. He remains behind to dismiss the people, and then goes alone up into a mountain to pray. The disciples' boat is tossed by waves and contrary winds, and then late at night they see Jesus walking toward them over the water. After they cry out in fear, Jesus tells them not to be afraid.

> And Peter, making answer said: Lord, if it be thou, bid me come to thee upon the waters. And he said: Come. And Peter going down out of the boat, walked upon the water to come to Jesus. But seeing the wind strong, he was afraid: and when he began to sink, he cried out, saying: Lord, save me. And immediately Jesus stretching forth his hand took hold of him, and said to him: O thou of little faith, why didst thou doubt? And when they were come up into the boat, the wind ceased. (Matt. 14: 28-23)

Peter's walk on the water shows both the power of faith and the danger of doubt. More importantly for Motes's story, it shows how completely the disciple depends on Jesus. Jesus, and Jesus alone, holds Peter above the water. He can do no more than believe in Him.

Motes does not want to follow Jesus, for that might mean depending only on Him—like Peter walking on the water. And depending on Jesus has its dangers. Christ Himself tells the people to count the cost before they become his disciples. "There's no peace for the redeemed." Motes would rather stand on his own feet than be supported by Jesus; he wants to keep his feet "on the known track," and not to walk over uncharted water.

Having decided not to shoot himself in the foot after all, Motes goes off to war. Although he sees the war as "a trick to lead him into temptation" (p. 23), he is sure he will be able to return uncorrupted. He plans to continue to avoid Jesus by avoiding sin. "He had a strong confidence in his power to resist evil; it was something he had inherited, like his face, from his grandfather." He looks forward to temptation, for he knows just what he will say when it comes.

> He meant to tell anyone in the army who invited him to sin that he
> was from Eastrod, Tennessee, and that he meant to get back there
> and stay back there, that he was going to be a preacher of the
> gospel and that he wasn't going to have his soul damned by the
> government or by any foreign place it sent him to.

When the offer to sin does come, in the shape of a trip to a brothel,
he tries to tell his buddies just that. But he does not finish, and his
friends tell him that "nobody was interested in his goddam soul
unless it was the priest."

> [H]e managed to answer that no priest taking orders from no pope
> was going to tamper with his soul. They told him he didn't have
> any soul and left for their brothel. (P. 24)

In what the soldiers tell him Motes sees another way of escape
from Jesus, one even better than avoiding sin. He can just forget all
his grandfather told him—forget Jesus and forget the soul He died
to save.

> He took a long time to believe them because he wanted to
> believe them. All he wanted was to believe them and get rid of it
> once and for all, and he saw the opportunity here to get rid of it
> without corruption, to be converted to nothing instead of to evil.
> (P. 24)

Motes is converted to the Nothingness the existentialists were proclaiming in place of God. After he has thought about it long enough,
he decides he is free of Jesus.

> He had all the time he could want to study his soul in and decide
> it was not there. When he was thoroughly convinced, he saw that
> this was something he had always known. The misery he had was
> a longing for home; it had nothing to do with Jesus.   (P. 24)

In his half-sleep Motes recalls his visit to Eastrod after his discharge. No one is left, and his house is falling down. All that is left
is the chifforobe in the kitchen, his mother's prized possession, and
he leaves a note warning that anyone who takes it will be "HUNTED
DOWN AND KILLED" (p. 26). He has taken only two mementos of

Eastrod into the army with him: his mother's Bible and her spectacles. When he reads the Bible, he wears the glasses. "They tired his eyes so that after a short time he was always obliged to stop" (p. 23). When he gets back to Tennessee, the Bible and the glasses are still in the bottom of his duffel bag. "He didn't read any book now but he kept the Bible because it had come from home. He kept the glasses in case his vision should ever become dim" (p. 25). It is revealing that he keeps these objects even when denying what they stand for. Throughout *Wise Blood*, Motes carries with him the idea of a Redeemer, even when he proclaims that it is simply excess baggage, just as he carries the Bible and the glasses. He is often unexpectedly reminded of Jesus, just as he later discovers the glasses after he has forgotten that he has them.

The glasses contribute something to the paradoxical treatment of vision in *Wise Blood*. They do Motes no good when he reads the Bible, and though he puts them on before answering the soldiers who invite him to the brothel, they are no help. But when he is repacking his duffel bag in preparation for his flight from Sabbath Lily, he rediscovers them and puts them on. In the mirror on the door he sees a blurred face. The image first reveals something about his own plan for escape: the glasses appear to be hiding "some dishonest plan that would show in his naked eyes" (p. 187). Then he sees his mother's face in his own, looking out of the mirror at him. Before he can take the glasses off, the door opens as Sabbath Lily enters with the mummy, and he is presented with another image of what he is trying to escape—both the Redeemer and the burden of the past.

The thought of his mother is terrible for Motes, and not only because she is part of the past he wants to be free of. His mother, like his grandfather, reminds Motes that Jesus died to redeem him. She seems to have been one of the redeemed for whom Motes says there is no peace (p. 140). While remembering the note he has left in the chifforobe, Motes decides that his mother will rest easier in her grave knowing that it is guarded.

> If she came looking any time at night, she would see. He wondered if she walked at night and came there ever. She would come with that look on her face, unrested and looking; the same look he had seen through the crack of her coffin. (P. 26)

The sixteen-year-old Motes had seen her in her coffin wearing an expression that made it appear that "she wasn't any more satisfied dead than alive, as if she were going to spring up and shove the lid back and fly out and satisfy herself" (p. 27). While Motes promises a church peaceful and satisfied where the dead stay dead, these redeemed who may rise from their coffins seem terribly threatening. The grandfather is like a wasp with Jesus like a stinger in his head; the mother becomes like a huge bat in Motes's dream, ready to fly out as the casket lid comes down.

As the casket closes, Motes dreams that he is being shut inside it.

> From inside he saw it closing, coming closer closer down and cutting off the light and the room. He opened his eyes and saw it closing and he sprang up between the crack and wedged his head and shoulders through it and hung there, dizzy. . . (P. 27)

As he hangs from the berth, Motes sees the porter and calls to him for help.

> "I'm sick!" he called. "I can't be closed up in this thing. Get me out!"
> The porter stood watching him and didn't move.
> "Jesus," Haze said, "Jesus."
> The porter didn't move. "Jesus been a long time gone," he said in a sour triumphant voice. (P. 27)

Motes has not escaped the memory of Jesus. Even though he has told the women in the dining car that he would not care about Jesus even if He were on the train, he calls on Him here. That at least is the literal meaning of his profanity—and the meaning the porter who taunts him with his own doctrine plays off. In much the same way, when his next mode of transportation comes to seem like a coffin, Motes will want to be saved—or at least wonder why no one is trying to save him—even though he has preached against the very idea of salvation and Redemption.

## A Nameless Unplaced Guilt

When Motes finally gets to Taulkinham, he tries to put all that he has remembered in his coffinlike berth behind him. He tries to cut himself off from all that came before his conversion to nothing— Eastrod, his call to preach, the memory of Original Sin, and the promise of Redemption. In the city he sets out to prove his perfect freedom and cleanness, but whichever way he turns he is confronted with the things he is trying to escape.

As soon as he leaves the train station in Taulkinham, Motes finds that he has not escaped his vocation. He looks like a preacher. He catches a yellow cab at the station and asks the driver to take him to see Mrs. Leora Watts, who has, according to a message he has just read in a men's room stall at the depot, "the friendliest bed in town" (p. 30). The cab driver is surprised at his passenger's destination, since Leora Watts "don't usually have no preachers for company." Motes denies that he is a preacher, but the cab driver is not convinced. "You look like a preacher," he tells Motes. "That hat looks like a preacher's hat" (p. 31). The hat is indeed the sort "an elderly country preacher would wear" (p. 10). Motes tells the driver that the hat is just a hat, but the driver is not satisfied. "It ain't only the hat . . . It's a look in your face somewheres." Motes's face recalls his grandfather's, but the resemblance is not something Motes wants to cultivate.

There is nothing Motes can say to make the driver believe he is not a preacher. The driver does not disapprove of Motes's destination. He can see why a preacher would want to make the visit.

> "I understand," the driver said. "It ain't anybody perfect on this green earth of God's, preacher nor nobody else. And you can tell people better how terrible sin is if you know from your own personal experience." (P. 32)

But Motes, unlike the driver, does not believe in sin. He is going to Mrs. Watts to prove just that point. He tells the driver that he does not believe in anything, but that does not make the driver change his mind about Motes's calling.

> "That's the trouble with you preachers," he said. "You've all got too good to believe in anything." (P. 32)

Motes will not believe in anything because he wants to think himself good and clean.

Motes's hat continues to mark him as a preacher. After telling her that he has come for "the usual business," Motes asks Mrs. Watts to understand that he is "no goddam preacher" (p. 34). But she, like the cab driver, can see he is marked as a preacher. When Motes returns for a second night, Mrs. Watts looks at Motes, says "That Jesus-seeing hat!" and takes it from him. She later cuts an obscene shape in it, and Motes has to buy a new one. He tries to buy one completely different from the old one, picks out "a white panama with a red and green and yellow band around it." But by the time he puts it on, it is not much different from the elderly preacher's hat.

> He went outside and took the red and green and yellow band off it and thumped out the crease in the top and turned down the brim. When he put it on, it looked just as fierce as the other one had. (P. 111)

Sabbath Lily has to tell Motes to take off the new hat just as Mrs. Watts takes the old one from him (p. 170). Sabbath Lily can also see Motes's call—and, like Mrs. Watts, she does not like it. When Motes is getting ready to leave and is talking about how he wants nothing but the truth, she snaps back at him, "Preacher talk. . . . Where were you going to run off to?" (P. 189).

By the time he is involved with Sabbath Lily, Motes is not denying his call. He is acting it out in reverse. He preaches against everything that his grandfather taught him, but he preaches in just the way the old man did. Even in making his car his pulpit, he is following the example of the grandfather who climbed on top of his Ford to threaten young Hazel with Redemption. Even as he tells the people outside the theaters, "where you come from is gone," he is acting out a memory of Eastrod.

In Taulkinham Motes denies his home. Before his conversion to nothing, he planned to tell anyone who invited him to sin that he was from Eastrod, Tennessee, before going on to talk about his soul. But now that he preaches that neither that past nor the future have any significance, he does not talk about Eastrod. Reminders of Tennessee come to him all the same. Enoch Emery recognizes him, and asks if he comes from Melsy, which is the nearest railroad stop to Eastrod and the place where Motes boarded the train (p. 57). Motes says no. But all the same, he cannot escape reminders of home. His own actions recall his grandfather; his mother's glasses are in his baggage; and his childhood returns to him in memories.

What Motes wants most to escape from in the city is the memory of sin and Redemption. It is to forget them that he begins to commit blasphemy and practice fornication. By committing the worst sins he will prove he does not believe in sin. He will avoid Jesus by proving that he does not believe in sin instead of by avoiding sin. But while walking through the streets of Taulkinham he meets Hawks, who accuses him of the very sins he has committed. And the preacher's accusation drives Motes to a defense that does not help him. "If I was in sin I was in it before I ever committed any. There's no change come in me" (p. 53). Motes's last words as he leaves Hawks are, "I don't need Jesus . . . What do I need with Jesus? I got Leora Watts" (p. 56). But in fact when he returns to Leora Watts he is again reminded of the sin he was in before he committed any.

Throughout *Wise Blood* Motes's sexual experiences are less significant as actual sins than as reminders of another sort of sin. Motes's real sin—the sin he cannot forget being in—is not his fornications with Leora Watts or Sabbath Lily Hawks or the woman at the whorehouse that the Lapsed Catholic boy takes him to. Sexuality is more important as a reminder of a vague sense of guilt that does not result from any particular act. In the last chapter of *Wise Blood*, Motes practices extreme penances—blinding himself, walking with rocks and broken glass in his shoes, binding himself with barbed wire. He says he does it because he is not clean, but never gives any sign that he wants to atone for any particular act. Earlier in the novel we learn that Motes practiced similar penances—walking with stones in his shoes—as a child. The childish penances are linked to sexuality, but sex does not seem to be the cause of the guilt.

As Motes is getting ready for his second night with Leora Watts, O'Connor describes the first time he saw a naked woman. A carnival had come to Melsy, and Motes's father took him to it. There is an extra charge for one of the sideshows: "the barker said it was so SINsational that it would cost any man that wanted to see it thirty-five cents" (p. 60). Hazel's father sends him off to look at the monkeys and furtively goes into this show.

Hazel soon leaves the monkeys and follows his father. He does not know for certain what is inside.

> It's something about a privy, he was thinking. It's some men in a privy. Then he thought, maybe it's a man and woman in a privy. She wouldn't want me in there. (P. 61)

He is following his father, but thinking of what his mother would have to say about it.

Young Motes talks the barker into letting him in for fifteen cents. At first all he can see are the backs of men. Once he climbs up on a bench, he sees that they are

> looking down into a lowered place where something white was lying, squirming a little, in a box lined with black cloth. For a second he thought it was a skinned animal and then he saw it was a woman. She was fat and she had a face like an ordinary woman except there was a mole on the corner of her lip that moved when she grinned, and one on her side.
>
> "Had one of themther built into ever' casket," his father, up toward the front, said, "be a heap ready to go sooner." (P. 62)

Motes recognizes his father's voice without looking, and crawls out of the side of the tent, "because he didn't want to pass the barker." He goes to sit in the far corner of his father's truck.

When he gets home, Motes's mother can see that he feels ashamed of something.

> He moved behind a tree and got out of her view, but in a few minutes, he could feel her watching him through the tree. He saw the lowered place and the casket again and a thin woman in the casket who was too long for it. Her head stuck up at one end and her knees were raised to make her fit. (Pp. 62–63)

The woman in the casket takes her place in the pattern of premature burial imagery that recurs throughout *Wise Blood*. Motes's father can just joke about death and sex, but for Motes himself both are more serious. The idea of lying alive in a coffin will continue to haunt him, as will the guilt his mother sees in him now.

As Motes stands against the tree, his mother approaches with a stick and asks him three times, "What you seen?"

> "What you seen," she said, using the same tone of voice all the time. She hit him across the legs with the stick, but he was like part of the tree. "Jesus died to redeem you," she said.
>
> "I never ast him," he muttered.
>
> She didn't hit him again but she stood looking at him, shutmouthed, and he forgot the guilt of the tent for the nameless unplaced guilt that was in him. In a minute she threw the stick away from her and went back to the wash-pot, still shut-mouthed. (P. 63)

The next day young Motes takes the shoes he normally wears only to revivals and during the winter and fills them with rocks. He walks for a mile in the rock-filled shoes and then soaks his feet in a creek, thinking, "that ought to satisify him. Nothing happened. If a stone had fallen, he would have taken it as a sign" (pp. 63-64). He walks on the rocks for another half mile on the way home.

It is the nameless unplaced guilt—the guilt of Original Sin—that the young Motes is trying to work off during this stony walk, and it is the same unplaced guilt that the older Motes tries to deny feeling. He is in it before he has committed any sins of his own. It is passed down to him: he feels it first when he hears his father's voice in the tent. And it is from this guilt, as his mother and his grandfather remind him, that Jesus died to save him. Motes, fearing the promised salvation, constantly claims to be free of all guilt, but especially from this, for if he is in sin before committing any, there is no way to avoid Jesus. Neither sinning nor avoiding sin will do any good. Throughout the novel, the scenes in which Motes is confronted with sexuality have more to do with Original Sin than with the fornication of which Hawks accuses him.

### The Getaway As Tomb

All the things Motes uses in Taulkinham to prove his freedom and cleanness quickly come to seem confining themselves. Sex is no exception. Motes is not driven to either Leora Watts or Sabbath Lily by lust. Neither woman is physically appealing. Motes wants to use sex to exercise his freedom—to prove he does not believe in sin. But from the first moment, he feels trapped. When he comes to Leora Watts, he says nothing until she grabs his arm and asks, " 'You huntin' something?' ... If she had not had him so firmly by the arm, he might have leaped out the window" (p. 34). The prostitute, like the train to Taulkinham, makes him feel so confined that he wants to jump out a window.

Motes continues to feel trapped by his sexual involvements. He suffers a good deal of humiliation with Mrs. Watts.

> Since the night before was the first time he had slept with any woman, he had not been very successful with Mrs. Watts. When he finished, he was like something washed ashore on her, and she had made obscene comments about him, which he remembered off and on during the day. (P. 59)

Later she cuts an obscene shape in Motes's hat while he is asleep. He plans to ruin Sabbath Lily because "he wanted someone he could teach something to" (p. 110). He wants to be in control. When it becomes clear that Sabbath Lily is more in control of their relationship than he is, Motes loses interest. After Sabbath Lily accomplishes the seduction Motes has planned, Motes awakens thinking of escaping to a new city. Proving that he does not believe in sin by practicing what it is called only makes him feel trapped.

Blasphemy proves to be no more liberating than fornication. Motes is no more able to control his church than to dominate in his sexual involvements. While he preaches earnestly and energetically, few listen to him and he makes no converts. He cannot keep the doctrines he denies from reappearing. He finds himself unwittingly promising salvation to bastards, and he sees his only disciple bringing Redemption and Jesus back into his church—the church he has founded to avoid them both. When he is standing on the nose of his Essex, he can escape from neither the role his grandfather left him nor the doctrines the grandfather preached.

Even the Essex, Motes's last means of proving his freedom, comes to seem confining. Vehicles have let Motes down before. The train is confining from the first and like a coffin when he is shut in the sleeping car. In any case, the train follows its own schedule, not Hazel Motes's. After Motes gets off to take some air at a junction stop, the train leaves while he is looking the other way, and he has to wait six hours for the next one. But, despite all the evidence to the contrary, he believes that the car whose course he directs himself will take him anywhere he wants to go. It is of course an illusion from the first, but despite what mechanics tell him—despite the times the horn will not work or the car will not even start—Motes believes the car is his way of escape until it is wrecked. But in a dream he does get an inkling that it is not really his way out.

On the night Hoover Shoats appears, Motes cannot make his escape in the Essex. He wants very much to get away from his saccharine disciple, but the car runs jerkily at first, allowing Shoats to get in with Motes, and then will not start at all after Motes has stopped it to shove Shoats out. Motes has to push it to the curb, with Shoats's help, and then can do nothing to get away from him. He will not walk away from the car because he fears it will be stolen. Motes decides to spend the night in the Essex, and once Shoats has left after making some threats about competition, he falls asleep.

Haze stayed in his car about an hour and had a bad experience in it: he dreamed he was not dead but only buried. He was not waiting on the Judgment because there was no Judgment, he was waiting on nothing. Various eyes looked through the back oval window at his situation, some with considerable reverence, like the boy from the zoo, and some only to see what they could see. There were three women with paper sacks who looked at him critically as if he were something—a piece of fish—they might buy, but they passed on after a minute. A man in a canvas hat looked in and put his thumb to his nose and wiggled his fingers. Then a woman with two little boys on either side of her stopped and looked in, grinning. After a second she pushed the boys out of view and indicated that she would climb in and keep him company for a while, but she couldn't get through the glass and finally she went off. All this time Haze was bent on getting out but since there was no use to try, he didn't make any move one way or the other. He kept expecting Hawks to appear at the oval window with a wrench, but the blind man didn't come. (P. 161)

The car that Motes thinks will take him anywhere becomes a coffin, just as the berth on the train to Taulkinham did. This second dream of premature burial shows Motes, at least unconsciously, realizing that his car—and the kind of freedom it represents—will let him down and finally imprison him.[22]

While Motes's first dream of being buried alive is full of memories of his family, who told him that Jesus would save him, this dream is full of images from Taulkinham—of all the things that cannot save him. Many eyes look in at him, but they cannot help, no matter whether they look at him with reverence, like Enoch Emery, "the boy from the zoo," or merely with curiosity, like the few people who have briefly listened to him outside the movie theater, or with mockery, like Hoover Shoats, whose white hat is recalled by the canvas hat in the dream. One of Motes's other ways of escape is recalled by the woman who offers to come in and keep him company. Though Motes has tried to prove his freedom by using Leora Watts and Sabbath Lily, he comes to feel trapped in both his sexual involvements. Here the woman cannot get into the car and coffin with him, and certainly cannot get him out.

In the dream Motes both wants to be saved and remembers the doctrines he has preached from atop the car that has now become his coffin. He is not lying in his tomb waiting for the Last Judgment and the Resurrection of the Dead, for he has preached that there is no Judgment and the dead stay that way. He is waiting for nothing—the nothing he was converted to long before. The last time he thought he was trapped in a tomb, he called on Jesus for help, but he is more consistent now. But somehow he is not satisfied. Since "there was no use to try," he makes no attempt to escape from the coffin, but he is bent on getting out: he wants the salvation he cannot achieve by himself. He later escapes from the coffin that his car and his faith in his freedom have become only with the assistance of a highway patrolman.

At the end of his dream Motes wonders why Hawks does not come to save him. The preacher is the only figure in the dream whom Motes imagines having a wrench to break the car's window, and he never comes to use it. Motes has wondered before "why the preacher didn't welcome him and act like a preacher should when he sees what he believes is a lost soul" (p. 145), and his attempts to prove to Hawks that he does not believe in Jesus have also been attempts to get Hawks to try and save him. In his dream Motes realizes both that if anyone will save him, it will be someone who preaches that "Jesus is a fact," and that Hawks is a fraud.

When Motes finally shakes off the dream, he finds that the Essex will now run without any trouble and drives home. Most of the dream has had no effect on him. The dream shows how much of his own situation he is aware of on some level, but he does not begin a new life. He is not transformed into a new man, as Poe's narrator is after waking from his dream of premature burial. Motes does pick Hawks's lock and sees for himself that the preacher is not blind, but he continues to believe his Essex is his way of escape, not his tomb.

## The Blind Leading the Blind

Motes desperately wants to escape the Redeemer who might free him from the tomb, but Jesus is the one thing he cannot escape. No matter where he goes he finds himself hearing the doctrines he wants to leave buried in Eastrod. All the freaks and charlatans he meets in Taulkinham bring him reminders of the Incarnate Savior. Asa Hawks, the fraud, tells him that Jesus is a fact and taunts him with the promise that Jesus loves him. Enoch Emery, the idiot, brings him a reminder that Jesus is flesh. And Hoover Shoats, the con man, reminds him that Jesus is a person, not just an idea or a way of saying something. Motes is tormented by these reminders of an incarnate redeemer until he loses his entombing car and goes home to blind himself and accept the role of Jesus's disciple. In his blindness he himself brings reminders of Jesus and an offer of grace to Mrs. Flood, his uncomprehending landlady.

Mrs. Flood is sitting on her porch when Motes returns to the boardinghouse after seeing his Essex destroyed. He mixes the lime at the spigot by the front steps, and then starts inside. As Motes passes her, Mrs. Flood asks him what he is going to do with the lime. He replies "Blind myself," and goes into the house. Mrs. Flood remains on the front porch, rocking a cat. She wonders what reason Motes could have for doing such a thing. She herself is a sensible person, who cannot see any point in a person's blinding himself.

> [I]f she had felt that bad, she would have killed herself and she wondered why anybody wouldn't do that. She would simply have put her head in an oven or maybe have given herself too many painless sleeping pills and that would have been that. Perhaps Mr. Motes was only being ugly, for what possible reason could a person have for wanting to destroy their sight? A woman like her, who was so clear-sighted, could never stand to be blind. If she had to be blind she would rather be dead. It occurred to her suddenly that when she was dead she would be blind too. She stared in front of her intensely, facing this for the first time. She recalled the phrase, "eternal death," that the preachers used, but she cleared it out of her mind with no more change of expression than the cat. She was not religious or morbid, for which every day she thanked her stars. She would credit a person who had that streak with anything, though, and Mr. Motes had it or he wouldn't be a preacher. He might put lime in his eyes and she wouldn't doubt it a bit, because they were all, if the truth was only known, a little bit off in their heads. What possible reason could a sane person have for wanting to not enjoy himself anymore?
> She certainly couldn't say. (Pp. 210–11)

Like the choragos in Sophocles, who tells Oedipus, "You were better dead than alive and blind," Mrs. Flood does not understand why someone would choose the penance of blindness rather than the escape of suicide.[23] She has no clue to Motes's reasons. There is no way for her to know that for Motes the choice has never been between enjoying himself and not enjoying himself anymore. (As his dutiful fornications show, Motes does not have much talent for enjoying himself.) The alternatives Motes has been faced with are freedom with its anguish or discipleship with its burdens. He can either suffer alone and pointlessly while proclaiming his perfect freedom, or suffer to some end after having accepted that he is not alone in the universe. The biblical story that lies behind Motes's self-blinding allows the reader to see it as an act of love. In one of her lectures O'Connor recalls reading a newspaper story about a preacher who wired a lamb to a cross as part of his Lenten revival. She admits that the preacher may have been just a showman, but says that she prefers to think that the crucified lamb was as close as the revivalist could get to the Eucharist. His self-blinding is as close as Hazel Motes, who is cut off from the Church and its sacraments, can get to Jesus's love and forgiveness.[24]

To Mrs. Flood, however, Motes's self-blinding is only a mystery. It soon becomes a mystery she wants to fathom. Motes continues to live in her house, and the sight of his ruined eyes—he will not hide them with dark glasses—constantly makes her wonder what a person might want beyond simply enjoying himself. Though Mrs. Flood does not like to look at Motes's scarred eyes, she becomes fascinated by them.

> If she didn't keep her mind going on something else when he was near her, she would find herself leaning forward, staring into his face as if she expected to see something she hadn't seen before. (P. 213)

Just as Motes stared into Hawks's dark glasses as if he wanted to see through them, Mrs. Flood now stares into Motes's sightless eyes. In both cases the blind eyes seem to contain a hint of something that will not fit into the sighted person's simple view of the world. The story of Hawks's self-blinding, false though it is, shakes Motes's confidence in his freedom from Redemption; Motes's ruined eyes trouble Mrs. Flood's placid selfishness.

After staring into Motes's face, Mrs. Flood gets a "sense that he was cheating her in some secret way" (p. 213). She decides to let him stay, despite his refusal to wear dark glasses, so that she can find out just how he is swindling her. Mrs. Flood feels entitled to all that comes her way. She sees it as only right that she take a larger and larger share of the disability check Motes gets from the government. It is only her own coming back to her.

> She felt justified in getting anything at all back that she could,

money or anything else, as if she had once owned the earth and been dispossessed of it. She couldn't look at anything steadily without wanting it, and what provoked her most was the thought that there might be something valuable hidden near her, something she couldn't see. (P. 214)

She is only exercising her right of ownership when she steams open Motes's government envelope to see how much he gets—she raises the rent soon afterwards—and when she arranges for the Welfare people to send Sabbath Lily to a detention home. She is not going to let her tax money be wasted—not on trash like Sabbath Lily. Even after she has made sure that Motes will not squander the money that is rightfully hers, Mrs. Flood still has the feeling that something is being kept from her. Looking steadily into her boarder's eyes makes her want something, but she cannot tell what it is.

To Mrs. Flood, it seems that Motes can see something with his blind eyes. She cannot rid herself of the idea, even though she is sure Motes is totally blind. (Once he removes the rag he uses for a bandage, there can be no doubt.) The more she takes the blind man's money, the more she feels that he is somehow holding something back from her.

[S]he didn't get rid of the feeling that she was being cheated. Why had he destroyed his eyes and saved himself unless he had some plan, unless he saw something that he couldn't get without being blind to everything else? (P. 216)

By "saved himself," Mrs. Flood means "not gone ahead and killed himself if he felt that bad," but her question also suggests the real reason for Motes's self-blinding. Motes's act is his acceptance of the salvation he has been trying to avoid. Until Motes's blind but seeing eyes raise the question for her, salvation is not something Mrs. Flood has thought about. Her sense that Motes has something valuable makes her begin to face the religious and morbid ideas she has avoided.

Mrs. Flood is sure that Motes sees something because he looks as if he is pressing on towards some goal. "His face had a peculiar pushing look, as if it were going forward after something it could just distinguish in the distance" (p. 214). Though she observes him closely, she cannot make sense of what Motes sees. Motes is not doing what she would do if she were blind—"she would have sat by the radio all day, eating cake and ice cream and soaking her feet" (p. 217).   Motes, however, shows no interest in food or in any other pleasure.   He does not do anything except walk, first back and forth in his room, and then around four or five blocks near the house. Mrs. Flood cannot make sense of it.

> He could have been dead and get all he got out of life but the exercise.  He might as well be one of them monks, she thought, he might as well be in a monkery.  She didn't understand it.  She didn't like the thought that something was being put over her head.  She liked the clear light of day.  She liked to see things. (P. 218)

(No doubt Motes would have been better off in a monastery, where he would have had an abbot to limit the severity of his penances.) Motes's indifference to everything around him forces Mrs. Flood to imagine what might be going on inside his head.  Though she has been content with the material world she can see by the clear light of day, she has to imagine that Motes can perceive what is hidden from her in the darkness of his mind.

She has trouble imagining what it would be like inside the blind man's head.

> She could not make up her mind what would be inside his head and what out.  She thought of her own head as a switchbox where she controlled from; but with him, she could only imagine the outside in, the whole black world in his head and his head bigger than the world, his head big enough to include the sky and the planets and whatever was or had been or would be.  How would he know if time was going backwards or forwards or if he was going with it?  She imagined it was like you were walking in a tunnel and all you could see was a pinpoint of light.  She had to imagine the pinpoint of light; she couldn't think of it at all without that.  She saw it as some kind of a star, like the star on Christmas cards.  She saw him going backwards to Bethlehem and she had to laugh. (P. 219)

Like Motes when he was still behind the wheel of his car, Mrs. Flood believes she is in control of her own fate.  But when imagining Motes's mind, she has to include more than just the ego at the switch. Motes's dark world may include everything, but most importantly, it includes some goal, something beyond the self that gives direction to everything else. Mrs. Flood is sure Motes is going somewhere, so there must be some pinpoint of light in Motes's darkness. The image of the star of Bethlehem—which Mrs. Flood, with appropriate banality, takes from a Christmas card—shows the goal Motes has found in the darkness. Motes has denied most strenuously the doctrine of the Incarnation. Now, in Mrs. Flood's imagination, he is moving toward the star that first announced that God had taken flesh and come down to save His people.

Though Mrs. Flood does not realize it, she has penetrated Motes's secret. What he now has is the Redeemer he has been running from. Motes has often denied the importance of history. In his sermons he has rejected all of the story of Salvation from the Fall to Judgment. Now, at least in Mrs. Flood's mind, he is traveling back to the point that gives meaning to the whole stretch of time. The birth of Christ makes the Fall at the beginning fortunate and the Judgment at the end a prelude to glory. Motes has accepted the involvement in history and the Redemption that he has tried to escape. What he has is the Jesus whose birth is still recalled by the stars on Christmas cards.

Mrs. Flood does not yet realize all this. Motes's actions still make no sense to her. He will not do any of the things she thinks would amuse him—strum a guitar, for instance. She is even more perplexed when she discovers that he is throwing his money into the trash. (He spends nothing on himself and has a good third of his check left every month despite Mrs. Flood's gouging.) When Mrs. Flood asks how he could leave his money in the wastebasket, he replies, "It was left over . . . I didn't need it" (p. 220). She is appalled.

> She dropped onto his straight chair. "Do you throw it away every month?" she asked after a time.
> "Only when it's left over," he said.
> "The poor and needy," she muttered. "The poor and needy. Don't you ever think about the poor and needy? If you don't want that money somebody else might."
> "You can have it," he said.
> "Mr. Motes," she said coldly, "I'm not charity yet!" She realized now that he was a mad man and that he ought to be under the control of a sensible person. (P. 220)

Motes's self-blinding has not convinced Mrs. Flood that Motes is mad, but his indifference to money does. But her thought that Motes should be under the care of a sensible person, like herself, also marks the beginning of a shift in her desires. She has wanted what Motes has—his money, his secret possession. Now she is beginning to want Motes himself. She has looked steadily into his face long enough to wish to possess him.

Mrs. Flood begins to think of how to attract Motes's attention. Since the blind man cannot appreciate her Grecian nose or the hair she has clustered like grapes on her brow and over each ear, she decides she must be interested in what he is interested in. She carries out this plan by suggesting to Motes that he begin preaching again. People would like to see a blind preacher, especially if he had a Seeing-Eye dog. She does not realize that Motes's interest is not in preaching, but in Jesus. She goes on to tell Motes why she has not gone in for religion herself.

> "For myself," she continued, "I don't have that streak. I believe that what's right today is wrong tomorrow and that the time to enjoy yourself is now so long as you let others do the same. I'm as good, Mr. Motes," she said, "not believing in Jesus as many a one that does."
> "You're better," he said, leaning forward suddenly. "If you believed in Jesus you wouldn't be so good."
> He had never paid her a compliment before! "Why Mr. Motes," she said, "I expect you're a fine preacher! You certainly ought to start it again. It would give you something to do. As it is, you don't have anything to do but walk. Why don't you start preaching again?"
> "I can't preach any more," he muttered.
> "Why?"
> "I don't have time," he said, and got up and walked off the porch as if she had reminded him of some urgent business. He walked as if his feet hurt him but he had to go on. (P. 221)

Mrs. Flood thinks Motes a fine preacher because he seems to be reassuring her of her goodness, but, in fact, what he means is that believing in Jesus involves accepting one's own sinfulness. The believer cannot think himself too good: he must be bad enough to need a savior. Motes has given up telling people that they are clean. He is now devoting his time to working out his own sinfulness.

Mrs. Flood soon discovers why Motes walks with a limp. His shoes are filled with gravel and broken glass and fragments of a rock. Penance has been the urgent business he has hurried off to see to. She cannot understand it. If she were blind, she would spend the day soaking her feet, not walking in shoes filled with rubble. She still wonders what his purpose is.

> Who's he doing this for? she asked herself. What's he getting out of doing it? Every now and then she would have an intimation of something hidden near her but out of her reach. "Mr. Motes," she said that day, when he was in her kitchen eating his dinner, "what do you walk on rocks for?"
> "To pay," he said in a harsh voice.
> "Pay for what?"
> "It don't make any difference for what," he said. "I'm paying." (P. 222)

Motes is repeating his childhood penance. And once again, he is not trying to atone for any particular sin. He is trying to expiate the nameless, unplaced guilt. Motes no longer proclaims his innocence.

When Mrs. Flood continues to ask him about what he is paying for—"But what have you got to show that you're paying for?" — Motes replies, "Mind your business. . . . You can't see." Throughout *Wise Blood*, there is an opposition between the physically blind, who can see spiritual things, and the spiritually blind, who take pride in their clear vision. Just as Oedipus's blindness gives him insight— just as Paul's blindness gives way to spiritual vision after the scales fall from his eyes—the blind in *Wise Blood* see more than the sighted. When Motes taunts Hawks on his blindness, the fake blind man replies, "I can see more than you . . . You got eyes and see not, ears and hear not, but you'll have to see some time" (p. 54). Once Motes does blind himself, he comes to see what he has been blind to: he sees that he is not sinless and self-sufficient, the master of his fate. After Motes accuses her of spiritual blindness, Mrs. Flood asks him the question that has been troubling her since he walked up the steps with the bucket of lime.

> "Do you think, Mr. Motes," she said hoarsely, "that when you're dead, you're blind?"
> "I hope so," he said after a minute.
> "Why?" she asked, staring at him.
> After a while he said, "If there's no bottom in your eyes, they hold more."
> The landlady stared for a long time, seeing nothing at all. (P. 222)

Motes seems to be envisioning a spiritual sight that continues after death, but Mrs. Flood still cannot understand.

After this conversation Mrs. Flood becomes even more obsessed by Motes. "She began to fasten all her attention on him, to the neglect of other things" (p. 223). She begins to follow him on his walks and to fix him special meals and carry them to his room. She tells him that she is the only person he has to look after him. "No one . . . has your interest at heart but me. Nobody would care if I didn't" (p. 223). Motes does not appreciate these attentions. They distract him from the business he is embarked on. He would prefer bad food to good. After a time he abruptly tells Mrs. Flood that he will be getting his food elsewhere—at a diner, run by a foreigner, that Mrs. Flood calls a dark and filthy place. She takes some comfort from the idea that when winter comes Motes will be forced back to her. "Where will you eat when winter comes, when the first wind blows the virus into you?" Motes catches influenza even before winter arrives, and Mrs. Flood has "the satisfaction of bringing his meals to his room." Her wish to possess Motes is growing, but she still cannot understand the mystery hidden by Motes's blind eyes and his strange penances.

One morning she enters Motes's room earlier than usual and is appalled to discover that Motes has been practicing another penance. Motes's shirt is open and she can see that he has three strands of barbed wire wrapped around his chest. She drops her tray in horror and asks Motes why he does such things. "It's not natural." Motes replies that it is natural.

> "Well, it's not normal. It's like one of them gory stories, it's something that people have quit doing—like boiling in oil or being a saint or walling up cats," she said. "There's no reason for it. People have quit doing it."
>
> "They ain't quit doing it as long as I'm doing it," he said.
>
> "People have quit doing it," she repeated. "What do you do it for?"
>
> "I'm not clean." (P. 224)

Until he lost his Essex, Motes always claimed to be clean. Now he admits that he is not. Through these horrible penances, he accepts his sinfulness, and, implicitly, the Savior whose blood will wash him clean.

Mrs. Flood will take only the literal meaning of Motes's explanation. With blood on his bed and nightshirt, he is not physically clean. Motes tells her that that is not the kind of clean he means, but

Mrs. Flood tells him there is only one kind of clean. Then, as if to prove it, she gets a broom and dust pan to sweep up the dishes she has broken. While she cleans she pronounces her verdict of Motes's way of cleaning himself.

> "It's easier to bleed than sweat, Mr. Motes," she said in the voice of High Sarcasm. "You must believe in Jesus or you wouldn't do these foolish things. You must have been lying to me when you named your fine church. I wouldn't be surprised if you weren't some kind of a agent of the pope or got some connection with something funny." (P. 225)

There is a great deal of truth in Mrs. Flood's rebuke. Motes would not do this if he did not believe in Jesus. The Church Without Christ disappeared when its only pulpit went over the embankment. Motes now is connected with something funny, something as scandalous as Christ. He is trying to do one of the things that Mrs. Flood says people have stopped doing. He is trying to be a saint, or at least to sanctify himself.

While Motes is still weak from the influenza, Mrs. Flood decides that it is time to get him to marry her.

> Her first plan had been to marry him and then have him committed to the state institution for the insane, but gradually her plan had become to marry him and keep him. Watching his face had become a habit with her; she wanted to penetrate the darkness behind it and see for herself what was there. (P. 225)

Now she has the sense that if she does not get Motes now, while he is weak, she will lose him entirely. Mrs. Flood's wish to possess everything she looks at long enough has transformed her greed for Motes's money into a desire for Motes himself. Staring into the mystery of Motes's eyes has transformed her greed into something less and less selfish. To begin with she wanted part of her tax money back; now she wants someone to take care of. But she still seems to think of everything she sees, even Hazel Motes, as part of the rightful inheritance she has been cheated of. She decides to "keep" Motes, as one keeps an object.

Mrs. Flood makes her proposal to Motes on one of the coldest days of the year. She asks Motes if he hears the wind outside, and reminds him that not all blind men are fortunate enough to have a warm place to stay and someone to take care of them. Then she tells him that she cannot keep climbing stairs the way she has been. Motes is alarmed by the tone of Mrs. Flood's voice, and as she continues, he gets out of bed and begins putting his clothes on over his nightshirt.

> "I been thinking," she went on, watching him as he went on with what he was doing, "and I see there's only one thing for you and me to do. Get married. I wouldn't do it under any ordinary condition but I would do it for a blind man and a sick one. If we don't help each other, Mr. Motes, there's nobody to help us," she said. "Nobody. The world is an empty place." (P. 227)

Motes himself had preached that the world was an empty place—though he never admitted that we could help each other. Now it is not so empty for him. It is filled with the Jesus for whom Motes is performing his penances. He does not answer Mrs. Flood; he puts on his rock-filled shoes.

Mrs. Flood turns her proposal into an ultimatum.

> I can't allow you to stay here under no other circumstances. I can't climb these stairs. I don't want a thing . . . but to help you. You don't have anybody to look after you but me. Nobody to care if you live or die but me! No other place but mine!

Motes preached that there was no place for you to be; all that matters is escape. Mrs. Flood believes she has a place for Motes—an island of security in the empty world. When Motes begins feeling for his cane, Mrs. Flood asks if he is going to try to run off again.

> "Or were you planning to find you another rooming house?" she asked in a voice getting higher. "Maybe you were planning to go to some other city!"
>
> "That's not where I'm going," he said. "There's no other house nor no other city."
>
> "There's nothing, Mr. Motes," she said, "and time goes forward, it don't go backward . . ." (P. 228)

The last time Motes was getting ready to escape from this room, he did believe that there was another house and another city. He would go off, find a new woman in a new city, and begin to preach the Church Without Christ with nothing on his mind. Now he knows that no such fresh start is possible. What he has now is a goal. He is going somewhere.

In telling Motes that time goes forward, not backward, Mrs. Flood shows some dim awareness of what Motes's goal is. When imagining the darkness inside Motes's head, she thinks of him going back in time toward the pinpoint of light that announced the birth of Jesus. Motes's goal now is the Jesus whose birth that light heralded. Motes's refusal to marry now is thus not another Adamic American's attempt to escape from domesticating women. He is not going off to start afresh and create himself anew. His rejection of Mrs. Flood's offer has more to do with Paul's advice to the Corinthians concerning marriage (I Cor. 7: 25-29). Paul advises those who are not married to remain single, since "the time is short," and believers will be better able to prepare for the end if they are not burdened by the cares brought by a wife or husband. For Motes, the end is near, and he does not have time for a wife, any more than he has time to preach.

When Motes walks out of Mrs. Flood's house, she tells him that he "needn't return to a place you don't value . . . the door won't be open to you," but she is sure he will return. "He'll be back," she muttered. "Let the wind cut into him a little" (p. 228). When he does not come back that night, despite a driving icy rain, Mrs. Flood finds herself thinking in a new way and altering her plans.

> [A]wake at midnight, Mrs. Flood, the landlady, began to weep. She wanted to run out into the rain and cold and hunt him and find him huddled in some half-sheltered place and bring him back and say, Mr. Motes, Mr. Motes, you can stay here forever, or the two of us will go where you're going, the two of us will go. She had had a hard life, without pain and without pleasure, and she thought that now that she was coming to the last part of it, she deserved a friend. If she was going to be blind when she was dead, who better to guide her than a blind man? Who better to lead the blind than the blind, who knew what it was like? (P. 229)

Mrs. Flood has been transformed. She is no longer the emotionless woman who sat rocking on her porch while Motes carried his lime upstairs. Nor is she the selfish woman who treated the whole world as her natural possession and feared being cheated of any part of her own. She is, for the first time, ready to offer an unselfish love to another person.

But the most significant part of Mrs. Flood's transformation comes in her recognition that she needs a guide. She needs someone to lead her through the dark after death. In having Mrs. Flood wonder who can better lead the blind than the blind, who know what it is like, O'Connor is playing with Christ's warning against the teaching of the Pharisees: "Let them alone: they are blind, and leaders of the blind. And if the blind lead the blind, both fall into the pit" (Matt. 15:14; see also Luke 6:39, where the reference is to teaching disciples, not the Pharisees). In *Wise Blood*, where the sighted are spiritually blind and the blindness allows a new vision, the blind can lead the blind.

To find the guide she needs, Mrs. Flood goes searching for Motes, and when she does not find him she calls the police, and asks them to bring back her blind tenant, who has not paid his rent. Two days later, two policemen find Motes lying in a drainage ditch, and Motes has his last encounter with the law. Motes's suit has suffered a good deal since he bought it on the way to Taulkinham, so the patrolmen are not sure at first if he fits the description of a blind man in a blue suit, but they finally decide that it "might have uster been blue." They watch him, trying to decide if he is dead or unconscious.

> His hand was moving along the edge of the ditch as if it were hunting something to grip. He asked them in a hoarse whisper where he was and if it was day or night.
>
> "It's day," the thinner one said, looking at the sky. "We got to take you back to pay your rent."
>
> "I want to go on where I'm going," the blind man said.
>
> "You got to pay your rent first," the policeman said. "Ever' bit of it!"
>
> The other, perceiving that he was conscious, hit him over the head with his new billy. "We don't want to have no trouble with him," he said. "You take his feet." (Pp. 230–31)

In his blindness, Motes has wanted both to continue moving toward his destination and to pay, to get clean. The lawmen unknowingly see to it that both purposes are fulfilled. When he dies in the squad car on the way back to Mrs. Flood's, he has finished paying—it don't matter what for, he has paid, "ever' bit of it." And as the landlady soon perceives, he is traveling on toward his destination.

The patrolmen do not notice that Motes is dead, and Mrs. Flood has them put him on her bed. She sits next to him and begins to tell him that she will take care of him whatever way he chooses to have it, "upstairs or down. Just however you want it and with me to wait on you, or if you want to go on somewhere, we'll both go." Then Mrs. Flood begins to notice something in his "stern and tranquil" face.

> She had never observed his face more composed and she grabbed his hand and held it to her heart. It was resistless and dry. The outline of a skull was plain under his skin and the deep burned eye sockets seemed to lead into the dark tunnel where he had disappeared. She leaned closer and closer to his face, looking deep into them, trying to see how she had been cheated or what had cheated her, but she couldn't see anything. She shut her eyes and saw the pinpoint of light but so far away that she could not hold it steady in her mind. She felt as if she were blocked at the entrance of something. She sat staring with her eyes shut, into his eyes, and felt as if she had finally got to the beginning of something she couldn't begin, and she saw him moving farther and farther away, farther and farther into the darkness until he was the pin-point of light. (Pp. 231-32)

Mrs. Flood has always liked to see things and prided herself on her clear vision, and so been troubled by the idea that there is something hidden from her that the blind man sees. Now in what is her last chance to plumb the mystery of her tenant's empty eyes, she stops trying to see with her ordinary sight. She closes her eyes and tries to see with a different sort of vision. What she sees is the pinpoint of light that she had imagined giving a direction to the empty darkness of Motes's head. Motes is moving farther and farther into the dark until he is one with the point of light, and that light is the star that proclaims the entry of Jesus into the world.

What Mrs. Flood sees through her closed eyes shows Motes moving toward the Jesus he has avoided for so long. It also shows the beginnings of a desire for Jesus in Mrs. Flood. She is blocked at the entrance of the tunnel and feels she is at a beginning she cannot begin, but nevertheless she sees where Motes is going—toward the star of Bethlehem—and she wants to go where he is going. She cannot look steadily at anything without wanting it, and now she is looking steadily at the pinpoint of light that blazed as a star to announce the Incarnation. Her goal and her desire is becoming the Jesus toward whom Motes is traveling. In Motes's blindness and penances, there is an offer of grace for Mrs. Flood. Even if no scales have fallen from his eyes, this Paul has brought the gospel to at least one gentile.

# Conclusion

After reading one of O'Connor's stories, one is often left most strongly with a visual image or the memory of a grotesque or violent plot. What sticks in the mind is the image of welts rising on a tattooed back or of a man preaching against Jesus from the hood of an old car. O'Connor's works are full of ideas. They are animated by Christian doctrines and address many of the issues that agitate modern culture. But they never show the least tendency to become tracts or essays instead of stories. (As her letters and lectures show, O'Connor could state her positions on both religious and cultural matters in plain prose when she chose to.) Her exploration of the mystery of the Incarnation is always the story of a tattooed man, never a précis of the Baltimore catechism; the vehicle for her attack on the American Adam figure is always the story of a man with a beat-up car, never an analysis of Emerson or Cooper.

By embodying the most lofty Christian doctrines in stories that seem grotesque and violent, O'Connor reclaimed a large region of literature for the religious writer. In earlier centuries, especially in the Middle Ages, religious concerns were not separated—in literature or in life—from the grotesque or violent. In Dante or in the mystery plays, Christian doctrines are presented in images that may offend the nose or shock the eye. But in twentieth-century America the usual assumption is that religious matters must be discussed in gentle and decorous ways—and anything that is always gentle and decorous can, in the end, only seem trivial. When O'Connor follows the example of the Old Testament prophets and presents the Lord's message in harsh and violent images, she restores life and interest to religious literature. In her stories, the acceptance or rejection of the offer of grace does seem a matter of life and death, for it is presented with the same seriousness as other life and death matters. Thanks in part to O'Connor's example, fiction writers who see the world in the light of the Christian mysteries can no longer be expected to observe any stifling decorum.

O'Connor's techniques have, of course, influenced writers who do not share her faith. The use of violence and the grotesque in much recent fiction seems heavily indebted to O'Connor's work. Violence has, of course, been one of the hallmarks of modern fiction throughout this century, but in O'Connor's work unexpected violence not only shocks the reader, it also marks those moments when a character is confronted with the offer of grace. Many recent writers use unexpected violence in a similar way, marking some epiphany for a character, often one that is in no way religious.

While O'Connor's fiction has been influential in many ways, her criticism has not yet received the attention it deserves. Indeed, many critics seem unwilling to grant it serious attention even when studying O'Connor's own works. O'Connor's critical writing does build on authorities no longer in fashion—the New Critics, Maritain, and Aquinas—but it nevertheless contributes a great deal to the theory of fiction. In arguing for the possibility of an anagogical dimension in fiction, O'Connor provides a justification for finding several meanings in a single text. Much of post-structuralist criticism has been directed to the same end, but O'Connor, unlike more recent critics, does not abandon the idea of stable reference. The post-structuralist argues that words refer only to other signs—never to things—and that the critic can create unlimited meanings from the unending deferral of reference. The critic may create many meanings, but none of them will be stable, and the idea of communication disappears. O'Connor, building on Aquinas, justifies polysemous meanings, not by abandoning the idea of reference, but by extending it. The word does refer to the thing, and the thing can then refer to still more things. The text can contain many meanings, but it cannot be made to bear whatever meaning the critic chooses to create. O'Connor does not, of course, address the post-structuralists on their own ground, but her criticism remains a refreshing, and to me much more plausible, contrast to the schools of thought that have dominated critical theory during the last twenty years.

In both her letters and her fiction, O'Connor strongly attacks some of the traditions that have dominated American culture, and her voice should be given great attention now that the canon of

American literature is being subjected to more scrutiny. The version of the canon that was in place until recently was dominated by the Transcendentalist tradition and figure of the American Adam.* Even critics who saw the limitations of this figure accepted the idea that its history was the main line of American literature, a literature that was thus not only male-dominated, but mostly made up of books about boys or solitary men. There are many grounds on which this tradition deserves attack, but O'Connor's was most basic. She attacks the whole tradition that grew from Emerson because it denies Original Sin and thus the need for Redemption, which to her were basic facts about the universe. She also saw that, in reality, an Adamic man would not in fact keep his innocence long, but would instead become diabolical, like Mr. Shiftlet.

Though O'Connor's attack on the American Adam figure and the tradition that springs from it is at root theological, it also takes aim at the treatment of women in that tradition. In much American literature, women only appear as threats to the man who wants to move ever onward, and the hero's triumph is to escape the woman's attempts to entrap and domesticate him. O'Connor sees that in escaping women the Adamic figure is also trying to escape other things—God and guilt and history—but she strongly attacks the portrayal of women merely as a threat to a man's freedom. When O'Connor's would-be Adams—Mr. Shiftlet and Hazel Motes—flee from domesticating females, they are acting in the best tradition of the American hero. But in both Sabbath Lily Hawks and Lucynell Crater, O'Connor shows how cruelly this tradition treats women, who become nothing more than objects men manipulate in order to prove their illusory freedom. It would be stretching the term to call O'Connor a feminist, but she shares with recent feminist critics a concern for the female figures so often excluded by canonical American fiction.

Like her exploration of the Christian mysteries, O'Connor's attacks on the American literary tradition are always embodied in physical images. The American Adam tradition takes the form of a man driving an old car into the sunset, leaving an abandoned idiot girl sleeping at a lunch counter; the denial of Original Sin implicit in the tradition becomes a man claiming that his broken-down car will take him anywhere he wants to go. In O'Connor fiction the physical world and the world of the spirit or the intellect are not separate, for physical acts reveal the action of ideas—or the presence of grace. And often all the elements are working at once: the wreck of Hazel

---

* Harold Bloom still makes Emerson the presiding figure over the authentic American tradtion.

Motes's Essex is at once part of an attack on a philosophical move-ment, an echo of a biblical story, and the turning point in the life of a man who has become vivid in the reader's mind.   O'Connor claimed that fiction should be read as the sacred text is read.   Her fiction often recalls scripture—in its violent and gritty details, in its fusion of many meanings into a single image, and in its wisdom and power.

# Appendix:
# The *Wise Blood* Manuscripts

O'Connor worked on *Wise Blood* for many years, and the novel went through many drafts before it reached its final form. Some drafts are lost, but many drafts and fragments from various versions of *Wise Blood* are preserved in the Flannery O'Connor Memorial Room in the Ina Dillard Russell Library at Georgia College. Furthermore, early versions of three chapters from *Wise Blood* were published as the short stories "The Train," "The Peeler," and "The Heart of the Park." One other published story, "A Stroke of Good Fortune," originated as part of *Wise Blood,* but corresponds to nothing in the final version of the novel. A chapter from the final version was published as the story "Enoch and the Gorilla" after *Wise Blood* was finished. An examination of the development of *Wise Blood* through draft after draft shows O'Connor slowly realizing what ideas she wants to embody in her novel and how she will present them.

On January 20, 1949, O'Connor sent a draft of nine chapters to Elizabeth McKee, her agent, who then sent them to John Selby at Reinhart.[1] This draft includes the chapters published as stories before the appearance of the complete novel. When this draft is compared with the finished novel, one is struck by several things that are not present in the final version. Haze—in some of the stories his last name is not yet Motes—has a sister, Ruby. Part of the plot concerns her realization that she is pregnant and her contemplation of an abortion. Leora Watts has a larger role, and Haze talks with her at some length. But what is even more striking is the realization of what is not present. There is no hint that Asa—who also appears with a different last name—is not a real blind man. Nothing is said about self-blinding. The Essex appears only briefly, and carries little symbolic value. Motes is not tormented by the idea that he has been redeemed. He does not found a church and is not driven to become a preacher. There are no references to St. Paul.

Only a few scraps remain of the drafts O'Connor wrote between the nine chapters she sent to Elizabeth McKee in 1949 and the final draft. But a comparison of the 1949 version and the final draft shows how O'Connor transformed an intriguing but chaotic earlier manuscript into a powerful and coherent novel. In 1949, after having sent McKee the manuscript, O'Connor went to live with the Robert Fitzgeralds, and while there she read Fitzgerald's translation of *Oedipus Rex*. Oedipus gave O'Connor the action her novel turns on: a self-blinding that brings insight. Even more importantly, once O'Connor discovered the gesture with which Haze's quest would culminate, she also introduced the ideas and images that give his bizarre actions in Taulkinham meaning: the biblical story of St. Paul, the automobile as embodiment of freedom, and the terrifying threat of Redemption.

In the first chapter of *Wise Blood*, Motes is clearly tormented by the idea of Redemption. In "The Train,"[2] which corresponds to the first chapter of the 1949 draft, Redemption does not haunt Hazel Wickers. Wickers talks with Mrs. Wallace Ben Hosen, (an earlier version of Mrs. Wally Bea Hitchcock) who was born a Hitchcock, but he does not say to her, "I bet you think you been redeemed." Nor does he tell anyone in the dining car that he would not care about Jesus, not even if He were on the train, or say that he would not want to be redeemed if his neighbors have been. More importantly, when Wickers lies in his coffin-like berth, he does not remember a grandfather who threatened him with the promise of Redemption. (There is a very brief description of the grandfather in the chapter that became "A Stroke of Good Fortune.") There is no description of a conversion "to nothing instead of to evil." And when he awakes from his terrifying dream, he does not call on the Jesus he has rejected.

Motes's endless running is propelled by the grandfather's descriptions of the Jesus who will "chase him over the waters of sin." Wickers, on the other hand is not escaping either the threat of Redemption or the memory of a call. Unlike Motes, Wickers does not look like a preacher. His hat is subjected to some abuse in the course of the 1949 draft, but no one calls his hat a preacher's hat or says that he looks like a preacher. (Motes looks like a preacher even to the cab driver who takes him to Leora Watts.) What is more, Wickers is not embarked on an aimless escape. He is coming to Taulkinham to see his sister Ruby, not just to do some things he has never done before.[3]

As the 1949 draft goes on, Haze sees his sister and in her apartment building he meets Leora Watts. The two women make him think about the idea of his cleanness in different ways. Haze does protest often that he is clean, just as Motes in the final version does. He at first refuses Leora because, he says, he is clean. There is a description of a trip to a brothel he made while in the army. He jumps out a window after saying to the whore, "Listen, I'm clean, I'm shielded by Jesus." When he does begin to commit fornication with Leora Watts, it is also to prove that he is clean. Like the Motes of the final draft, this Haze sins to show he does not believe in sin. He even tells Leora Watts at one point, "I'm not doing this because it's fun . . . I'm doing it to prove I'm clean." Haze is confident that he is clean in part because his family's blood, which he had feared bore some stain, is coming up again in Ruby's child. As some other drafts show, Ruby's contemplation of an abortion leads him to question his denial of the reality of sin.

As in the final version of *Wise Blood*, Haze in this draft meets a street-corner evangelist in front of a peeler stand. ("The Peeler" in *Complete Stories* corresponds to this chapter of the 1949 draft, which became chapter three of the final version. Haze is named Motes, but the preacher's name is Asa Shrike.) Shrike is not an obvious fraud, like Hawks. He does not say things like, "If you won't repent, give up a nickel, wouldn't you rather have me beg than preach?" The exchanges between Motes and the preacher are not so fully developed as they are in the final version, but they contain the seeds of most of what finally appeared in the novel. What is missing is Motes's announcement that he is founding his own church. Haze warns the people coming out of the auditorium away from the blind man, but he does not preach his own attack on Jesus. He does not assume the role of Saul as Christ's persecutor. The rest of the chapter, which describes Haze's feeling the nameless, unplaced guilt after seeing the woman in the box at the carnival, is much like the final version. This Haze is troubled by the idea of guilt and cleanness, but he is not also tormented by the idea of Redemption, as is Motes in the final version.

In the 1949 draft there are chapters very much like chapters four and five of the final version. ("The Heart of the Park" in *Complete Stories*, corresponds with the eighth chapter of the draft and chapter five of the published novel.) They do not appear in their final order—Motes buys the Essex before meeting the blind preacher—but they are otherwise fairly close to the final version. Most of the description of Haze's buying his Essex is in this early version. But the scene where Motes buys his Essex from Slade's is the part of *Wise Blood* where the car has the least symbolic value. Since Motes has not yet begun to preach on it—or about it—the car stands for fairly little. It is only after Haze drives out of the city, and is first stopped by the promise of Jesus' love on the roadside sign, that the car clearly becomes more than a way to get around Taulkinham. This scene does appear in the 1949 draft; it is the first hint of symbolic patterns that the car will finally take part in. (Because he buys the car before he meets the preacher in this version, Haze cannot react to the promise of Jesus's love by going to find Hawks and prove he does not believe in sin. He goes home to his sister's.)

Except for changes in names and some minor details, the description of Motes's visit to Enoch in the park is much like chapter five of the published novel. Haze, however, tells the woman and the Frosty Bottle and the owl in the cage, "I ain't clean," not "I AM clean . . . If Jesus existed I wouldn't be clean," as Hazel Motes does in the final version. (See *Complete Stories*, p. 89, and *Wise Blood*, p. 91). Haze in the 1949 draft is troubled by the idea that he may not be clean; Hazel Motes knows he must be clean because otherwise he has been redeemed.

As the 1949 draft continues, Haze goes to see the blind preacher in his room, but their confrontation does not get very far. O'Connor had at this point decided that Haze would try to prove his cleanness by seducing the preacher's wife. (Sabbath is Asa's wife, not his daughter, in this draft.) At the end of the nine chapters O'Connor mailed at the beginning of 1949, there is a note in which she described the direction she expected the rest of the novel to take. The rest of the novel was to be built around Haze's seduction of Sabbath Lily.

> Hazel Motes moves into the same house with the blind man and his wife. He is convinced now he isn't clean and is trying to find out just how unclean he is. He figures that if he can commit the worst sin he can think of, he'll prove that he doesn't believe in Jesus. He decides the worst sin he can commit is to seduce the blind man's fifteen-year-old wife. Everything he does in preparation for the sin strengthens his belief in Jesus, so that by the time he gets ready to seduce her, he sees the action as certain damnation. Whether he will finally seduce her or not, I don't know. This

is the general pattern that the rest of the novel will be worked around.

Motes's plan to seduce Sabbath Lily, of course, only plays a secondary role in the final version of *Wise Blood*. Just as she eliminated the Ruby plot, O'Connor recast the plot involving Motes and the young girl after she discovered a symbolic pattern that would direct her novel to some coherent ending.

Between the writing of the 1949 draft and the final version, O'Connor came to see what would give her novel a direction. (The last chapter of the 1949 draft is very weak; when Haze confronts the blind preacher he has very little to say to him.) The Oedipus story gave her the idea of self-blinding, and in the juxtaposition of a false blind man and a true one she found a way to show her hero assuming the role he had earlier rejected. In Saint Paul she found a model for an enemy of Christ who is dogged by Redemption, and in his violent conversion a way of representing her hero's transformation. In the automobile she found an embodiment for the idea that man is so free that he needs no Redeemer. The completed novel owes its power to the fusion of these elements. The draft O'Connor finished in January of 1949 was chaotic and not shaped by any unifying pattern. John Selby at Rinehart was not completely unreasonable in demanding drastic changes. Over the next two years, O'Connor pruned away what did not fit her final conception, and strengthened the rest by giving it an underlying structure—the story of Saint Paul—and a dominant image—the automobile.

In any case, the manuscripts show that O'Connor consciously fused the story of Saint Paul and the automobile in *Wise Blood*. There are no references to Saint Paul in the 1949 draft. The car only appears briefly. In the street preacher's blindness, and in the scene in which Haze is stopped by a roadside sign, there is the germ of the novel that would grow once O'Connor began thinking about Oedipus and Saint Paul.

# Notes

## Introduction: An Incarnational Art (pp. 1–9)

[1] Joseph Conrad, *Joseph Conrad on Fiction*, ed. Walter F. Wright (Lincoln: University of Nebraska Press, 1964), p. 160.

[2] O'Connor underlined this quotation from Gregory in her copy of Aquinas. *Introduction to St. Thomas Aquinas*, ed. Anton C. Pegis (New York: The Modern Library, 1948).

[3] The most egregious examples of turning O'Connor's stories into facile allegories can be found in James A. Grimshaw's *The Flannery O'Connor Companion* (Westport, Conn.: Greenwood Press, 1981). Grimshaw, for instance, turns "The Life You Save May Be Your Own" into an allegory of the devil gaining another damned soul: "Delivering Lucynell to the roadside café, The Hot Spot (hell), does not give Shiftlet (the devil) satisfaction" (p. 43). Of course this allegory does not fit very well. Lucynell the idiot girl is described as "an angel of gawd," which seems a strange thing to call a damned soul, and besides as an idiot she is incapable of the reflection necessary for mortal sin and therefore beyond any danger of damnation. Shiftlet himself is a wicked man, but he is not the devil himself. O'Connor describes him as, "of the devil, because nothing in him resists the devil:" but the two are not one and the same. Reducing "The Life You Save May Be Your Own" to this schematic allegory misses the real interest of the story, which shows a man resisting an offer of grace—an opportunity to live for something beyond himself—in order to live out the story of the solitary moving male so celebrated by our culture.

[4] Flannery O'Connor, "The Catholic Novelist in the Protestant South," *Mystery and Manners: Occasional Prose*, selected and edited by Sally and Robert Fitzgerald (New York: Farrar, Straus, and Giroux, 1969), pp. 202-3. All subsequent references will be to this edition.

[5] "Hate" is the word O'Connor used to describe Hawthorne's attitude toward the Transcendentalists. Hawthorne's view of them was in fact much more ambiguous, but O'Connor's very exaggeration is revealing. *The Habit of Being: Letters,* edited and with an Introduction by Sally Fitzgerald (New York: Farrar, Straus, Giroux, 1979), p. 145. All further references to O'Connor's letters will be to this edition.

[6] Recognizing that O'Connor used Motes and his Essex to embody the tradition of the innocent, ever-moving male also explains some of the other changes made between the earlier drafts and the final version of the novel. In a very interesting paper on the *Wise Blood* drafts ("Carnal Knowledge: The Terrors of Sexuality in the *Wise Blood* drafts," delivered at the MLA Convention in 1984), Sarah Gordon notes that the roles of the female characters diminish considerably from the many early drafts to the final version. Motes's sister Ruby disappears; Leora and Sabbath Lily become much less important. Gordon attributes this transformation to O'Connor's having succumbed to the strictures of her patriarchal Church and reduced woman to the role of temptress. I cannot agree with this interpretation. To begin with, I cannot imagine anything less tempting than Leora and Sabbath Lily as they appear in the final version. What is more, Motes's temptation is always purely intellectual. He does not enjoy sin; neither woman attracts him physically. He sins to prove he is free. As the drafts go on, I believe O'Connor came to realize that her novel would be stronger if she allowed Motes to try to live out the male-dominated myth she wished to attack. The women's roles grow smaller because seen from the point of view of an Adamic American male, they cannot do anything else.

**One: The Burning Bush and the Illustrated Man (pp. 11–53)**

[1] "The Grotesque in Southern Fiction," *Mystery and Manners* , pp. 40-41.

[2] Flannery O'Connor, "Parker's Back," *The Complete Stories* (New York: Farrar, Straus and Giroux, 1971), p. 510. All subsequent references to O'Connor's stories will be to this edition.

[3] Ray Bradbury, "The Illustrated Man," *The Vintage Bradbury* (New York: Vintage Books, 1965), pp. 252-65; first published in *Esquire,* July 1950. This story should not be confused with the book *The Illustrated Man,* in which a tattooed man appears in the frame that links a number of separate short stories. The story "The Illustrated Man" does not appear in the book of the same name.

[4] Letter to "A," July 17, 1964. *The Habit of Being,* p. 593.

⁵ The similarities between the two characters begin with their names: Bradbury's hero is William Philippus Phelps; O'Connor's, Obadiah Elihue Parker. The commonplace last name begins with P; the middle name is odd and polysyllabic.

⁶ For O'Connor's admiration for Saint Thomas, see her letter to "A" of August 9, 1955. "I feel I can personally guarantee that St. Thomas loved God because for the life of me I cannot help loving St. Thomas" (*The Habit of Being*, p. 94). She quotes Aquinas and Maritain throughout her letters.

⁷Saint Thomas Aquinas, *Summa Theologica*, Q. 1. Art. 10. I have quoted from *Introduction to St. Thomas Aquinas*, edited by Anton C. Pegis (New York: The Modern Library, 1948), which is the selection from Aquinas that O'Connor used. O'Connor marked a number of passages in her copy, including one on the page where Aquinas describes the four senses of Scripture: *"On the contrary, Gregory says: Holy Scripture by the manner of its speech transcends every science, because in one and the same sentence, while it describes a fact, it reveals a mystery* (p. 72). O'Connor's markings are described in Arthur F. Kinney's, *Flannery O'Connor's Library: Resources of Being* (Athens: University of Georgia Press, 1985), p. 72.

⁸See, for example, Dante's description of the four levels of interpretation in the section of the *Convivio* reprinted in *Literary Criticism of Dante Alighieri*, trans. and ed. Robert S. Haller (Lincoln: University of Nebraska Press, 1973), p. 112.

⁹ Although Aquinas, like many recent critics, provides a justification for polysemous readings, his theory is diametrically opposed to the post-structuralist version of interpretation. Aquinas claims that many meanings may be found in a text because the word refers to the thing and the thing then refers to still more things. The post-structuralists claim that infinite meanings may be created in a text because the word never refers to the thing at all and exists only in shifting and unstable patterns of difference with other words.

¹⁰Joseph Conrad, Preface to *The Nigger of the "Narcissus,"* in *Joseph Conrad on Fiction*, ed. Walter F. Wright (Lincoln: University of Nebraska Press, 1964), p. 160.

¹¹William K. Wimsatt and Cleanth Brooks, *Literary Criticism: A Short History* (New York: Alfred A. Knopf, 1959), p. 684.

¹² Preface to *The Nigger of the "Narcissus,"* in *Joseph Conrad on Fiction*, p. 162.

[13] Preface to *The Nigger of the "Narcissus,"* in *Joseph Conrad on Fiction,* p. 161.

[14] O'Connor says much the same thing, connecting Conrad and Saint Augustine, in a letter written to "A" on January 13, 1956 (*The Habit of Being,* p. 128).

[15] But, as O'Connor goes on to explain, belief in the goodness of the world does not make it more difficult to depict what is not good:

> This in no way hinders [the artist's] perception of evil but rather sharpens it, for only when the natural world is seen as good does evil become intelligible as a destructive force and a necessary result of our freedom.

[16] O'Connor is always careful, however, to make clear that such a gift does not confer any moral distinction on the artist. She often quotes Aquinas's dictum that "Art does not require rectitude of the appetite." In other words, she believes one can be a good artist and a bad human being.

[17] Since O'Connor also identified deformed people in real life with the grotesque characters—the prophet-freaks—of her fiction, one wonders to what extent she considered herself a freak. Did she find in her crutches and constant worries about her illness some kinship with the tattooed man? Since some of her grotesques—like Hulga in "Good Country People" or Asbury in "The Enduring Chill"—are sickly intellectuals, it seems likely.

[18] For Lewis's description of how the aesthetic longing he calls joy led him back to Christianity, see *Surprised by Joy.*

[19] Sally Fitzgerald describes Parker as a loaf of bread that is consecrated in the course of the story.

[20] O'Connor discusses how she uses objects as signs of spiritual states in "Writing Short Stories," *Mystery and Manners,* pp. 98-99, where her immediate subject is Hulga's wooden leg in "Good Country People." As "Good Country People" progresses, more and more details accumulate that reveal the leg as a sign of Hulga's spiritual deadness—"when the Bible salesman steals it, the reader realizes that he has taken away part of the girl's personality and has revealed her deeper affliction to her for the first time."
O'Connor goes on to say, "If you want to say the wooden leg is a symbol, you can say that. But it is a wooden leg first, and as a wooden leg it is absolutely necessary to the story. It has its place on the literal level of the story, but it operates in depth as well as on the surface." In the same way, Parker's tattoos are absolutely necesssary to the story on the literal level, but they also reveal a great deal more. The literal contains the spiritual senses.

21 It is difficult to decide which version of the Bible to cite when discussing O'Connor. Her own Bibles were, of course, Catholic versions—either the Rheims-Douay version or the new translation of the Vulgate by Ronald Knox. The Bible, however, that influenced the language of her region so heavily, and which we must imagine her characters knowing, is the King James version. I have taken my quotations from the Rheims-Douay version. None of the passages I discuss is significantly different in the King James version.

22 O'Connor owned a copy of Thomas Merton's *The Sign of Jonas* (New York: Harcourt Brace, 1953); see Kinney, *Flannery O'Connor's Library*, p. 62. Merton's book may have encouraged her to think about Jonah.

23 *Summa Theologica*, Q.1. Art. 10; in Pegis, *Introduction to St. Thomas*, p. 18.

24 Theodore Ziolkowski, "Some Features of Religious Figuralism in Twentieth-Century Literature," *Literary Uses of Typology from the Late Middle Ages to the Present*, ed. Earl Miner (Princeton: Princeton University Press, 1977), p. 357. Ziolkowski goes on to say that, beyond a form, the "prefigurative patterns" supply "further dimensions of meaning that enhance the contemporary work" (p. 358).

25 Flannery O'Connor, *The Presence of Grace and Other Book Reviews*, compiled by Leo J. Zuber, ed. Carter W. Martin (Athens, Georgia: The University of Georgia Press, 1983), p. 128. The book under review is F. W. Dillistone's *The Novelist and the Passion Story*.

26 Timothy Ware, *The Orthodox Church*, (Penguin Books, 1984), p. 38.

27 Parker, who accepts the physical representation of the Divine but realizes that it is"just a picture," here represents the Catholic position. In a letter O'Connor describes old Tarwater in *The Violent Bear It Away* as a "crypto-Catholic." "When you leave a man alone with his Bible and the Holy Ghost inspires him, he's going to be a Catholic one way or another, even though he knows nothing about the visible Church. His kind of Christianity may not be socially desirable, but it will be real in the sight of God" (*The Habit of Being*, p. 517). In the same way, Parker after his conversion is a natural Catholic even though he knows nothing of the visible Church, and has expressed his faith in a way few would call desirable.

28 C. S. Lewis, *The Allegory of Love: A Study in Mediaeval Tradition* (Oxford: Oxford University Press, 1936), pp. 322–23. For a Catholic critique of Lewis's discussion, see Christopher Derrick's *C. S. Lewis and the Church of Rome* (San Francisco: Ignatius Press, 1981).

[29] Even into this century, some Protestant scholars have felt sympathy for the earlier Iconoclasts. See, for example, Walter F. Adeney's *The Greek and Eastern Churches* (first ed. 1909; reprinted: Clifton, N.J.: Reference Book Publishers, 1965), in which the chapters describing the Iconoclastic controversy are entitled, "The Iconoclastic Reforms" and "The Restoration of Image Worship."

[30] Significantly, the Protestant churches where the liturgical ritual is fullest are also those that seem least Protestant and closest to the Catholic Church. Episcopalians may burn incense and tolerate crossings and bowings, but not Baptists.

[31] For a discussion of how artists with a fully incarnational theology can treat sexuality, see Leo Steinberg's *The Sexuality of Christ in Renaissance Art and Modern Oblivion* (New York: Pantheon, 1983).

## Two: The Automobile and the American Adam (pp. 55–105)

[1] Her friend "A," for instance, evidently had to explain the difference between a fender and a bumper to her. See *The Habit of Being*, p. 148.

[2] For example, James L. Flink, *The Car Culture* (Cambridge, Massachusetts: The MIT Press, 1975) and George Pierson, *The Moving American* (New York: Knopf, 1973).

[3] Frederick Jackson Turner, "The Significance of the Frontier in American History," *The Frontier in American History*, (New York: Henry Holt and Company, 1920), p. 37. First published in *The Annual Report of the American Historical Association for 1893* (Washington, D.C.: American Historical Association, 1893), pp. 190-227.

[4] Pierson, *The Moving American*, p. 11.

[5] Professor Elaine Showalter of Princeton University pointed out to me that automobiles often appear as images of the female body. ("Fill her up" is the obvious example.) Like the West itself—the "Virgin Land"—an automobile can be a surrogate female presence, one that—unlike real women—cannot involve the male, through procreation, in history or the ties of society.

[6] Herbert Marshall McLuhan, *The Mechanical Bride: The Folklore of Industrial Man.* (New York: The Vanguard Press, 1951.) O'Connor writes about McLuhan's book in a September 1954 letter to "A." She had lent her friend her copy, and was driven to defend the book when it was returned almost immediately. *The Habit of Being*, p. 173.

7 "No Particular Place to Go," by Chuck Berry. This song has been used in television commercials for automobiles.

8 For a discussion of car songs and the frontier tradition, see Warren Belasco's "Motivatin' with Chuck Berry and Frederick Jackson Turner," *The Automobile and American Culture*, ed. David L. Lewis and Laurence Goldstein. (Ann Arbor: The University of Michigan Press, 1983), pp. 262-79. Belasco's arguments from etymology are at times a bit far-fetched—I don't know what role the classics played in Chuck Berry's education, but I suspect he wasn't thinking of the Latin *amabilis* when he named his heroine Maybellene—but what he says about the significance of the car in rock 'n' roll seems completely valid.

9 Bruce Springsteen, "Thunder Road," *Born to Run* (Columbia Records, 1975). Springsteen's use of religious imagery is much richer and more complex than I have discussed here. In "Adam Raised a Cain," he even writes a rock song about Original Sin.

10 Flannery O'Connor, *Wise Blood* (New York: Farrar, Straus and Giroux, 1962), p. 113. All references to *Wise Blood* are to this edition.

11 David L. Lewis, "From Rumble Seats to Rockin' Vans," in Lewis and Goldstein, *The Automobile and American Culture*, pp. 123-33.

12 The folk song "900 Miles."

13 Leroy Carr's "How Long, How Long Blues."

14 "Downbound Train," *Born in the U.S.A.* (Columbia Records, 1984).

15 Henley's "Invictus."

16 It is interesting that the *roman fleuve* in which a society, almost more than any of its members, is the real subject, has become much more popular in England than in America. Faulkner is of course a significant exception.

17 O'Connor only mentions Fiedler once, and Lewis not at all, in her published letters. Arthur F. Kinney's catalog of the books from O'Connor's collection, now in Russell Library at Georgia College, *Flannery O'Connor's Library: Resources of Being*, lists nothing by Lewis, and Fiedler appears only in the introduction to a book by Simone Weil. Kinney's catalog, however, does not include all the books O'Connor owned, much less all those she read or heard about. There are some other books by Americanist critics in the O'Connor Collection at Georgia College, notably Richard Chase's *American*

*Novel and Its Tradition* (Garden City, N.Y.: Doubleday/Anchor, 1957).

[18] *The Habit of Being*, p. 413. It is unfortunately impossible to tell which of Fiedler's works O'Connor is referring to. From the date, October 1960, it would seem likely that she is talking about *Love and Death in the American Novel*.

[19] Leslie A. Fiedler, *Love and Death in the American Novel*, Revised Edition (New York: Stein and Day, 1982), p. 25.

[20] Nina Baym, "Melodramas of Beset Manhood: How Theories of American Fiction Exclude Women Authors," *The New Feminist Criticism: Essays on Women, Literature, and Theory,* ed. Elaine Showalter (New York: Pantheon, 1985) pp. 68-80. First published in *American Quarterly* 33 (1981).

[21] As Fiedler and some of the other critics describe it, male American authors were involved in a struggle much like that of their heroes to escape the constraints imposed on them by a feminine society. The nineteenth-century male writer fights and ultimately wins a long battle with the hordes of scribbling women who filled the early best-seller lists with romantic Richardsonian melodramas. And, according to Fiedler, he also fights a female audience:

> In America . . . the late start of the novel and the lack of distinguished figures in its early years helped create simultaneously the genteel, sentimental, quasi-literate, female audience (female in sensibility whatever the nominal sex of the readers who composed it) and a product which satisfied it. *Against* this audience and in competition with the writing which satisfied it, our best fictionists from Charles Brockden Brown to Edgar Allan Poe to Hawthorne and Melville have felt it necessary to struggle for their integrity and their livelihoods. (*Love and Death in the American Novel*, p. 93)

Fiedler sees these male authors keeping their integrity by writing stories about the struggles of men against society rather than the struggles of men and women in it. But one might describe the efforts of male American writers as the attempt to import a best-selling formula from another genre. The sentimental audience relished stories of the wandering man alone against the world in nonfiction; the writers Fiedler lists tried to make it accept him in fiction.

[22] Baym does discuss some works—notably some of Willa Cather's— "which project a version of the particular myth we are speaking of but cast the main character as a woman. When a woman takes the central role, it follows naturally that the socializer and domesticator will be a man" (p. 74).

The Cougar ad I discussed earlier shows that the gender of the protagonist can also be reversed in popular culture. But these inversions of the myth are always surprising. And Baym contends that male theorists reject the female versions of their hero: "Instead of being read as a woman's version of the myth, such novels are read as stories of the frustration of female nature."

[23] Fiedler, "Come Back to the Raft Ag'in, Huck Honey," *A Fiedler Reader* (New York: Stein and Day, 1977), originally published in *The Partisan Review,* June 1948, p. 5. Fiedler at times seems to blame women for the boyishness of American heroes: "The acceptance by the male of the female image of him first as seducer and blackguard and then (in America) as Bad Boy follows naturally upon the female's acceptance of the male's image of her as sexless savior and (in America) eternal Mama" (*Love and Death in the American Novel,* p. 90).

[24] R. W. B. Lewis, *The American Adam: Innocence, Tragedy, and Tradition in the Nineteenth Century* (Chicago: The University of Chicago Press, 1955). All italics are Lewis's.

[25] Wallace Stevens, "Sunday Morning," *The Collected Poems of Wallace Stevens* (New York: Knopf, 1954), p. 66.

[26] Walt Whitman, "Song of the Open Road," *Complete Poetry and Prose* (New York: Library of America, 1982), pp. 297-307. There are also passages in this poem where Whitman sounds less Adamic. (For instance, he carries men and women with him: "it is impossible for me to get rid of them.")

While examining the Quaker State ad in *The Mechanical Bride,* McLuhan asks if Whitman gave "America the poetry of the open road."

[27] Joni Mitchell, "Woodstock" (New York: Siquomb Music, 1969).

[28] It is interesting that the twentieth-century author who uses the Adam story to emphasize that we are fallen and out of the Garden should have begun life in California—as far as the attempt could be taken to reverse the expulsion from Eden by westward movement. Steinbeck, unlike any of the Adamic writers Lewis discusses, remembers Adam's sons.

[29] For a statement of Unitarian beliefs that makes explicit the link between the rejection of Original Sin and the rejection of the Trinity, see William Ellery Channings's discourse of 1826, *Unitarian Christianity Most Favorable to Piety (The Works of William E. Channing, D.D., Seventh Complete Edition* (Boston: James Munroe and Company, 1847), vol. 3, p. 181:

[W]e find Trinitarianism connecting itself with a scheme of administration, exceedingly derogatory to the Divine character. It teaches, that the Infinite Father saw fit to put into the hands of our first parents the character and condition of their whole progeny; and that, through one act of disobedience, the whole race bring with them into being a corrupt nature, or are born depraved. It teaches, that the offenses of a short life, though begun and spent under this disastrous influence, merit endless punishment, and that God's law threatens this infinite penalty; and that man is thus burdened with a guilt, which no sufferings of the created universe can expiate, which nothing but the sufferings of an Infinite Being can purge away. In this condition of human nature, Trinitarianism finds a sphere of action for its different persons. I am aware that some Trinitarians, on hearing this statement of their system, may reproach me with ascribing to them the errors of Calvinism, a system they abhor as much as ourselves. But none of the peculiarities of Calvinism enter into this exposition. I have given what I understand to be the leading features of Trinitarianism all the world over. . . .

Denying the thesis concerning the "condition of human nature," Channing can find no "sphere of action" for the Son.

[30] *Love and Death in the American Novel,* p. 24.

[31] "Self-Reliance," from Ralph Waldo Emerson, *Essays and Lectures,* ed. Joel Porte (New York: Library of America 1983), p. 275. Emerson's italics.

[32] Hunter S. Thompson, *Fear and Loathing in Las Vegas: A Savage Journey to the Heart of the American Dream* (New York: Popular Library, 1971).

[33] Mark Twain, *The Adventures of Huckleberry Finn,* ed. Leo Marx (Indianapolis: Bobbs-Merrill, 1967), p. 328.

[34] Even Jim is fleeing women: the owner who he fears will sell him South is Miss Watson. Jim's goal, however, is reunion with a woman—with his wife and children in a free state.

[35] Fiedler, "Come Back to the Raft Ag'in, Huck Honey," *A Fiedler Reader,* pp. 3–13.

[36] In the first chapter of *What Was Literature? Class Culture and Mass Society,* Fiedler discusses how the tradition of a white man and a colored man standing alone together against the world has continued. (New York: Touchstone, 1984). He extends "colored" to include Vulcans, so as to take account of Mr. Spock and Captain Kirk.

[37] The homoerotic element is the one aspect of the myth of the ever-moving

American hero that O'Connor does not make much use of.

[38] Thompson's own book on the Hell's Angels (*Hell's Angels: A Strange and Terrible Saga* (New York: Ballantine, 1967) includes an interesting analysis of motorcycle gang members as Anglo-Saxon Americans who have followed the dream of moving on for three centuries, and then found themselves at the Pacific coast, only able to ride up and down the highways.

[39] Hunter Thompson also declares himself the heir of the striving male of popular literature. *Fear and Loathing* ends with Thompson conning an airport drugstore into giving him some amyls. "I took another big hit off the amyl, and by the time I got to the bar my heart was full of joy. I felt like a monster reincarnation of Horatio Alger.... a Man on the Move, and just sick enough to be totally confident." And aside from his complete freedom from conventional work-ethic morality, Thompson's hero does fit the Alger mold: he is the boy alone making his way through the big world.

[40] John Steinbeck, *Travels with Charley in Search of America* (New York: Viking, 1962); Robert Pirsig, *Zen and the Art of Motorcycle Maintenance*, (New York: Morrow, 1975); *Blue Highways: A Journey into America*, (Boston: Little, Brown, 1982). The romantic names that Steinbeck and Least Heat Moon give their vehicles are revealing. Steinbeck calls his camper, Rocinante, after Don Quixote's horse: the quest may be crazy but it is noble nonetheless. Moon names his van Ghost Dancing—the frontier myth lives on in his imagination from the Indian perspective. The real Ghost Dancers believed their ritual would bring a time when all would be set right: Do Americans think that driving will do that for them?

[41] "Howl" and "Footnote to Howl," *Collected Poems 1947-1980* (New York: Harper and Row, 1984), pp. 134, 135. For Ginsberg's version of the dream of movement, see "The Green Automobile," p. 83.

[42] George Pierson mentions that the pioneer was "auto-mobile" (The Moving American, p. 239). Flink and other writers on the automobile often use the term "self-propelling" when describing the kind of vehicle they are talking about.

[43] See "Introduction to *A Memoir of Mary Ann*," *Mystery and Manners*, p. 219.

[44] As Lewis points out several times in *The American Adam*, Catholics are naturally not part of either the party of Memory, with the old Calvinists, nor of the party of Hope, with those who denied sin entirely. They are at home in the party of Irony. Lewis sees Catholic tendencies in the other members of his party of Irony—even Melville. In identifying "communion" as the

concern which linked together the party of Irony—communion in contrast to the solitude of the new Adam, "the simple genuine self against the whole world," or of the old Calvinist alone before God, he does make it sound like the natural home for a Catholic in the American debate.

[45] O'Connor had a number of books on Hawthorne in her library (see Kinney's *Resources of Being*, pp. 121-22). For the most part, the passages she marked in these works have to do with Hawthorne's sense of sin. She puts a check in the margin where Henry James says that " To [Hawthorne] . . . the consciousness of sin was the most importunate fact of life"; she underlines a passage where Mark Van Doren quotes Melville on Hawthorne's "Calvinistic sense of Innate Depravity and Original Sin." She does not appear to have annotated Hawthorne's own works.

[46] Among the literary manifestations of the idea of the black as truly evil is Poe's *Narrative of Arthur Gordon Pym*. Poe shows his Antarctic blacks—who have not even white teeth to mitigate their darkness—as completely fiendish.

[47] "The Regional Writer," *Mystery and Manners*, p. 59.

[48] The nation as a whole seems never to have been affected by its unjust victories—not over the Indians it robbed, nor over the Mexicans whose nation it dismembered, nor over those smaller neighbors who did not show enough deference to our leadership later on.

[49] William Faulkner, "The Bear," *Go Down, Moses* (New York: The Modern Library, 1942), p. 195.

[50] Robert Penn Warren, "Homage to Emerson, On Night Flight to New York," *Selected Poems 1923-1975* (New York: Random House, 1976), p. 153.

[51] *The Habit of Being*, p. 396.

[52] Robert Penn Warren, *All the King's Men* (New York: Harcourt Brace, 1981), p. 61.

[53] Burden, in the section of *All the King's Men* describing the drive west, often sounds like Hazel Motes talking about freedom and his Essex, and both are echoes of the existentialists.

[54] See "The Last American Hero," Tom Wolfe's essay on Johnson, in *The Purple Decades, A Reader* (New York: Farrar, Straus, Giroux, 1982) p. 27.

[55] Shiftlet's question and Mrs. Crater's response recall Proverbs 31:10: "Who

can find a virtuous woman? For her price is far above rubies." Lucynell's price is a man who will stay in one place—and a car has to be thrown in on her side of the bargain, p. 149.

### Three: "Nobody With a Good Car Needs to Be Justified" (pp. 107–195)

[1] I am thinking primarily of *The Conversion of Saint Paul* in the Ceraci Chapel, Santa Maria del Popolo, Rome. There is another version of the same subject, also with a prominant horse, in the Odescalchi collection, Rome. Both are reproduced in the museum exhibition catalog, *The Age of Caravaggio*, John P. O'Neill, ed. (New York Metropolitan Museum, 1985), pp. 40, 41.

[2] See Appendix: The *Wise Blood* Manuscripts.

[3] See the discussion of Unitarianism in the preceding chapter, p. 85.

[4] Whether Oedipus blinds himself to atone for his incest or for his hubris in demanding to know who killed his predecessor or in trying to escape the fate the oracle decreed for him, he had *done* something.

[5] T. S. Eliot, *The Waste Land and Other Poems* (New York: Harcourt Brace, 1934). O'Connor had many of Eliot's works in her library. See Kinney's *Flannery O'Connor's Library: Resources of Being*.

[6] The women at the movie theater are not alone in missing what Motes is up to. I have talked with graduate students in English, who after seeing John Huston's version of *Wise Blood* could say, "I suppose a lot of those preachers are like that." That what Motes *says* has more in common with Jean-Paul Sartre than with Jimmy Swaggart does not seem to have registered. A preacher is a preacher, even if he denies every Christian doctrine.

[7] Motes's proclamation that his car has made him free catches the American myth of freedom and movement perfectly. There are many who would agree with Motes. I have seen John Huston's film version of *Wise Blood* twice, and both audiences cheered when Motes said that "Nobody with a car needs to be justified." The punk group Gang of Four sings a song containing several allusions to *Wise Blood*, and in it they reproduce Motes's confidence in his ability to control his fate as long as he keeps driving: "A man with a good car needs no justification / Fate is in my hands and in the transmission" ("A Man With a Good Car," *Hard* (Warner Brothers Records, 1983).

[8] Sabbath Lily is wrong in believing that it is written that a Bastard Shall Not Enter the Kingdom of Heaven. In fact Deuteronomy says "A bastard shall

not enter into the congregation of the Lord" (23:2)—that is, into the assembly of Israel. This prohibition, which comes in a passage that also bars eunuchs and Moabites from the Assembly, does not refer to the Kingdom of Heaven. And it is in any case a part of the Old Law from which Christ frees us. (The Moabites are accepted from the Book of Ruth onwards; The Lord sends Philip to preach to the Ethiopian Eunuch (Acts 8: 27-39). In any case the scriptural and theological question is not what is really on Sabbath Lily's mind.

[9] I had always taken Sabbath Lily's "warf" as a fine example of Flannery O'Connor's use of dialect, but the new Library of America edition of her work, which unfortunately did not appear until after this study was almost complete, shows that it was in fact a typographical error. The word is warp.

[10] Evidently Ben Griffith asked O'Connor about a Wordsworth influence in *Wise Blood*. In her reply, she says, "I have been exposed to Wordsworth's 'Intimation' ode but that is all I can say about it. I have one of those food-chopper brains that nothing comes out of the way it was put in" *(The Habit of Being,* p. 68). Some of the ode seems to have come out of the chopper as Onnie Jay's Mood, Melody, and Mentality.

[11] Though our automobiles are associated with the feeling of freedom, they paradoxically also involve us even more deeply in law. For most of us, traffic regulations are the laws we most often encounter—and most often break. Hazel Motes is not at all unusual in finding that freedom can quickly bring one face to face with the law.

[12] Sally Fitzgerald thinks that the officer is in some sense an angel. Whether or not one wants to imagine him as literally one of the heavenly host, it is certainly true that he plays the role of an *angel*—that is of a *messenger* from the Lord. He presents the message in the only form Motes will hear it. As for his being literally one of the company of heaven—the question really does not matter, but I suspect that if our guardian spirits ever do take human form, they are more likely to appear to us like the messenger who stops Motes than to blow-dry their ethereal hair and assume the form of Michael Landon. The road out of Taulkinham is a highway to heaven only because of the wreck. O'Connor always shows a God who is loving, but by no means gentle. In much of American popular culture He is gentle and not much else.

[13] Liverani, Mariella. "Paolo, Apostolo, Santo, Martire—Iconographia." *Bibliotheca Sanctorum,* vol. 10 (Rome: Instituto Giovanni XXIII della Pontificia Università Lateranense, 1968) pp. 211–27.

[14] Little, Lester K. "Pride Goes Before Avarice: Social Change and the Vices in Latin Christendom." *American Historical Review,* 76 (1971), 16-49.

[15] *The Conversion of Saint Paul,* from the Digby MS in *Medieval Drama.,* ed. David Bevington (Boston: Houghton Miflin, 1975), pp. 664-86.

[16] In Matthew, and with few variations in the other synoptic Gospels, Jesus says no more than "Take ye, and eat, This is my body," when giving his disciples the bread He has blessed. It is when giving them the cup that he explains that by his sacrifice he is establishing a new covenant and bringing the forgiveness of sins. The covenants of the Old Testament (Exodus 24: 6-8) were sealed in the blood of animals; the new covenant, in Jesus' own blood.

[17] Flannery O'Connor, *Everything That Rises Must Converge* (New York: Farrar, Straus and Giroux, 1965). Introduction by Robert Fitzgerald, p. xxvi.

[18] Jean-Paul Sartre, *Being and Nothingness: An Essay on Phenomenological Ontology,* translated by Hazel E. Barnes (New York: Philosophical Library, 1956), p. 441.

[19] Jean-Paul Sartre, "Existentialism is a Humanism," *Existentialism from Dostoevsky to Sartre,* ed. Walter Kaufmann, (New York: Meridian, 1956), p. 292.

[20] Robert G. Olson, *An Introduction to Existentialism* (New York: Dover, 1962), p. 52.

[21] Edgar Allan Poe, *Poetry and Tales* (New York: The Library of America, 1984), pp. 666–79.

[22] There is a similar identification of the automobile with the tomb in "The Life You Save May Be Your Own." Mrs. Crater tells Shiftlet he can stay

> "...if you don't mind sleeping in that car yonder."
> "Why listen, lady," he said with a grin of delight, "the monks of old slept in their coffins!"
> "They wasn't as advanced as we are," the old woman said.
> (*Complete Stories,* p. 149)

For Shiftlet, of course, sleeping in the car is not a *memento mori* but a first step on his way to appropriating the vehicle and making his escape from Mrs. Crater and Lucynell; he never escapes the tomb of his freedom.

Mrs. Crater, like Mrs. Flood in *Wise Blood,* has no patience for the idea of penance.

[23] Fitzgerald and Fitt's translation of *Oedipus,* Exodus, l. 139.

[24] O'Connor evidently felt that she had not made Motes's reasons for

blinding himself believable enough. In a letter to "A" (10 November 1955) she discusses a writer who claimed that his purpose was "to explain the reasonable man to himself." She goes on to say that her idea of the "reasonable man" is not the legal one.

> Mine is certainly something else—God's reasonable man, the prototype of whom must be Abraham, willing to sacrifice his son and thereby show that he is in the image of God Who sacrifices His Son. All H. Motes had to sacrifice was his sight but then (you are right) he was a mystic and he did it. The failure of the novel seems to be that he is not believable enough as a human being to make his blinding himself believable for the reasons that he did it. For the things I want them to do, my characters apparently will have to seem twice as human as humans (*The Habit of Being*, p. 116).

In an earlier letter she rejects the accusation that there is a lack of love in *Wise Blood*. "It seems to me the form of love in it is penance, as good a form as any other under Mr. Motes's circumstances" (p. 40).

### Appendix: The *Wise Blood* Manuscripts (pp. 201–205)

[1] For the letter that accompanied the MS, see *The Habit of Being*, p. 8.

[2] As much as possible, I will try to refer to the published stories taken from the early drafts, since they are readily available in *Complete Stories*.

[3] Haze's sister in Taulkinham is only briefly mentioned in the published version of "The Train."

# Works Cited

Adeney, Walter F. *The Greek and Eastern Churches*. First published 1909; reprinted: Clifton, N.J.: Reference Book Publishers, 1965.

Aquinas, St. Thomas. *Introduction to St. Thomas Aquinas*. Edited by Anton C. Pegis. New York: The Modern Library, 1948.

Baym, Nina. "Melodramas of Beset Manhood: How Theories of American Fiction Exclude Women Authors." *The New Feminist Criticism: Essays on Women, Literature, and Theory*. Edited by Elaine Showalter. New York: Pantheon, 1985. Pp. 68-80. First published in American Quarterly 33 (1981).

Belasco, Warren. "Motivatin' with Chuck Berry and Frederick Jackson Turner," *The Automobile and American Culture*. Edited by David L. Lewis and Laurence Goldstein. Ann Arbor: The University of Michigan Press, 1983. Pp. 262-79.

Bevington, David, ed. Medieval Drama. Boston: Houghton Miflin, 1975. See "The Conversion of St. Paul," from the Digby MS.

Bloom, Harold. Introduction to *Robert Penn Warren: Modern Critical Views*. Edited by Harold Bloom. New York: Chelsea House Publishers, 1986.

Bradbury, Ray. "The Illustrated Man." In *The Vintage Bradbury*. New York: Vintage Books, 1965. Pp. 252-65. First published in *Esquire*, July 1950.

Chase, Richard. *The American Novel and Its Tradition*. Baltimore: The Johns Hopkins University Press, 1957.

Conrad, Joseph. *Joseph Conrad on Fiction*. Edited by Walter F. Wright. Lincoln: University of Nebraska Press, 1964.

Dante Alighieri. *Literary Criticism of Dante Alighieri*. Trans. and ed. Robert S. Haller. Lincoln: University of Nebraska Press, 1973.

Derrick, Christopher. *C. S. Lewis and the Church of Rome*. San Francisco: Ignatius Press, 1981.

The Dominican Nuns of Our Lady of Perpetual Help Home. Atlanta, Georgia. *A Memoir of Mary Ann*. Introduction by Flannery O'Connor. New York, Farrar, Straus and Cudahy, 1961.

Eliot, T. S. "Ulysses, Order, and Myth." In *Forms of Modern Fiction*. Edited by William Van O'Connor, 120-24. Bloomington, 1959. Originally published in the *Dial*, 1923.

Emerson, Ralph Waldo. "Self-Reliance." In *Essays: First Series, Essays and Lectures*, 275. New York: Library of America.

Faulkner, William. "The Bear," *Go Down, Moses*. New York: The Modern Library, 1942.

Fiedler, Leslie. "Come Back to the Raft Ag'in, Huck Honey." *A Fiedler Reader*. New York: Stein and Day, 1977. Pp. 3-13. Originally published in *The Partisan Review*, June 1948.

—*Love and Death in the American Novel*. Revised Edition. New York: Stein and Day, 1982.

—*What Was Literature? Class Culture and Mass Society*. New York: Touchstone, 1984.

Flink, James L. *The Car Culture*. Cambridge, Massachusetts: The MIT Press, 1975.

Gill, Andrew and Jon King (Gang of Four). "A Man With a Good Car," *Hard*. Warner Brothers Records, 1983.

Ginsberg, Allen. *Collected Poems 1947-1980*. New York: Harper and Row, 1984.

Gordon, Sarah. "Carnal Knowledge: The Terrors of Sexuality in the *Wise Blood* Drafts." Paper delivered at the MLA Convention in 1984.

Grimshaw, James A. *The Flannery O'Connor Companion*. Westport, Conn.: Greenwood Press, 1981.

Kinney, Arthur F. *Flannery O'Connor's Library: Resources of Being*. Athens: University of Georgia Press, 1985.

Lewis, C. S. *The Allegory of Love: A Study in Mediaeval Tradition*. Oxford: Oxford University Press, 1936.

—*Surprised by Joy: The Shape of My Early Life*. London: Geoffrey Bles, 1955.

Lewis, David L. "From Rumble Seats to Rockin' Vans." In *The Automobile and American Culture*. Edited by David L. Lewis and Laurence Goldstein, 123-33. Ann Arbor: The University of Michigan Press, 1983.

Lewis, R. W. B. *The American Adam: Innocence, Tragedy, and Tradition in the Nineteenth Century*. Chicago: The University of Chicago Press, 1955.

Little, Lester K. "Pride Goes Before Avarice: Social Change and the Vices in Latin Christendom." *American Historical Review*, 76 (1971): 16-49.

Liverani, Mariella. "Paolo, Apostolo, Santo, Martire—Iconographia." *Bibliotheca Sanctorum*, vol. 10. Rome: Instituto Giovanni XXIII della Pontificia Università Lateranense, 1968. Pp. 211-27.

Marx, Leo. *The Machine in the Garden: Technology and the Pastoral Ideal in*

*America.* New York: Oxford University Press, 1964.

McLuhan, Herbert Marshall. *The Mechanical Bride: The Folklore of Industrial Man.* New York: The Vanguard Press, 1951.

Merton, Thomas. *The Sign of Jonas.* New York: Harcourt Brace, 1953.

Moon, Least Heat. *Blue Highways: A Journey into America.* Boston: Little, Brown, 1982.

O'Connor, Flannery. *The Complete Stories.* New York: Farrar, Straus & Giroux, Inc., 1971.

—*Everything That Rises Must Converge.* Introduction by Robert Fitzgerald. New York: Farrar, Straus & Giroux, Inc., 1965.

—*The Habit of Being: Letters.* Edited and with an Introduction by Sally Fitzgerald. New York: Farrar, Straus, & Giroux, Inc., 1979.

—*Mystery and Manners: Occasional Prose.* Selected and edited by Sally and Robert Fitzgerald. New York: Farrar, Straus & Giroux, Inc., 1969.

—*The Presence of Grace and Other Book Reviews.* Compiled by Leo J. Zuber. Edited by Carter W. Martin. Athens, Georgia: The University of Georgia Press, 1983.

Olson, Robert G. *An Introduction to Existentialism.* New York: Dover, 1962.

O'Neill, John P., ed. *The Age of Caravaggio.* Metropolitan Museum Catalog. New York: Metropolitan Museum, 1985.

Pierson, George. *The Moving American.* New York: Knopf, 1973.

Pirsig, Robert. *Zen and the Art of Motorcycle Maintenance.* New York: Morrow, 1975.

Poe, Edgar Allan. *Poetry and Tales.* New York: The Library of America, 1984.

Sartre, Jean-Paul. *Being and Nothingness: An Essay on Phenomenological Ontology.* Translated by Hazel E. Barnes. New York: Philosophical Library, 1956.

—"Existentialism Is a Humanism." *Existentialism from Dostoevsky to Sartre.* Edited by Walter Kaufmann. New York: Meridian, 1956.

Smith, Henry Nash. *Virgin Land: The American West as Symbol and Myth.* New York: Vintage Books, 1950.

Springsteen, Bruce. "Adam Raised a Cain." *Darkness on the Edge of Town.* Columbia Records, 1978.

—"Downbound Train." *Born in the U.S.A.* Columbia Records, 1984.

—"Thunder Road." *Born to Run.* Columbia Records, 1975.

Steinbeck, John. *Travels with Charley in Search of America.* New York: Viking, 1962.

Steinberg, Leo. *The Sexuality of Christ in Renaissance Art and Modern Oblivion.* New York: Pantheon, 1983.

Stevens,Wallace. *The Collected Poems of Wallace Stevens.* New York: Knopf, 1954.

Thompson, Hunter. *Fear and Loathing in Las Vegas: A Savage Journey to the Heart of the American Dream.* New York: Popular Library, 1971.

—*Hell's Angels: A Strange and Terrible Saga.* New York: Ballantine, 1967.

Turner, Frederick Jackson. "The Significance of the Frontier in American History," 37. In *The Frontier in American History*. New York: Henry Holt and Company, 1920. First published in *The Annual Report of the American Historical Association for 1893*, 190-227. Washington, D.C.: American Historical Association, 1893.

Twain, Mark. *The Adventures of Huckleberry Finn*. Edited by Leo Marx. Indianapolis: Bobbs-Merrill, 1967.

Ware, Timothy. *The Orthodox Church*. Penguin Books, 1984.

Warren, Robert Penn. *All the King's Men*. New York: Harcourt Brace, 1981.

—*Selected Poems 1923-1975*. New York: Random House, 1976.

Whitman, Walt. *Complete Poetry and Prose*. New York: Library of America, 1982.

Wimsatt, William K., Jr. and Cleanth Brooks. *Literary Criticism: A Short History*. Chicago: University of Chicago Press, 1983.

Wolfe, Tom. "The Last American Hero," 27. In *The Purple Decades, A Reader*. New York: Farrar, Straus, & Giroux, Inc., 1982.

Ziolkowski, Theodore. *Fictional Transfigurations of Jesus*. Princeton: Princeton University Press, 1972.

—"Some Features of Religious Figuralism in Twentieth-Century Literature." *Literary Uses of Typology from the Late Middle Ages to the Present*. Edited by Earl Miner. Princeton: Princeton University Press, 1977.

# Other Books from
# Loyola University Press
# in Literature and Religion

**Walker Percy and the Postmodern World**
*Mary K. Sweeny*

How do Walker Percy's works dramatize his concern with the death of the modern age? The answers lie in the pages of this book.
**Hardcover $12.95  ISBN 0-8294-0541-0**

**Heaven and Hell on Earth:**
**An Appreciation of Five Novels of Graham Greene**
*K. C. Joseph Kurismmootil, S.J.*

*Brighton Rock, The End of the Affair, The Power and the Glory, The Heart of the Matter,* and *A Burnt-Out Case* reflect Greene's perception of Heaven and Hell's coexistence on earth.
**Hardcover $12.95  ISBN 0-8294-0378-7**

**Eros and the Womanliness of God:**
**Andrew Greeley's Romances of Renewal**
*Ingrid H. Shafer*

This insightful interpretation uncovers the ways in which Greeley's romance novels have injected a feminine element into the general conception of a male God.
**Hardcover $12.95  ISBN 0-8294-0519-4**

**Dostoevsky and the Catholic Church**
*Denis Dirscherl*

Dirscherl examines Dostoevsky's fiction, and finds a piquant animosity toward the West and especially the Roman Catholic Church.
**Hardcover $12.95  ISBN 0-8294-0502-x**

**Dark Prophets of Hope:**
**Dostoevsky • Sartre • Camus • Faulkner**
*Jean Kellogg*

Here are the common threads of existentialism in the fiction of four great authors.
**Paperback $7.95 ISBN 0-8294-0243-8**

**Pleasures Forevermore:**
**The Theology of C. S. Lewis**
*John Randolph Willis, S.J.*

The theological foundation beneath C. S. Lewis's writing is uncovered.
**Hardcover $12.95 ISBN 0-8294-0421-x**

**The Vital Tradition:**
**The Catholic Novel in a Period of Convergence**
*Gene Kellogg*

Here is the "all encompassing" history of Catholic thought vividly represented in fiction.
**Hardcover $8.95 ISBN 0-8294-0192-x**

**Gerard Manley Hopkins—a tribute**
*W. A. M. Peters, S.J.*

A plauditory look at one of the finest poets ever.
**Hardcover $12.95 ISBN 0-8294-0421-x**

**A Commentary on the Sonnets of G. M. Hopkins**
*Peter Milward, S.J.*

Complete and concise annotations on all of Hopkins' sonnets of fourteen lines or less.
**Paperback $6.95 ISBN 0-8294-0494-5**

**Readings of the Wreck:**
**Essays in Commemoration of the Centenary of G. M. Hopkins'**
*The Wreck of the Deutschland*
*edited by Peter Milward, S.J. and Raymond Schoder, S.J.*

A number of excellent scholars delve into Hopkins' seminal poem.
**Hardcover $8.95 ISBN 0-8294-0249-7**

**Shakespeare's Religious Background**
*Peter Milward, S.J.*

A detailed analysis of the turbulent times of religious upheaval in which Shakespeare lived.
**Hardcover $12.95 ISBN 0-8294-0508-9**

### The Art of G. K. Chesterton
*Alzina Stone Dale*

Filled with many previously unpublished sketches, drawings, and cartoons by the famous Chesterton.
**Hardcover $24.95 ISBN 0-8294-0516-x**

### G. K.'s Weekly, A Sampler
*Lyle W. Dorsett*

Thirty issues of *G. K.'s Weekly* from 1925 to 1936 are presented here, preserved and unedited.
**Hardcover $24.95 ISBN 0-8294-0531-3**

### Pilgrim in Love:
### An Introduction to Dante and His Spirituality
*James Collins*

Various myths about the man behind *The Divine Comedy* are shattered in this insightful account.
**Hardcover $12.95 ISBN 0-8294-0453-8**

### God's Plenty:
### Chaucer's Christian Humanism
*Ruth M. Ames*

In this book you will find a different Chaucer than you are used to—a gregarious soul that could not be smothered by the "Dark Ages."
**Hardcover $12.95 ISBN 0-8294-0426-0**

### Hilaire Belloc's Prefaces:
### Written for Fellow Authors
*selected by J. A. De Chantigny*

The versatility of Belloc's genius is explored through the prefaces he wrote for other authors.
**Hardcover $10.95 ISBN 0-8294-0209-8**

### More Than the Ear Discovers:
### God in the Plays of Christopher Fry
*Stanley Wiersma*

A penetrating investigation of Fry's prophetic vision of our society.
**Hardcover $12.95 ISBN 0-8294-0442-2**

**Fiction, Film, and F. Scott Fitzgerald**
*Gene Phillips, S.J.*
A fascinating look at the Hollywood adaptations of F. Scott Fitzgerald's fiction.
**Hardcover $12.95 ISBN 0-8294-0500-3**

**Hollywood and the Catholic Church:**
**The Image of Roman Catholicism in American Movies**
*Les and Barbara Keyser*
Roger Ebert gives this perceptive analysis of Hollywood's stereotyped image of Catholicism a "thumbs up!"
**Hardcover $12.95 ISBN 0-8294-0468-6**

These books are available at finer bookstores everywhere or directly from:

Loyola University Press
3441 North Ashland Avenue
Chicago, Illinois 60657
FOUNDED IN 1912

(800) 621-1008
in Illinois (312) 281-1818
Call us for a free catalog